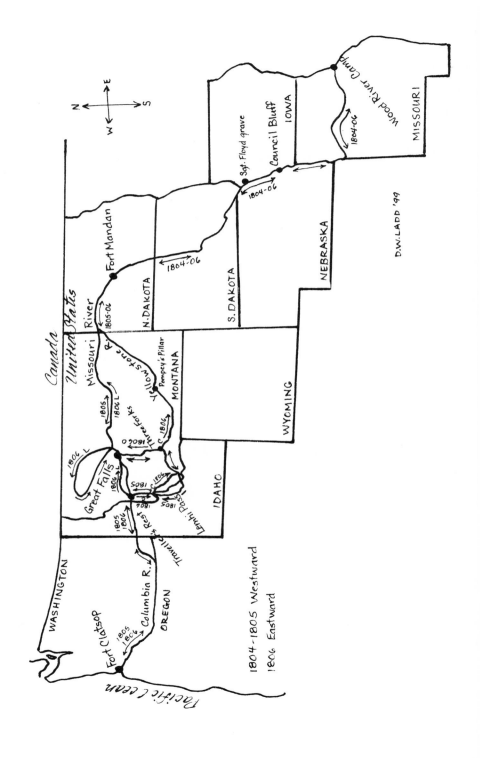

Canada

United States

Missouri River

Fort Mandan

Yellowstone R.

Pompey's Pillar

Great Falls

Three Forks

Lemhi Pass

Traveler's Rest

Columbia R.

Fort Clatsop

Pacific Ocean

WASHINGTON

OREGON

IDAHO

MONTANA

WYOMING

N.DAKOTA

S.DAKOTA

NEBRASKA

IOWA

MISSOURI

Council Bluff

Sgt. Floyd grave

Wood River Camp

1804-06

1804-06

1804-06

1805-06

1805

1804 L

1806 L

1804 L

1805

1805 1806

C.1806

O.1806

C.1805 1806

1805 1806

1805 1806

1804-1805 Westward

1806 Eastward

D.W. LADD '99

N
E
W
S

Lewis & Clark
On The Upper Missouri

— BY THE DISCOVERY WRITERS —
- Jean Clary
- Diann Ladd
- Pat Hastings
- Jeanne O'Neill
- Katie White
- Riga Winthrop

With a Foreword by Dale A. Burk

Lewis & Clark on the Upper Missouri

–By The Discovery Writers–

- Jeanne O'Neill
- Jean Clary
- Patricia B. Hastings
- Diann Ladd
- Katie White
- Riga Winthrop

With a Foreword by Dale A. Burk

Published in the United States of America

Copyright 1999 by Dale A. Burk

ISBN 0-912299-85-1 (Hardcover)
ISBN 0-912299-84-3 (Softcover)

Library of Congress Catalog Card No. 99-75624

STONEYDALE PRESS PUBLISHING COMPANY
523 Main Street • Stevensville, Montana 59870
Phone: 406-777-2729

Table of Contents

Cover Painting: This huge and exquisitely done 60x30-inch canvas by artist Robert F. Morgan of Helena, Montana, is titled "CAPTAIN LEWIS AND PARTY AT FIELD'S GULCH (Gates of the Mountains) on the upper Missouri River, breaking camp the morning of July 20, 1805, on the party's upriver journey.

Dedication

To DALE BURK, our publisher

Whose vision, perseverance, skill and grace kindled the fires of imagination. Writing became creation, enriching an adventure into the past.

Acknowledgments

•*Lynette Adkison, Dillon-area Lewis and Clark Bicentennial Coordinator for the Bureau of Land Management and the Montana Department of Fish, Wildlife & Parks, for information on Beaverhead County*

•*Fred Allendorf, Professor of Biological Sciences, University of Montana, Missoula, Montana*

•*Phil and Shirley Althen of Stevensville, Montana, for their generosity in sharing their files and their knowledge of the Lewis & Clark Expedition*

•*Dr. Robert Bergantino of Butte, Montana, for sharing his incredible knowledge of the route of the Lewis & Clark Expedition*

•*Clint Blackwood, Executive Director, Montana Lewis & Clark Bicentennial Commission*

•*Marshall Bloom, authority on Trout, Hamilton, Montana*

•*Chuck Campbell, retired faculty of University of Montana, and Suzie Campbell, who directed us in our research of the Blackfoot River journey of Captain Lewis in July of 1806*

•*Chris Clancy, Fisheries Biologist, Montana Department. of Fish, Wildlife and Parks, Hamilton, Montana*

•*Patrick Clary, M.D., Dover, New Hampshire, for present-day medical information.*

•*Carol Cotton, Valley County Pioneer Museum, Glasgow, Montana*

•*Wayne F. Curtis, Consultant for Montana Power Company, who supplied us with information on the company's hydroelectric developments on the Upper Missouri River*

•*Judith Deitz, Coordinator of the MonDak Heritage Center, Sidney, Montana*

•*Monte Dolack of Missoula, Montana, for permission to use his painting "White Cliffs" in our color section.*

•*Richie Doyle, for his presentation of Captain Clark and his patience and generosity in answering questions and supplying references*

•*Glenn Erickson, Montana Fish, Wildlife and Parks, Helena, Montana*

•*Duncan Gilchrist, author and authority on Bighorn Sheep, Corvallis, Montana*

•*Elizabeth Goldman, Dover, New Hampshire, for research about communicable diseases*

•*Margaret Gorsky of the U.S. Forest Service, Northern Region office, Missoula, Montana,*

•*Ella Mae Howard of Great Falls, Montana, for assistance with information on the portage of the Great Falls of the Missouri River*

•*Jodi Hunt, for time and patience spent proofreading*

•*George Knapp and Chuck Sundstrom for the presentation of the Traveling Trunk and cooperation with us in obtaining information*

•*Kim Lacey of the Glasgow Chamber of Commerce*

•*Kirby Lambert, curator, and Diane Keller of the Montana Historical Society in Helena, Montana, for both their advice and assistance*

•*Billie Linkletter and Millie Guest of Stoneydale Press, for their availability and assistance*

•*Jeff Marks, Professor of Ornithology, University of Montana, Missoula, Montana*

•*Sterling D. Miller, Resource Specialist, National Wildlife Federation*

•*Joan McDougal, Beaverhead Museum in Dillon, Montana, for generous assistance with research*

•*Steve Morehouse, Bureau of Land Management, Dillon, Montana, for firsthand information on Lewis and Clark in Beaverhead County*

•*Robert F. Morgan, artist and historian, Clancy, Montana, not only for his powerful visual images on canvas but his incredible knowledge of the details of the Corps of Discovery's travels on the Upper Missouri*

•*John Ormiston, U.S. Forest Service wildlife biologist of the south zone of the Bitterroot National Forest, Sula, Montana*

•*Terry Peterson, Helena, Montana, for help with statistics and communicable diseases.*

•*Jim Potter, Director of University Relations, University of Montana, Havre, Montana*

•*Mike Ryan, Archeologist, Beaverhead National Forest, Dillon, Montana*

•*Julianne Ruby, Librarian, Lewis & Clark Trail Heritage Foundation, Inc., Great Falls, Montana*

•*Viola Squires, Beaverhead Museum in Dillon, Montana, for generous assistance with research*

•*Elmer Sprunger of Bigfork, Montana, for his painting reproduced in this book*

•*Staff of the North Valley Library in Stevensville, Montana: Patty Jo Thomas, Bill Stout and Nina Packer for their cooperation and assistance in locating references*

•*Dr. Gene Swanzey of Hamilton, Montana, our mentor and friend, for his encouragement and expertise as we traveled with Lewis and Clark on the Upper Missouri*

•*Vern Sylvester of Stevensville, Montana, for his expertise on the geography of Montana*

•*Robert Timmerman of Hamilton, Montana, for assistance in research on the Fort Peck Dam.*

•*To our family and friends, particularly our husbands, whose patience, support and encouragement made the journey a pleasant and intriguing adventure*

•*Jane Warner, Librarian, Fort Clatsop National Monument, Astoria, Oregon*

•*Clark W. Whitehead, Recreation Staff, Bureau of Land Management, Lewistown District Office, Lewistown, Montana*

•*Any person not mentioned who contributed in any way to the publication of Lewis & Clark on the Upper Missouri, be it a word of encouragement, a clipping from a newspaper, question, or a pat on the back – we thank you*

•*And to the members of our Scripture Study Group, who listened, offered encouragement and support, and traveled the Upper Missouri with us as we prepared this book, and, most important, prayed with us. We thank you.*

Foreword

The story of Lewis & Clark on the Upper Missouri is largely one of Lewis & Clark in Montana. But not completely so! There were other "Montana" river drainages involved: the Bitterroot, Clark Fork, Blackfoot, as well as Camp Creek and Lolo Creek, and their waters do not drain into the Missouri; indeed, all are headwaters tributaries of the mighty Columbia and they all, ultimately, flow into the Pacific Ocean. Also, the term Upper Missouri must include a portion of the "Big Muddy," the Missouri, as it flows through Mandan Country, what is still Mandan country but is now known as North Dakota.

So, partially of necessity to define a geographical region directly tied to the geography and chronology of the Lewis & Clark Expedition, the authors of this volume have called the "Upper Missouri" as those parts of the Missouri River drainage from the Expedition's winter encampment at the Mandan village upstream to the Continental Divide whence they passed from the Missouri River drainage into that of the mighty Columbia. These authors, the self-named "Discovery Writers," six ladies out of Stevensville, Montana, whose earlier volume "Lewis & Clark In The Bitterroot" detailed the largely overlooked story of the Corps of Discovery's two jaunts through that awesome part of America's geography, also wanted to call their new book "Lewis & Clark on the Upper Missouri" because that's exactly what it covers..

As they did in their earlier volume, the authors of this book have tried to treat their subject in a manner exactly the opposite of what most often has been done in writings about the Lewis & Clark Expedition. For sure their first volume was among the first to take a minute and specifically "local" working of a significant part of the expedition, examine it in detail, and set it in the context of the greater journey rather than visa-versa. The specifics written of herein are a variety of detailed aspects of the Corps of Discovery's journey(s) on the Upper Missouri (there were two, after all, the outward bound and the return trip). The context is, of course, that their travels in this region are but part of the greater whole, a journey that ultimately crossed and re-crossed an entire continent.

Still, it is the specific, and the effort to relate, along the route, what happened then, what has happened since, and what the situation is now that makes this volume significant. It gives us comprehension, continuity, and context. We see, perhaps even experience, and understand that the Lewis & Clark Expedition not only was set in the context of its time and place, but in the context of our time and place. What they did, what they saw, what they recorded, what they hoped for and achieved or failed, are not only their legacy but ours as well. They did not, in the true meaning of the word, "discover" much that was not already known to native peoples along the route. But none of the earlier "knowing" made as profound a subsequent impact on what would follow, and change things for everyone and everything, as the fact that the Lewis & Clark Expedition had made its grueling way up the main Missouri River in the spring and summer of 1805.

From that point onward, the region and what was there would be known to people elsewhere who not only could, but would, come to it, claim it, use it, change it, sometimes desecrate it, but for sure take it, forever. That is at once a comprehension of context that is both profound and inescapable and, I believe, one that Meriwether Lewis himself articulated, perhaps without really knowing it, as he sat on a group of rocks below the Great Falls of the Missouri and penned these words on June 13, 1805: "on some rocks under the centre of the falls, enjoyed the sublime spectacle of this stupendous object which since the creation had been lavishing its magificence upon the desert, unknown to civilization."

It was, ultimately, on this very spot, a place Meriwether Lewis himself, that agent and harbinger of the "civilization" that had sent him, presented the most lavish description of natural beauty to the found in his journals, this "sublime spectacle", the Great Falls of the Missouri, that the context of time and place and circumstance, as well as the inevitable impact of making such places known to civilization as understood by Captain Lewis, would be played out. Here, at the Great Falls of the Missouri and the series of falls nearby, civilized man would, little more than a century later, build not one but several dams and while the waters still flow and the spectacle of a grand river is still to be found and in a very real way it is still stupendous, even awe-inspiring, it is no longer sublime. Indeed, when one visits the rocks under the center of the falls, as I did this fine June morning and have on numerous other occasions, and reaches into Lewis' words and truly comprehends how this particular spectacle had touched his soul, that this was the grandest, the best, the most awesome nature feature that he saw and wrote about on the entire trip, it brings to mind that rather than sublimity we can only recall his notion of ultimate sublimity with an inescapable feeling of sadness.

Which brings us to a couple of other points the Discovery Writers place in context for us, given the fact that we enjoy the perspective of almost two hundred years of context building. These are primarily those of relating what was found, and written of, then to what is found today, once again the notion of context in the face of unrelenting change in both the natural and human environments. From the river itself to flora and fauna, to people and time and circumstance, from junctions of streams like the Marias and the Missouri, the Sun and the Missouri, the Dearborn and the Missouri, the Jefferson, Madison and Gallatin, the Beaverhead and the Big Hole (Wisdom) Rivers, and the places where towns and cities would develop, Loma, Fort Benton, Great Falls, Toston, Helena, Three Forks, Whitehall, Twin Bridges, and Dillon, among others, we find that these places are part of the legacy of the Lewis & Clark Expedition.

There is one other significant aspect of the journey that any serious aficionado of the Expedition looking at the story of the Lewis & Clark Expedition on its upriver journey into the Upper Missouri must ponder — and that is the fact that, on that leg of their journey, they never came in direct contact with the Blackfeet, even though they spent five months or more in the heart of that nation's country. The Discovery Writers do deal with this fact, or phenomenon, in their text, and well they should for it had to be incredible luck, the hand of Providence, or simple fate that no such encounter ever took place. Not that either the two leaders or the members of the Corps minded; their trip through the Upper Missouri was sufficiently wrought with physical agony, geographic and other natural obstacles of overwhelming power (like waterfalls and grizzly bears and prickly pear cactus and sharp rocks and vicious thunderstorms and rattlesnakes galore) that they were undoubtedly relieved that they hadn't had to deal with an Indian nation that was known to be not only hostile but inalterable in its attitude toward outsiders.

Even so, it was within the confines of the uppermost reaches of the Upper Missouri that the Expedition experienced its most significant encounter with native people, the Shoshone, Sacajawea's people. In fact, the very uppermost part of the region, the true headwaters, the crown of the continent, above the famous Beaverhead Rock, above where present-day Dillon is located, where Horse Prairie Creek springs forth just under the Continental Divide and one passes into the Lemhi of present-day Idaho. Here, atop the continent, Hugh McNeal exulted on August 12, 1805, as he stood astride a rivulet near the top that literally and figuratively represented the Expedition's triumphant ascendance of the Upper Missouri and proclaimed "thanked his god that he had lived to bestride the mighty and heretofore deemed endless Missouri."

It was a sentiment that rings as true to those who make that same journey today, albeit under more favorable and certainly less arduous circumstances, as it did for Hugh McNeal and Meriwether Lewis when he wrote it in his journal that "the road took us to the most distant fountain of the waters of the Mighty Missouri in surch of which we have spent so many toilsome days & wristless nights." The comments are also sentiments of context, ones that place the story of Hugh McNeal, Meriwether Lewis, William Clark and the entire Corps of Discovery simultaneously in their time and in ours. It's a story that is, at once, theirs and ours, and you'll find it both revitalized and enjoyed within the pages that follow, as you set out on your own "wristless" journey....

Dale A. Burk
Great Falls, Montana
June 24, 1999

Chapter One

FROM WINTER CAMP: OFF TO THE UPPER MISSOURI

Dreams are the seeds from which ideas grow into grand adventures. One such dream of Thomas Jefferson, third president of the United States, led to the grandest of American adventures. Jefferson envisioned a United States extending to the shores of the Pacific Ocean. In 1801 Jefferson was occupied in the planning of an expedition that would transverse the northwest territory beyond the Mississippi River, through the valleys drained by the Missouri River, over the Continental Divide to the Pacific. Three previous expeditions, planned and equipped by Jefferson, had failed, but now he had the power and influence of the presidency to push his plans through, and word was out that the British were about to explore, claim and colonize this vast wilderness south of Canada for their own commercial interests, namely the very lucrative fur trade. Jefferson, an embodiment of the Age of Enlightenment and a student of the voyages of the British explorer, Captain James Cook, designed this fourth expedition in the hope of locating a passage to the Pacific Ocean, the fabled Northwest Passage, and of extending scientific knowledge of the land, its resources, geography, of the flora and fauna and of the native people who inhabited this wilderness. Together with his private secretary, young, able Meriwether Lewis, who was eager to lead the excursion into the western wilderness, Jefferson engineered the plan that would culminate in the historical epic of America, the Lewis and Clark Expedition.

Although Jefferson's preoccupation with science and the extension of knowledge also prompted his interest in this expedition, as president of the young republic his primary concern was to lay claim to and secure this unknown territory for America and for American commerce. Commerce, not war, he was confident, was the engine that would bring the Indians into peaceful coexistence with each other and with the Americans who would soon be pushing westward.

The plan, evolved by President Jefferson and Meriwether Lewis, was for this Expedition to travel up the Missouri River to its headwaters, cross the Continental Divide over mountains which they believed could be portaged in a single day, then follow the Columbia River down to the Pacific Ocean. Jefferson tutored young Lewis in the natural sciences, provided him with available maps and instruction on all that was then known about the lands of the upper Missouri and sent him to Philadelphia for intensive study under the most advanced

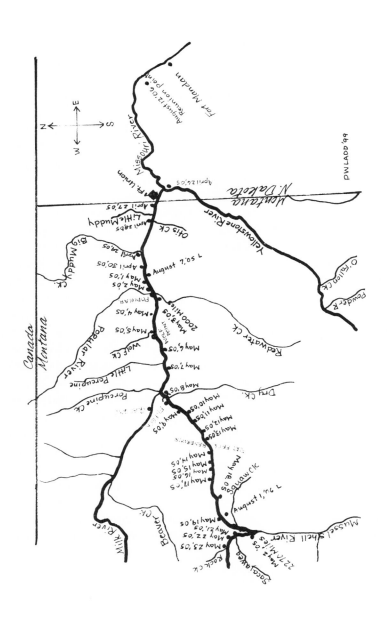

scientists and medical doctors of that time. Jefferson, himself, used his political skills to persuade Congress to fund this Expedition by appealing to the commercial interests of its representatives. Congress did so, but quite meagerly.

The area west of the Mississippi River to the Rocky Mountains was territory called Louisiana, owned by the French but under Spanish administration. The Expedition would need permission to cross this land. While Jefferson was dealing to obtain the important port of New Orleans and so secure that port for American commerce, fate dropped Louisiana into the President's hands. When Napoleon offered to sell Louisiana to the United States in 1803, Jefferson jumped on the offer and bought the Territory for $15,000,000. It was even more expedient then that an expedition be sent to explore this new territory. Thus, this Expedition would be traveling on United States territory at least to the Continental Divide, i.e. to the Rocky Mountains.

In what was probably the most brilliant decision of his career, Meriwether Lewis invited his friend and former Army captain, William Clark, to join him in this adventure. When Clark accepted, the indomitable joint command of Lewis and Clark was born. The two young men complemented one another. Both were tall, strong, hardy and athletic. Both had military and wilderness experience. Lewis was cool and detached; Clark, warm and gregarious. Lewis was educated, skilled in descriptive and literary writing. Clark's raw intelligence was shaped and honed by experience and by self-instruction. Lewis preferred solitary walking, observing and writing. Clark enjoyed associating with the men and with the Indians. Lewis was the engineer; Clark, the cartographer. While Lewis was moody and probably suffered from what would now be diagnosed as "bi-polar disease," Clark was the balance: steady, sanguine and grounded. Both men were excellent hunters, although Clark was the more experienced frontiersman and the better boatman. Together they commanded through discipline and constant surveillance while exhibiting a unified leadership in which they asked no more of their men than they were willing to do themselves. However, both men were always in authority, ever the leaders. Although Lewis had requested a captaincy for William Clark, the Secretary of War conferred the lower rank of lieutenant on the thirty-five year old former army captain, which frustrated and disappointed Meriwether Lewis. However, when he asked Clark to keep the matter secret, which they both did, and accept the title of captain, a disgruntled Clark agreed, so eager was he to partake in this great adventure. William Clark was always referred to as "Captain Clark."

Winter Camp

By the fall of 1803, preparations for the Expedition were underway. The two captains had enlisted a core group of soldiers and recruits to join the Expedition and had also hired a civilian, George Droulliard, interpreter, hunter

William Clark   *Meriwether Lewis*
Illustrations by Diann Ladd.

and guide. They camped that winter on the Wood River in Illinois Territory across from the mouth of the Missouri River and named their camp, Camp Dubois. Throughout the winter, the two captains prepared the men for the Expedition, shaped them under military discipline, and eliminated the misfits. Included in the group, all skilled frontiersmen, were craftsmen, hunters, woodsmen and boatmen. From rough, unruly, wild and sometimes rebellious recruits, the men developed into a unit ready and able to undertake the rigors and hardships of this unprecedented excursion. Under the captains' leadership a *esprit de corps* would generate which would hold this group together under the most trying circumstances.

On May 14, 1804, all was ready. The men pushed the boats into the Missouri, a little flotilla consisting of two fifty-five foot keelboats and two pirogues which carried all the provisions for the journey. Besides the recruits, George Droulliard, Captain Clark's black servant, York, Captain Lewis' Newfoundland dog, Seaman, the boats carried a crew of French engages, or hired boatmen. They then *proceeded on* to make and record history on their journey into the northwest wilderness.

Up The Missouri

Going against the current of the mighty river, especially during spring runoff, was a herculean job. Fallen trees and swollen waters challenged the men rowing the fifty-five-foot keelboat and the two pirogues. When necessary, they "poled", meaning they pushed a wooden pole against the river bottom, then walked from bow to stern in the icy water. When poling didn't work it was necessary for them to "cordell" which involved walking in the muddy and clogged shallows or on the bank pulling the boat by long towlines. This was excruciating labor and a test of the spirit, hardiness and stamina of the men selected by the captains. The hunters were kept busy supplying meat for the crew as each man ate eight to nine pounds of meat a day. The midsummer heat on the Great Plains became almost intolerable, and frequent violent storms threatened the boats. Progress was slow and at times dangerous, as when the keelboat struck a snag that turned it sideways in midstream. Only the quick action of the men saved it. The captains, following President Jefferson's orders, took observations, noted mileage, described the plants and animals they saw, the land and landmarks, the weather and the *"troublesome musquetoes, or misquetors"* which would remain their pesky companions through most of the journey.

The only fatality of the whole Expedition occurred when young Sergeant Charles Floyd died, apparently of appendicitis, near Sioux Falls, Iowa, August 20, 1804. Patrick Gass, a carpenter for the party, was selected to fill his position.

Traders were coming downstream, their boats loaded with furs. The captains and men gleaned every bit of information they could from them. The traders warned them of the fierce, war-like and powerful Teton Sioux Indians who controlled travel on the Upper Missouri, and who exacted a high price for the privilege of traveling through their territory. Jefferson had instructed Lewis to treat all the Indians he encountered in a friendly manner, instructing them of the sovereignty of the United States, and the President's desire for peace between the Indian nations. They were also to obtain all the information they could concerning the Indians' names, social structure, culture, food, diseases and treatment, and record the various tribal languages. As they counciled with the natives, offered them gifts and urged them to trade with the American traders, not the British and French, the captains were to invite the chiefs to visit Washington and meet their great father who now owned their land and would be their protector. This they did and endeavored to impress their hosts with a grandiose military show, including guns and flags all in the American style. Meanwhile, they were also to learn what the Indians had to give in trade and what goods they desired to have.

No problems occurred until September 26, 1804, when, near present-day Pierre, South Dakota, the Expedition encountered the Teton Sioux, or the Lakota, about whom they had been warned. These Indians, as did the other Indian tribes, entertained the captains and the men with Indian hospitality including smoking the pipe, feasting and dancing. Captain Lewis attempted to give them President Jefferson's message. However, the Lakota were suspicious of these white Americans whom they feared might attempt to usurp their power on the river. Unfortunately, there was no skilled interpreter present, and, consequently, two confrontations occurred which fortunately were resolved without bloodshed. The captains stood their ground against the bullying of the Teton chiefs who were refusing to allow the boats to pass. Finally, because of the fearlessness of the Americans, the Teton Sioux backed off and let them continue their journey. According to Bernard DeVoto, this bold stand by the captains and their men was probably communicated to the other Indians of the Plains, by what DeVoto called, "the Indian underground" and the Expedition continued upriver with no further interference.

On October 26, 1804, the Expedition reached the first of the Mandan villages in North Dakota. There they camped, as planned, while constructing their winter quarters on the north bank of the Missouri. This strongly built stockade was named Fort Mandan, in honor of their friendly neighbors.

The Big Muddy

As President Jefferson pondered the extent of his new acquisition, the Louisiana Territory, speculation ran rampant. The recent purchase was a great unknown area sparking the imagination to the possibilities that lay before him and the country. Jefferson's "givens" were few. He knew that a major river known as the "Missouri" ran into the Mississippi from the west. He also knew that another major river, the "Columbia," emptied into the Pacific. Could it be that these two great water highways were connected? Some said that a company of men could take a boat up the Missouri to its source, do a one-day portage, and then float down the Columbia to the Pacific. Nothing could have been further from the truth! As the men of the Corps of Discovery became intimately acquainted with this "Goliath" of a river they were to discover just how erroneous that statement was. They would learn the hard truth that the Missouri would not be quite so accommodating.

As the nineteenth century dawned this young country's waterways were truly its highways for transportation and freight. The horse was the only other means of getting from here to there. As the rivers and streams have always been vital to the Indian tribes, so it was in the time of Lewis and Clark; they were the lifeblood of this new nation as it began to grow westward.

As the Corps of Discovery encountered the many sides of the river's personality, they learned to show it respect, fear, wonder, and yes, even to curse its hellish nature. Although the Missouri was not always a gentleman, it still remained the highway to the West and for many years was the road of fur traders. The Missouri's watershed was the heart of the Louisiana Territory.

There is a powerful melancholy oozing up from the Missouri. And could anyone argue that it is not justified in its pensive flow? In the river's youth, it was abruptly uprooted from its straight trek to the Atlantic by the geological calamity of an ice age. "Big Muddy" sought the sea, but half a continent of clay and boulder hindered the journey so it accommodatingly turned to the south, then east, roguely dumping its muddy waters into the Mississippi. This *wild river has endured two centuries of unmerciful endeavors at taming it. Man has sought to harness the river's power with dams and revetments, and cleaned up its meandering shallow ways with deep channels to accommodate barge traffic. And to add insult to injury, the river has been violated with undisciplined growth and development along its banks for much of its length, as well as the devastation that pollution brings.*

The Missouri was named by the Indians who lived along its banks; the English translation of the Indian name is "Big Muddy" and it has the honor of being the longest river on our continent. At 2,625 miles it's almost five hundred miles longer than the Mississippi. For the record, the Missouri drains an area of approximately 95 million acres.

For all that man has sought to change Old Muddy, it still has a variety of tricks up its sleeves and will always be a vagabond in ever changing water levels which brings no permanence to the banks and sand bars. But change is one of the many lures of the Missouri. During a short trip the color, scenery and weather can run the gamut in variety.

The Missouri is indeed the longest of American rivers and represents time along its route that few other natural features can. In Montana alone, the river exposes almost two hundred million years of geological evidence. A floater can travel from Fort Benton one hundred fifty miles eastward along the Missouri and readily see evidence of the ancient past. The Missouri can take one on an excursion averaging thirty miles and forty million years a day!

There has been a long history of man's efforts at bending and contorting this great river to meet his needs. Although Lewis and Clark had the difficult experience of learning that the Missouri would not be the easy route to the Pacific that all had hoped for, it still had much to offer this young country. The fur trappers and traders were the first to reap the river's great bounties. With the fur trade came a need for military forts. Then as men and families began to stretch westward, the Missouri was the means of entry into the wilds that Lewis and Clark had explored. At first they came in anything that would float. They came in bullboats, canoes, pirogues and keelboats. Finally shallow-hulled and broad beamed steamboats traveled on the river bringing supplies to the towns that grew up around the forts.

The wide, shallow, slow moving Missouri has been dredged to meet the needs of commercial towboats changing it from a river with many shallow side channels into one deep, fast moving river. The Corps of Engineers has built a chain of huge dams and reservoirs which generate electric power and hold back floods while simultaneously providing fishing opportunities for anglers and a playground for boaters.

Along the upper Missouri, though, the river has maintained its wildness and most closely resembles the river Lewis and Clark saw. But the dams upstream, riverfront development and even cattle grazing along the banks which threaten the river's majestic cottonwood tree, all play a part in changing this great river. Even so, in its upper reaches, and in almost all of its headwater streams, the Missouri runs cold and clear just as it did in the time of the Lewis and Clark Expedition and in this region the Missouri boasts a world-class fishery for trout, whitefish, smallmouth bass, sauger, walleye, sturgeon and northern pike. But change is affecting the quality of the river's water and the environment along it.

As a new century dawns critical decisions must be made to protect this river that has given us so much. The conservation group, American Rivers, has perennially listed the Missouri among the United States' ten most endangered rivers. At the close of the twentieth century, 1999, it is listed as number two on that list. Over five hundred native wildlife species made their home along the "Big Muddy"; now, a hundred of those species are in decline. Development has destroyed habitat thus threatening extinction to many kinds of fish and birds.

As we look at the future of the Missouri, compromise is essential. Just as the U. S. Army Corps of Engineers built the dams and controls to meet the needs for hydroelectric power, flood control and navigation, so now, it must make room to protect historic resources, wetlands and riparian zones for wildlife and a booming recreational industry. Whatever is planned for the Missouri, renewal of this grandest of American resources is a must!

At the Mandan

The villages of the Mandan were centrally located on the northern plains. They ultimately became a significant trade center which saw a steady stream of Indians and white traders coming over land and by water to exchange goods and merchandise. The Spanish and French had been there, now Canadian traders (North West Company) and British traders (Hudson Bay Company) were regular visitors; merchants from St. Louis also came; and French-Canadian "free-traders."

The Arapahoe, Kiowa, Assiniboin, Crow and Cheyenne all made their way to the river villages to exchange and barter dried meat, dressed skins, knives, awls, bullets, dried roots and fruits, kettles, plumes, musical instruments and buffalo hides. Nearby, Arikara and Hidatsa came in bullboats bringing baskets of squash, corn, beans and pumpkins; from the west and southwest there were mules, horses and leather goods; from the north tribes brought ammunition and guns supplied by the British; and European goods were brought by both Indian and white middlemen.

The Missouri villages were a trading and cultural crossroads. They also were the site of the large summer rendezvous, where the tribes met not only to trade, but to visit, court, gossip, horse race, wrestle, dance, visit and exchange information. A fluent sign language was developed to enable trade between tribes speaking different languages. An interim of peace, or a "treaty," was often made between warring tribes to allow trading. It usually included travel time back home, at which time their peace agreement ended and disagreements would continue. There were well established Indian travel routes on the plains to their hunting grounds, trade areas and fairs. Author Thomas Mails says the routes which connected Indians to materials and supplies, and other Indians, are some of our present day paved highways.

There had previously been one-half century of trade contact with outsiders when Lewis and Clark arrived at the Mandan Villages. The white man's world already had intersected the Indian's. The Mandan, unfortunately, were greatly affected in a way other than by trade. Well over one-half of their population died during the 1751 and 1803 smallpox epidemics. (Warfare then further decimated the already depopulated and weakened tribe.) There had been nine large Mandan settlements. When Lewis and Clark arrived there were two remaining. The Expedition noted the uninhabited villages remaining on their way upriver to the villages. The Mandan would be ravaged again by smallpox in 1837, that time to near extinction. A letter written by a clerk working for the American Fur Company at Mandan during that time said,"At the moment I am writing, there are but 32 of these poor people in existense, and they mostly women and children."[1]

– – – – –

The Mandans were farmers. They regularly planted crops of corn, beans, squash, sunflowers, pumpkins and tobacco, which they traded. They were not hostile, nomadic horse raiders or plunderers, but were sedentary, raised crops, and warred defensively. They have been characterized as more similar to the peaceful, "town living" southern Pueblo than the Plains Indians.

They lived in circular earth lodges on top of the high bluffs above the Missouri River. Their dwellings had the look of being made entirely of dirt, but they were actually well constructed, roomy, post and beam structures, with beams and many rafters. The framed lodges were layered with secured willow branches, twigs, grasses, and finally covered with thick layers of sod with space left in the center for a smoke hole or chimney, which was also a light source. The distinctive earth domed villages made of fifty to sixty clusters of earth lodges were protected by eighteen-feet tall surrounding palisades and four-feet deep ditches (dry moats).

The Mandan had a "deluge" or flood story. The essence of the story was that a lone man survived rising flood waters, the Mandans were his descendants, and the lone man, at some point in time, had built a wall to protect them. That story was symbolized on the large, central plaza around which their earth lodges were built by a pole shrine to their cultural hero, "Lone Man." The shrine with

A representation of the historic Mandan home. (Photo courtesy Gordon Zimmerman)

a barrel-type enclosure (symbolizing the protective wall), was the focal point of their village.

The lodges around the shrine were the dwellings of ceremonial leaders, and important tribal members and officials. The largest (and sometimes rectangular) structure was the public Ceremonial Lodge, complete with tall poles and effigies hanging from them.

The nineteenth century artist, George Catlin, painted many Mandan village scenes showing the plaza, some of their ceremonies and religious rituals on the plaza; the shrine; the effigy poles; and their earth-domed lodges. Catlin is considered one of the finest visual recorders and reporters of the western Indians. He traveled and lived among many of the western tribes painting and writing about what he observed. Not only did he paint many Mandan village scenes, but he also produced portraits of some of the river valley chiefs and their family members.

– – – – –

Mandan corn fed the Corps over the winter in the river valley. Historian Stephen Ambrose maintains that without the availability of Indian corn the Expedition might not have survived that winter. Hunting was poor, and the animals were so thin the men complained that there was no fat and very little meat to subsist on. When the food supplies began to run short in December, John Shields, the blacksmith, began an operation of sharpening hoes, axes and similar implements in exchange for corn. The Indians brought their utensils in for repair and the Corps' corn supply increased handsomely. But it was Shields' battle axes which struck gold with the Indians. Lewis commented that the "Indians are pecuarly attached to [the] battle ax." Many months later Sergeant Ordway saw one of the axes in the possession of a Nez Perce Indian near the Pacific Coast. Lewis said about Shields, "We by the aide of our Blacksmiths procured corn sufficient for the party during the winter and about 70 or 90 bushels to carry with us." (January, 1805)

Northern Indians had developed a short corn which grew more quickly and needed less rain, enabling it to mature in the shortened growing season of the Northern territory. It was a hardy corn which would adapt to the harsh climates. Agronomists have recently gone back to Indian corn to restore some of its hardiness to recent crosses or hybridized corn.

The dwellings of farming tribes had storage bins for keeping their grains and other stores. These were jug shaped pits, five to six feet deep, four to five feet wide at the base, and lined with grass and corn cobs to maintain dryness. The dried vegetables (pumpkins, squash, etc.) were placed in the pit's center and surrounded by dried and shelled corn. Most dwellings had at least one or two of these caches.

─ ─ ─ ─ ─

An important addition to the Expedition was made at Mandan. Captain Clark said on November 4,

"A Mr Chaubonie, interpeter for the Gross Ventre nation came
to See us...this man wished to hire as an interpiter."

The new interpreter was Toussaint Charbonneau, a French Canadian who had worked for the North West Company before living among the Hidatsa as a free trader. He was the husband of two young Shoshoni girls, one of whom would accompany him on the journey. Lewis later characterized him as "a man of no particular merit," and most writers and historians seem to agree with that assessment. The young wife who accompanied him, however, became the heroine of the Expedition.

Sacajewa, a young Shoshoni, enters the Expedition's story with the delivery of her first child, little Jean Baptiste, born on February 11, 1805. Captain Clark would nickname him, "Little Pomp," his dancing boy, and he named a topographical feature on the Yellowstone after him (Pompey's Pillar).

─ ─ ─ ─ ─

During the winter of 1805 politics were rife at Mandan. There were political maneuvering, jealousies and intrigue between the Expedition and the French Canadian and British traders; among the Indian nations and tribes; among the free traders; and between Lewis and Clark and the Indians. Powers were shifting. Some old alliances were holding, but others were unstable and tottering. The river valley was caught in the incipient changing face of the west, and the developing forces of a new government.

The Mandan and Hidatsa villages were important to traders, and to the new government of the territory of the Louisiana Purchase, which Lewis and Clark represented. Some of the Indian leaders at the Mandan that winter whom Lewis and Clark met, traded and fraternized with were:

Black Cat, the Mandan chief who welcomed Lewis and Clark, visited often, wanted peace, and about whom Lewis said, "This man possesses more intelligence and firmness than any Indian I have met."

Sheheke (Big White) was the lower Mandan Village Chief. The Expedition camped across the river from his village. He went to Washington to meet President Jefferson with the Expedition on their return in 1806.

Chief Le Borgne (One Eye), the powerful and colorful Hidatsa chief who closely examined York, Clark's black slave, to find if he really was a black man or simply painted black. Charlie Russell painted the encounter, showing Le Borgne trying to rub York's color off as the Expedition and an intent Indian audience watches. Le Borgne's village was the largest of the three Hidatsa villages and he was considered an exceptional leader and militarily powerful.

Black Moccasin, Hidatsa chief of the Minnetarees, Metaharta of the Willows. Sacajewea and Charbonneau lived in his village before joining the

"York," by Charles M. Russell. Watercolor, 1908. Scene in a Mandan village along the Missouri River during the upriver part of the journey. (Courtesy of the Montana Historical Society)

Expedition. George Catlin painted Black Moccasin's portrait in 1832. Black Moccasin was at least 100 years old at that point. He queried Catlin about "Long Knife and Red Hair", the Indian names given to Lewis and Clark. Catlin later told Clark of Black Moccasin's conversation and showed Clark the portrait. Clark replied that Black Moccasin had been an old man when he and Lewis designated him as chief over thirty years ago.

Good feelings characterized the relationship between the Mandan and Hidatsa Indians and the Expedition during the long winter months of 1804 and 1805. They saw each other frequently and socially.

The Expedition hunted buffalo with the Mandans and were impressed with their riding and hunting skills. The Indians guided their swift horses with their knees leaving their hands free to shoot their bow and arrows. The Indian arrows were released with such power and accuracy that they usually penetrated the heart of the animal, often to the arrow's ending feather.

They danced many times with the Mandans. The Indians requested that Cruzatte bring his violin; and they were intrigued with York, who danced with fluid grace even though he was a large man.

They exchanged gifts with the Mandans throughout the winter. The chiefs slept and ate at the fort many times. The Indian women brought food to the

A view of the Missouri River in the Mandan country of North Dakota. Photo courtesy Gordon Zimmerman)

Expedition many times. The Corps was invited to participate with the Indians in the Buffalo Call Ceremony.

Lewis and Clark also gathered geographical information at Mandan. The Indians knew the territory the Expedition was about to enter, particularly the Hidatsa, who were nomadic raiders. The Captains spent time with them questioning and exploring their knowledge of the country west of the Mississippi and then evaluating what they heard. Chief Sheheke gave Clark "a sketch of the country as far as the high mountains, and on the south side of the River Rejone" (Yellowstone). If his sketch was a map it would, like most Indian maps, not be oriented on a north-south axis. They were usually oriented toward the sunrise and sunset, or sometimes simply in the direction traveled. They were invaluable, however, in providing landmarks, topographical and geographical information and estimated distances. Some of the Indians gave the Captains "charts of their ways" and vocabularies of their language, which undoubtedly were used in some way for Lewis and Clark's "Estimate of Eastern Indians." Based on the Indian information and what the Corps had seen, plus conversations with traders, Clark was able to produce some of the maps he would soon send back to Jefferson. The Indians also provided intelligence about other tribes the Corps was likely to meet on their journey.

The Mandan and Hidatsa were friendly and helpful to the Captains and Expedition, enabling them to endure a harsh winter and subsequently meet the territory ahead of them with useful information to guide them.

Chapter Two

FROM THE MANDAN TO THE MARIAS RIVER

Spring edged into the Great Plains, melting ice and nudging plants and animals awake. The men of the Expedition were anxious to be off on their westward exploration into the vast wilderness which Stephen Ambrose calls *terra incognita,* unknown land. On April 7, 1805, the keelboat, commanded by Corporal Richard Warfington and manned by the French *engages* turned downstream onto the Missouri River toward St. Louis. Aboard were valuable records of the trip so far, specimens of plants and animals, including a live prairie dog, a prairie hen and four magpies destined for President Jefferson. The red and white pirogues and six dugout canoes turned in the opposite direction against the current of the mighty Missouri. These boats carried thirty-three permanent members of the Corps of Discovery, (name given by Jefferson) including the Charbonneau family, Touissant, Sacajawea and two-month old Jean Baptiste. Captain Lewis wrote, *"This little fleet, altho'not quite so rispectable as those of Columbus or Capt. Cook, were still viewed by us with as much pleasure as those deservedly famed adventurers ever beheld theirs;......we were now about to penetrate a country at least two-thousand miles in width, on which the foot of civilized man had never trodden;...I could but esteem this moment of my departure as among the most happy of my life..."*

The powerful river kept the little flotilla alert with high and changing winds. On the 13th of April, 1805, a sudden squall nearly vanquished the white pirogue. When Charbonneau, who was at the helm, turned in the wrong direction, the pirogue almost upset, sending a shiver of fear through the party. Had the pirogue turned over, several of the party including Sacajawea and her baby would probably have drowned and important journals, instruments and supplies would have been lost. These winds were noted by Captain Clark *"dureing those winds we eat Drink & breeth...Sand."* However, wildflowers and game were abundant, and Captain Lewis remarked on the fat and succulent beaver. After transversing the Great Bend of the Missouri, the party continued upriver occasionally being helped by a friendly wind into which they could raise sail. On April 26, 1805, they reached the mouth of the river described and named by the Hidatsa Indians, the *Mee Ah-zah* (*ah-zah* meaning "river" in their language) and by the French Canadians, the *Roche Jaune* or River of Yellow Rock, the

Yellowstone. The Yellowstone River comes in from the south, is the main tributary to the Missouri and is described by David Lavender, in his book "The Way to the Western Sea," as *"truly majestic...strong and beautiful, curling lazily through a wide fertile plain streaked with magnificent stand of trees, their new leaves glistening in the sunlight."* The travelers camped and celebrated, a dram of whiskey to each person. Pierre Cruzatte, the boatman, took up his fiddle and the men danced and sang with *"much hilarity."*

Only a few miles from the junction of the Missouri and Yellowstone Rivers the Expedition entered present-day Montana. Montana historian K. Ross Toole wrote that *the Expedition traveled farther into Montana than into any other state and spent more time there than in any other area. Its most important discoveries and greatest crises occurred in Montana"* (Montana: An Uncommon Land)

Fort Union

Captain Clark noted that the confluence of the Missouri and Yellowstone Rivers "was a judicious position for the purpose of trade." In 1828, the American Fur Company, owned by John Jacob Astor, the robber baron of the fur trade, established Fort Union overlooking the junction of the two rivers. It was first called Fort Floyd, and trade was with the Assiniboins who lived on the land. The Blackfeet, who controlled the trade on the Missouri as far as the Three Forks, were allied to the British through Canada and employed a vendetta against all Americans whom they tracked and murdered when they found them on their land. However, Kenneth McKenzie, a henchman for Astor, sent Jacob Berger, who had traded for the British, to the feared Blackfeet. Berger succeeded in bringing the Blackfeet into the fort. Fort Union became a highly successful trading post employing over 100 workers until the Civil War. McKenzie, a vain dishonorable man, lived the life of royalty at the fort, served by liveried servants, partaking of expensive wines and foods and greeted by bagpipes upon entering the dining room. He entertained his visiting guests in extravagant fashion. Trade at Fort Union boomed, not only because of its geographical position, but also because McKenzie plied the Indians with alcohol even though it was illegal to do so. His homemade alcohol was doctored with river water, cayenne pepper, sage-brush, tobacco and a bit of strychnine. Thus, the Plains Indians were already in a weakened condition, when smallpox arrived on a steamboat and decimated the tribes in 1837.

As the fur-bearing animals became nearly extinct, so did Fort Union. It is now a National Historic Site. Several buildings have been reconstructed including a visitor center located in the Bourgeois House, the elegant white home of the fort's administrator. (McRae and Jewell, Montana Handbook)

From the Yellowstone to the Marias:

Captain Lewis noted that game was very abundant; deer, elk, buffalo and antelope, bear and the wolves. On April 29, 1805, the men encountered the first grizzly bear. The Hidatsa and Mandan Indians were terrified by this formidable beast and had warned the men of the monster. However, Captain Lewis was confidant that since his men were equipped with the most modern rifles the grizzly would present no problem. This particular bear was young, weighed about 300 pounds, and although he pursued Lewis for seventy to eighty yards, the captain was able to kill him. However, on May 11, 1805, William Bratton, a skilled hunter, encountered another grizzly and shot him. Bratton's grizzly did not die, but chased his attacker a considerable distance before a breathless and terrified Bratton reached the river and jumped into the safety of the pirogue. Captain Lewis immediately ordered a party to trail the bear, which they found a mile away, wounded and concealed in the brush. Lewis now concluded that he would rather fight two Indians than one bear.

Paddlefish In The Missouri

PADDLEFISH: The paddlefish is unique in that it is found only in the Missouri and Yellowstone rivers and in the Yangtze River in China. Large and flat-bellied, it is a freshwater relative of the sturgeon, looks like a shark with a long paddle-shaped snout which grows up to two feet in length and is believed to contain sensory receptors which aid in navigation and detection of plankton for food. Fossil evidence indicates the fish has existed for seventy-million years. Anglers use heavy-duty gear to snag the fish. The record catch is 142 pounds 8 ounces.

On May 14, 1805, a day so cold that moccasins froze near the fire, six hunters engaged a grizzly. Four shots struck the bear, two balls through his lungs. The enraged bear charged. More shots only slowed the bear temporarily. The men ran toward the river, pursued by the bear. Two men reached a canoe, four hid in the willows, reloaded their guns, shot and hit the bear again. The grizzly went directly toward them. Two men jumped twenty feet into the river, the bear followed. Fortunately, one of the hunters on shore aimed a direct shot into the bear's head, finally killing him. By now the party, including Captain Lewis had a deep respect for *ursus horribilis*. They named a nearby creek *"Brown Bear Defeated Creek,"* a name that did not stick. Many more encounters with grizzlies awaited them.

Game was plentiful; the men ate well. Although Sacajawea contributed edible roots "White apple, some wild licorice," a diet of nearly all meat was not healthy, and there were some indications that the men may have suffered from scurvy. Charbonneau contributed to the menu a *boudin blanc*, or white pudding, a sausage made from the intestine of the buffalo.

"That the cook makes love to, this he holds fast at one end with the right hand while with the forefinger and the thumb of the left he gently compresses it, and discharges what he says is not good to eat, but of which in the s[e]quel we get a moderate portion. About 6 feet of the lower extremity of the large gut of the Buffaloe the first morsel,,, the mustle lying underneath the shoulder blade next to the back, and fillets are next sought, these are needed up very fine with a portion of kidney suit; to this composition is then added a just proportion of pepper and salt and a small quantity of flour...all is compleatly filled with something good to eat, it is tyed to the other end, but not any cut off, for that would make the pattern too scant; it is then baptized in the missouri with two dips and a flirt, then bobbed into the kettle, for whence, after it be well boiled it is taken and fried in bears oil until it becomes brown, when it is ready to esswage the pangs of a keen appetite, or *such as travelers in the wilderness are seldom at a loss for."* – Lewis, May 9, 1805

Where were the Indians? The captains had gathered information from the Mandans and Hidatsa about the Indians inhabiting Montana. They hoped to avoid the Assiniboin who hunted in the lands bordering the Missouri and were reputed to be *"turbulent and faithless disposition"*. However, Indian sign did appear: timber rafts along the river, stick lodges and camps, a tepee pole and tepee ring, prayer cloth offerings. The Indians were around, probably watching the strangers, but they neither showed nor became a threat to the explorers. In late May some worn-out moccasins were brought to Sacajawea, who after examining them, assured the captains that they were not Shoshoni but possibly Atsina (known also as Gros Ventres). Did the Indians choose to observe the Expedition but not to encounter it? Were the travelers just lucky or, as DeVoto had observed, did news of the Teton standoff travel to these tribes who then avoided the Americans? The captains were anxious, however, to encounter the Shoshoni whom they hoped would provide horses to transport the Expedition across the mountains.

May 2, 1805. A Montana spring day. An inch of snow fell. Captain Clark mused that the green trees and flowers were covered with snow, an unusual sight for that southerner. Despite going against the river's current and transversing the sandbars, snags, sawyers and other debris, the Expedition made good time, averaging about seventeen to twenty miles a day. The captains were still confident that they would maintain their planned schedule, to reach the Pacific Coast and return to the Mandan Villages before the winter of 1805-06 set in.

As they traveled from Fort Mandan the explorers named the creeks and landmarks they discovered. Some names honored the members of the Expedition, some described an event or place on the journey. Unfortunately, few of these names have survived because of the delay in publishing the journals. On April 29, 1805, they camped on a creek they named Martha's, now called Big Muddy. Captain Lewis' dog, Seaman, caught and killed an antelope, and Captain Clark saw the first *"big- horned animal"*, the Rocky Mountain sheep.

May 3, 1805, was very cold and clear, the wind high. Sergeant Ordway reported ice. Captain Lewis named a "beautiful, bold running stream *Porcupine River* because of a large number of porcupines there. It is now called Poplar River. Clark named a tributary, "2,000 mile Creek" now called Red Water and noted that it was 1860 river miles above the mouth of the Missouri. Although wild roses were blooming the air was becoming more arid and the travelers observed alkali deposits.

Poplar, Montana, and Wolf Point, Montana

The small town of Poplar, like so many other river towns, began as a fur-trading post, expanded when the railroad went through in 1887 and is now the agency town for the Fort Peck Indian Reservation and home to a tribal community college, NAES.

Wolf Point also originated as a trading post, and provided jobs in felling trees to feed the voracious appetites of the steamboats traveling the Missouri River between Fort Benton and St. Louis. The name derives from a harsh winter in which the trappers poisoned and trapped an especially good harvest of wolves. However, the wolves froze before they could be skinned, and the trappers stacked the bodies along the river until spring. When they returned the local Indians had taken control and refused to allow the trappers to claim their booty, which became a pile of stinking carcasses and a landmark for the steamboat crews. Wolf Point is now a trading hub and also a center for the Sioux and Assinboine Indians on the Fort Peck Indian Reservation.

May 8, 1805. They passed the mouth of a river coming in from the north, near present-day Glasgow, Montana, which Captain Lewis likened to tea with milk in it, and which the Hidatsas had described and called *Ah-mah-tah,ru-shush-sher* or "The River that Scolds All Others." He named it "Milk River", a name it retains today. Lewis hoped that this river would reach beyond the 49th parallel to the Saskatchewan River in Canada and thus provide the United States claim to the rich Canadian fur trade. It did not, nor did any other rivers discovered by the explorers.

May 14, 1805, was a memorable day, one year since the Expedition had left Camp Dubois and the same day of the grizzly attack on the six hunters.

Rarely did both captains leave the fleet at the same time, but this day both were on the shore. Charbonneau was relieving Drouillard at the helm. A sudden wind struck up, hit the main sail of the boat turning it sideways and upsetting it. The captains, watching from the shore were helpless and horrified. Lewis reacted instantly and was ready to swim across the river which would have been a disaster, but fortunately, he recovered his common sense. Fortunately also, Cruzatte took charge, and while Charbonneau was crying to God for mercy, Cruzatte, shrieking like a devil, threatened to shoot him if he did not take up the tiller and right the ship. Charbonneau managed to do just that, and the pirogue made it safely to shore although almost swamped with water. Sacajawea, the heroine of the incident, while sitting in water and with baby in tow, both in danger of drowning, reached out and captured most of the articles floating in the river. Captain Lewis, who never did warm up to the young Indian mother as did Clark, later praised her, *"The Indian woman to whom I ascribe equal fortitude and resolution, with any person on board at the time of the accedent, caught and preserved most of the light articles which were washed overboard."* Lewis also declared that had the pirogue been lost he would have valued his life as little for the pirogue carried journals, instruments, maps and other valuable items. After a day like that the captains brought out the spirits and cheered the men with a gill (four fluid ounces) each.

"Burnt Lodge Creek" commemorated another adventure. On the night of May 17, 1805, the guard awakened the sleeping camp warning them of a burning tree which was about to topple onto the lodge where the two captains were sleeping in a leather tepee and with them George Drouillard and the Charbonneau family. In this way teen-age Sacajawea, the only woman in the camp, was safe, surrounded by the hunters. Quickly the men moved the tepee fifty yards away just before the tree crashed where they had been sleeping.

On May 19, 1805, Seaman, Captain Lewis' trusted and invaluable dog, swam into the river to retrieve a beaver, wounded by one of the men. The beaver bit the dog, cutting an artery. After much difficulty Captain Lewis stopped the flow of blood but feared for the life of his faithful dog. However, like the other members of the Expedition, Seaman, sturdy, healthy and spirited, survived the nearly fatal wound.

The party crossed the mouth of the Musselshell River, the name translated from the Hidatsa. This junction is now under the waters of Fort Peck Dam. A nearby creek they named for Sacajawea.

Fort Peck Dam
Fort Peck is an earth-filled dam or hydraulic fill dam and is reputed to be one of the largest in the world. In the 1930's the country was in the throes of the Great Depression. President Franklin Roosevelt through his public works

projects under the Rivers and Harbors Act spear-headed the construction of the dam by the U.S. Corps of Engineers. Its purpose was flood control, navigation, irrigation and hydroelectric generation.while also providing jobs for over 11,000 hungry desperate workers. The Fort Peck name is derived from an old Indian trading post built in 1867. After the homesteaders were evacuated and paid nearly nothing for their land, construction began: one railroad, two roads, 154 lines to transport electricity from Rainbow Dam at Great Falls. The winter of 1933-34 brought temperatures of sixty degrees below zero, but did not interrupt construction although flesh froze to metal on contact. A model town was built consisting of 261 temporary homes, twelve stores, forty-six bed hospital, school, movie theater, hotel and a military-type mall. There were also bunk-houses for the men and dormitories for the women. While the town was kept clean and safe, boom towns with names like Wheeler, Square Deal, New Deal, etc. mushroomed and provided gambling and bawdy entertainment for the workers.

One-hundred thirty million cubic yards of dirt were removed and replaced with four million cubic yards of gravel and 1.6 million cubic yards of riprap to establish the dam's embankment. Four tunnels were constructed underground, each a mile long, a herculean task. Each tunnel can carry twice the normal flow of the river and divert the river's water around the dam. The reservoir can store nineteen million acre feet of water, and its tributaries above the dam drain an area equivalent to the states of Virginia, Maryland and Delaware combined. The dam inundates much of the river trail of the Expedition and covers the mouth of the Musselshell River. It is 150 miles long and offers some of the best recreation in eastern Montana. In September, 1938, an inspection crew noted an irregularity. Within minutes railroad lines began to heave, timbers groaned and cracks appeared. The center core pool of the dam was settling. The dam broke. One hundred and eighty workers ran for their lives over the shifting mass. Eight men died; two are still buried under the dam. The decision to complete the dam involved major risk, but the risk was taken; the dam stands. The American Society of Civil Engineers has named Fort Peck Dam a National Civil Engineering Historical Landmark.

Early in May Captain Lewis had described the land as "...*butiful beyond description*," and even Patrick Gass wrote "*beautiful on both sides of the river.* But as the party entered the last days of May, they also entered the Missouri River Breaks, a section of the Missouri River that has earned the designation, "A Wild and Scenic River." High bluffs overlooked the river; the air was very dry. This was a tortuous journey for the men who pulled the pirogue and canoes over jutting rock, sandbars, and rapids often in ice cold water up to their waists. The wind hampered them, and their feet were cut and bruised. David Lavender aptly referred to these struggling men as *"human draft horses."* Lewis wrote that their labor was incredibly painful and great, but that they were faithful and bore it without a murmur. Clark called it *"the Deserts of America."* Lewis described it as a *"desert barren country,"* and Sergeant Gass wrote, *"the most dismal country I ever beheld."* These are the badlands of the Missouri River Breaks, an area rich in history and probably one of the least changed scenic trails over which the Expedition passed.

The Missouri River Breaks

The Upper Missouri National Wild and Scenic River is a 149 mile stretch of the Missouri River between Fort Peck Lake and Fort Benton. It is bordered by scenic white cliffs and badlands and is the only major portion of river protected and preserved in its natural free-flowing state. It is administered by the Bureau of Land Management.

As the Judith Basin in Central Montana opened up, large ranches were established, and gold was discovered. Thieves and rustlers such as Butch Cassidy and The Hole in the Wall Gang led by Kid Curry, followed, pushing stolen cattle into Canada and back. They would then disappear into the inaccessible badlands of the Missouri River Breaks. The hold these frontier outlaws had upon the territory was finally broken by Granville Stuart and the vigilantes.

"...Game is becoming more scarce," wrote Captain Lewis on May 24, 1805 *"particularly beaver, of which we have seen but few for several days the beaver appears to keep pace with the timber as it declines in quantity they also become more scarce".* Seaman became the hero of the Expedition on May 25, 1805, when a bull buffalo swam across the river, hauled himself over the white pirogue and headed for the camp, tramping within inches of the heads of the sleeping men. The sentry yelled out, and the bull veered toward the leather tepee. Seaman barked wildly at the dangerous animal, and it veered to the right and disappeared.

The same day Captain Clark reported to Captain Lewis that while he was walking he had observed mountains on either side of the river covered with snow and shining in the sun. "The Land of the Shining Mountains", a title aptly given to the state of Montana. The next day Lewis climbed to the highest part of the area and confessed to *"secret pleasure"* when he thought that he was so close to the headwaters of the *"heretofore conceived boundless Missouri."* Lewis reflected on the fact that these *"snowey barriers"* would present difficulties *"but as I have always held it a crime to anticipate evils I will believe it a good comfortable road untill I am compelled to believe differently."*

Charles M. Russell National Wildlife Refuge

Fort Peck is also the northern gateway to the Charles M. Russell National Wildlife Refuge, a million acre range habitat for big horn sheep, pronghorns, deer, coyote and elk, the only place in Montana where elk abound in their native prairie all year round. This sanctuary is also home to over 200 species of birds, also reptiles, fish and prairie dog towns. Everything that Lewis and Clark saw is there except the grizzlies which are now found in the western part of the state, and the Audubon subspecies of bighorn sheep.

Antelope.

A terrible stench assaulted the noses of the party on May 29, 1805, as they passed stacks of rotting buffalo carcasses being devoured by wolves. Captain Lewis suspected that they had come upon a *Pishkun* or buffalo jump where the Indians drove herds of bison over a cliff to their death and then salvaged the meat, skins, and bones. However, archeologists who have studied the site have concluded that these buffalo had drowned when the ice broke up, and the carcasses had been washed up on shore by the spring runoff. Captain Clark walked among the greedy wolves which were feeding upon the carcasses. The wolves were so glutted they paid no attention to him. He killed one by thrusting his espontoon through its ribs and into its heart. The creek nearby was named *Slaughter Creek*, now known as Arrow Creek. This is the only known "double-campsite" of the Expedition in Montana. May 29, 1805 and Lewis and party, July 19, 1806.

The river opened up, and as the party passed the White Cliffs, Captain Lewis described the awesome spectacle on May 31st, 1805. Here the nearly perpendicular cliffs of white sandstone and the figures formed by the elements, he portrayed as *"1,000 grotesque figures...elegant buildings... pyramids,...nitches and alcoves of various forms and sizes,... parapets with well-stocked statuary, vast ranges of walls of tolerable workmanship, so perfect indeed are those walls that I should have thought that nature had attempted to rival the human art of masonry had I not recollected that she had first begun her work."*

A romantic note on the journey was sounded when Captain Clark named a pretty clear sparkling river which emptied into the Missouri from the south, *"Judieth,"* after Miss Julia Hancock, who three years later would become Mrs. William Clark. This river is still called the Judith River.

But now a worrisome note appeared in Clark's journal. Sacajawea was very ill.

Until desecrated by unknown vandals in 1998, the Eye of the Needle along the upper Missouri River had stood for eons and was renowned as one of the most incredible views to be found along the entire length of the Missouri. (Photo by Pat Hastings)

Upper Missouri Attracted World-Class Artists

Europeans were fascinated by the American West. One of them was Prince Maximilian Wied Neuweid, a Prussian and a naturalist who came to the West to study the animals, some of the land's physical aspects, and the Indians. He brought with him a young Swiss artist, Karl Bodmer (1809-1893). Bodmer, like George Catlin before him, sketched and painted Indians from his own observations and experiences. He and Prince Maxmilian lived at Fort Clark for six months in 1833 and later at Fort McKenzie in the heart of Blackfeet country. During that time he produced over four hundred watercolors and sketches which he later turned into exquisite polychromic engravings to illustrate the two volume book or atlas, "Travels in the Interior of North America," written by Prince Maximilian.

Bodmer was a precise draftsman. His pictures are characterized by exceptional thoroughness, detail, and study. They are ethnological in scope and a significant record of the Missouri frontier. Not only did he sketch and paint the Indians, their daily life, customs and dress, but he also captured the landscape of the West – studies of the country side, the mountains, rivers, and terrain. He portrayed them with such accuracy that the terrain in his paintings is still identifiable today.

George Catlin (1796-1872) was American born (Wilkes Barre, Pennsylvania). He was personally motivated to capture the Indians and their culture for posterity. After traveling eight years in the West he painted leaders of forty tribes and their family members. His sketches and paintings captured facial likeness and detailed their clothing, adornments, and the distinguishing details of the various tribes leaving a comprehensive account of Indian tribes from the Great Plains to the Rocky Mountains. Catlin was the first to record the yearly ceremony, the okeepa, of the Mandans. He painted hunting scenes, Indian warfare, their daily life, and camp scenes. He wanted to produce "the literal and graphic delineation of the living manner and custom of an interesting race of people" who were being swept away by disease, war, and white settlement. For his study of western Indians Catlin used sketches and both watercolor and oil medium. He also wrote about his life among the Indians, publishing his "Letters and Notes on the Manners, Customs, and Conditions of the North American Indians" and also the "North American Indian Portfolio."

Bodmer and Catlin were the final recorders of some Indians. Their work gives us insight on a life and culture of the West that can no longer be found. Later artists who were born too late and missed that time period used their work as a reference.

The list of artists who painted the West is long. A few are:

•James Audubon (1785-1851) made American birds known to the world. He left a legacy of diverse plant and animal life painted in true color, in their natural setting, and scaled to life. His "Bird of America" and five volumes of "Ornithological Biography" were published, and part of his "Viviparous Quadrupeds of America" was completed before he became medically unable. The artist's bust is in the Hall of Fame of Great Americans. Carved on the plaque beneath are his words, "The production of nature...became my playmates...I felt that an intimacy with them...must

accompany my steps through life."

    •Paul Kane (1810-1871) painted Indians on both sides of the Rockies and produced some very significant works.

    •Alfred J. Miller (1810-1874) painted some important western events. The body of his work is largely romantic rather than scientific like Bodmer and Catlin's.

    •Edgard S. Paxson (1852-1919) painted almost without exception frontier subjects, historic events, and people involved in those events. He produced thirteen paintings of the Lewis and Clark Expedition, and four of Sacajawea. His most famous work is "Custer's Last Stand." During his life he made at least two thousand paintings – washes, oils, watercolors and "en grisaille" illustrations.

    •Joseph H. Sharp (1859-1953) painted Montana Indians in their daily life and routines documenting a culture in transition.

    •Olaf Seltzer (1877-1957) researched and recreated the Indian world of the past. Accuracy of detail was very important to him. He was greatly influenced by C. M. Russell.

    •Charles M. Russell (1877-1957) spent a lifetime sketching and painting scenes of western life. Many of his paintings express the drama of Plain's Indian life which he portrayed with compassion and realism. He lived with the Blackfeet (Bloods) during a winter, learning their language, customs, legends, stories, and religious rituals. He also visited and became friends with other western tribes, a fact reflected in the authentic detail of his paintings and sculptures that reveal features and items distinguishing various tribes. He painted the buffalo many times, as did Catlin and others, showing its importance in the Indian's life. Russell respected Native Americans and captured some of their spirit and lifestyle on canvas, his work usually telling a story rather than portraying a specific occurrence. He was considered the greatest painter of western art during the later part of his life.

Chapter Three

DECISION AT THE MARIAS

The Expedition was now in for a surprise, a puzzle that would delay and divide the men from their captains. A large full-flowing river joined the Missouri on the north side forming a junction at present-day Loma, Montana. This river had not been mentioned neither by the Hidatsa nor the Mandans, who had been correct, to this point on the river, on all the information they had given the captains. Their informers had been emphatic about a great falls on the Missouri River. When the white men found these falls it was a sure sign they were on the river which would bring them into the land of Sacajawea's people, the Shoshone. Of course the Hidatsa knew this territory. Did they not periodically hunt and raid the Shoshone of their people and their horses? What they did not mention was that at some point these plains Indians, who did not travel by water, rode their horses overland to the hunting grounds. Now, however, the captains were puzzled. Which river was the Missouri? And what was the other? Should they take the wrong fork, the delay would probably cost them all of the summer, and they could be stranded over the winter. A wrong decision could also cost the leaders the confidence of their men. The northern fork was muddied and roiling and resembled the Missouri they knew and on which they had been traveling for months. The southern fork was clear, rippled over smooth rocks, a sign to the captains that it had originated in the mountains. But Pierre Cruzatte, the experienced old riverman, was adamant that they should follow the north fork, and to a man the members agreed with Cruzatte. The captains pored over maps, analyzed their observations, weighed the evidence and came up with a joint decision. The south fork was the Missouri. However, they were judicious leaders who did not arbitrarily make a choice in conflict with their men. Consequently, the captains decided to send two scouting parties on one-day observations of both forks. They returned with no conclusive evidence. What now?

On June 4, 1805, Captain Clark, with Joseph and Reuben Fields, Sergeant Gass, George Shannon, the youngest member of the party, and Clark's servant, York, proceeded up the southern fork. Captain Lewis took with him, George Drouillard, Sergeant Pryor, Shields, Windsor, Cruzatte and LePage and ascended the north fork. The parties were to explore for a day and a half and return to camp. Captain Clark traveled forty-five miles upstream where he observed the *snowey* mountains, the Highwood Mountains to the southeast, and later the Big and Little Belts to the southwest and saw that the river was running swift and deep. He had seen enough. This was the Missouri as it " *ran south of west a long distance and had a strong rapid current.*" A dangerous encounter with a grizzly nearly cost Joseph Fields his life. *"So near that it struck his foot."* Clark and his men turned back to camp on June 5, 1805. Had he proceeded another ten miles Clark would have been the first to see the great falls of the Missouri.

Captain Lewis and his party travelled fifty-nine miles upstream of the north fork, a miserable and dangerous journey, as the rain had turned the clay soil

---

The American Bison

BUFFALO, MAINSTAY OF THE NATIVE AMERICAN: defined as genus, bison, a large shaggy-maned wild ox with short horns and heavy forequarters with a large muscular hump. The buffalo was the lifeblood of the American Indian. When the buffalo, which held a sacred place in Indian civilization was hunted to near extinction, the Indian lost not only his food supply but the increments of his culture. The cumbersome shaggy animal provided: Food, shelter, clothing, ceremonial ornaments and vessels, bedding, spoons, tools, thread, ornaments, jewelry, horse trappings, toys, jewelry, cradles, pouches, quivers, shields, belts and bands, drums and sticks, ropes and thongs, cinches and saddles, stirrups, quirts, splints, bull boats, weapons, powderhorn, medicine bags, sleds, medicine balls, pillows, whips and switches, fuel, glue, rattles, basins, fishooks, dice. etc.

LaBarge Rock stands as a sentinel among towering white cliffs, whose reflections literally shimmer, along a stunning beautiful wild section of the upper Missouri River. (Photo by Pat Hastings)

into gumbo, so slippery and greasy that footholds were precarious. Lewis, by his methodical observations and shrewd analysis, determined that this river was too far north to be the route to the Pacific. However, with gallantry he named it *Maria's* in honor of his cousin, Maria Woods. On the return both he and Private Windsor nearly lost their lives, Captain Lewis slipped on the edge of a bluff and only saved himself from a ninety-foot drop over a precipice with the help of his espontoon. He had barely reached a point where he could safely stand and was still shaken from this experience when he heard a cry. "Good God! Captain, what shall I do?" Windsor was dangling over a precipice and grabbing on to the edge by his left arm and left foot to keep himself from falling to his death below. Captain Lewis, with great presence of mind, spoke deliberately and calmly to the frightened Windsor, instructing him to reach for his knife with his right hand and dig a foothole into the bank for his right foot. The young soldier did so and was then able to climb on his knees to safety. Another very close call.

The party returned to camp two days late, exhausted and still not in accord as to which river was the Missouri. The captains did not take a vote, as they were absolutely sure that the south fork was the right one to take, but to a man the others in the corps agreed with Pierre Cruzatte that they should take the north fork. However, in tribute to their captains' leadership, the men agreed that they were ready to follow their leaders even though they were convinced that the captains were wrong. Lewis and Clark then determined to split the party again. Why? John L. Allen states that although the co-captains were assured that their conclusions were correct, it was important for them to maintain the confidence of their men. Captain Lewis would proceed on foot up the south fork in search of the Great Falls of the Missouri. Captain Clark, because he was the better waterman, would follow with the remainder of the party including a very sick Sacajawea. On the night of June 9, 1805, Lewis recorded that the men, after a draft of grog, were cheerful and danced and sang to Cruszatte's fiddling. What *esprit de corps!*

Note: The Marias River is not quite as significant as the Missouri, but during spring run-off when the Corps of Discovery observed it, the river was at peak stage. During any other season it would not have been so big as to be a challenge, although Tiber Dam now sits across the Marias River and controls its waters for irrigation.

Loma
Fort Peigan, a trading post was established here at the junction of the two rivers in 1831 by James Kipp of the American Fur Company. However, it lasted only one year when it was burned by the Indians and was replaced by Fort McKenzie. At Loma a ferryboat crossed the river for many years and a post office was opened in 1911. A highway sign reads, "Take a Break: Lewis

and Clark did in 1805."

For ten days the corps camped at the junction of the two rivers, mending their clothes and moccasins, nursing their bruised and bleeding feet, hiding the red pirogue and preparing a cache of goods to lighten the load. On June 10, 1805, Captain Clark reported that Sacajawea was very sick. After treating her to the best of his knowledge, and seeing no improvement he was anxious to release her to Captain Lewis' ministrations.

During this time the captains had been taking observations, studying and redrawing their maps, conferring together and coming to their decision; the south fork on the left was the Missouri. Consequently, they determined to proceed upriver, searching and expecting to find the Great Falls of the Missouri which were the undeniable characteristic of that river. Although Captain Lewis was suffering from a severe case of dysentery, he, with Drouillard, Gibson, Goodrich and Joseph Fields, set out by land to follow the south fork until they reached the Great Falls. Captain Clark, the better waterman, would conduct the remaining party members up the river, carrying their supplies and the very ill Sacajawea.

Point Decision, the junction of the Missouri and Marias Rivers near Loma, Montana. This was an important location for the Expedition on both its upriver journey in 1805 and on its return journey in 1806. Here the Missouri flows eastward, away from the photo point, while the Marias comes in from the left on the north side of the Missouri. (Photo by Pat Hastings)

June 11, 1805, Captain Lewis and his men set out, but after traveling about nine miles the captain became so violently ill that he could not continue. Ever ingenious, Lewis doctored himself with what was at hand, a concoction made from the bark of chokecherry, and did so successfully. On June 12, he and his men walked twenty-seven miles, an incredible hike for a man still weak from his previous day's illness. Lewis described a beautiful and picturesque view of the mountains, today's Big Belt and Little Belt ranges, covered with snow, an *"august spectacle"*. He also recorded *" more buffalo than he had ever seen before at a single view."* The men ate well with venison and fresh fish caught by that enthusiastic fisherman, Silas Goodrich.

June 13, 1805, was a most memorable day. On this day Captain Lewis walked ahead of the men, heard the roar of falling water, saw the spray ascending like smoke – and then before him, the Great Falls of the Missouri. He traveled seven miles after first hearing the sound before reaching the falls and then sat *"on some rocks under the centre of the falls, enjoyed the sublime spectacle of this stupendous object which since the creation had been lavishing its magnificence upon the desert, unknown to civilization."* That day he sat for hours just relishing the astonishing spectacle before him, and that evening after a sumptuous meal he wrote pages of description. The description of the Falls as written by Meriwether Lewis in the Journals is well worth reading by anyone interested in the Expedition, particularly in Montana. These falls, which for many years were spectacular in their natural beauty, will never be seen again for "progress" deemed them expendable in the name of hydroelectric power as they are now submerged or altered by the waters of Ryan Dam, an electricity- producing project of the Montana Power Company

---

Ryan Dam

The Ryan development, originally called Volta, is one of three early developments on the Missouri River near Great Falls (the others were Black Eagle, 1890-91 and Rainbow 1910). Ryan was completed in 1915 and named for John D. Ryan, first president of the Montana Power Company. The purpose of these dams was to provide electrical energy to the copper mines in Butte, Montana which were developed in response to the demand for copperwire caused by the spread of electrical technology in the United States and Europe. Although electricity had become available in the early 1880's, its use was limited until long-distance transmission technology became accessible in the mid 1890's. Other Montana Power Dams built on the Great Falls of the Missouri River are the Morony (1930) and the Cochrane (1958).

On June 14th, 1805, Joseph Fields was sent downriver to Captain Clark with a note dated "the great falls of the Missouri." Leaving the men to hunt and fish and to dry jerky in preparation for the arrival of Clark and the remaining party, Captain Lewis preceeded to go *"for a walk"* and observe what lay beyond the Great Falls. To his amazement there were five waterfalls in all extending over ten miles with rapids in between and bordered on each side with cliffs 150 to 200 feet high. He observed a small island covered with timber in which a tall cottonwood tree housed an eagle's nest. Ah! ha! The eagles nest described to him by the Hidatsas. When he climbed a hill which would someday support a smelter in the city of Great Falls, he observed the river which the Hidatsas had described and named Medicine River, the present-day Sun River. The Missouri then stretched to the south where flocks of geese swam and rested in the cool waters fed by mountain streams, while numerous herds of buffalo grazed on the bordering plains.

The Blackfeet

The Blackfeet are of Algonkin origin. There are three divisions or tribes of Blackfeet, the Piegan (PAY-gan), the Bloods and the Siksika. (Confusingly, Siksika is also the Blackfeet or nation proper, in addition to being a tribe.) Their territory at the time of the Lewis and Clark Expedition was in the northwest corner of the Great Plains. It was extensive, covering an area of approximately 140,000 square miles (in north-central Montana abutting the Rocky Mountains eastward, with a great portion being in Canada). The territory bordered on the main range of the Rockies, which was its western boundary. The waters of the Milk, Marias and Sun Rivers flowed through the territory, making it the richest beaver country in the West. The fertile mountain foothills were rich with timber and wildlife, good for raising horses and well supplied with buffalo. The Marias River Valley was about the center of the territory, which the Blackfeet protected and called their own.

The Blackfeet were a dominant military power, and were called names such as hostile, bloodthirsty and fear inspiring. They were feared by their neighboring tribes and were unwavering in their animosity to white trappers. Interlopers within their territory ,whether white or Indian, were met with hostility. They twice forced American trapping companies to abandon enterprises attempted within their region. They were the only tribe with whom the Corps of Discovery fought. Two young Blackfeet braves were killed in the encounter, and some historians feel that incident set the tone for following hostilities toward American trade companies and trappers.

The Blackfeet were nomadic buffalo hunters and part of the plains culture. They were not agricultural, but they gathered wild fruits and vegetables to supplement their diet. They owned many horses and acquired guns from the British sooner than many tribes, enabling them to become a dominant force on the plains. As part of the plains culture, they lived in skin covered tipis, dressed in clothing made from dressed skins of buffalo and deer, and used every part of the buffalo for some aspect of their daily living. Their tipis were painted and decorated. Many of their daily-used items were decorated with beadwork by the women, who were also skilled in porcupine quill embroidery.

The Blackfeet were an independent, disciplined people who operated under democratic leadership and government. Their leaders were dignified and the business-like manner of the camp's operation impressed traders who witnessed it. Artists Karl Bodmer, George Catlin and Paul Kane painted depictions of Blackfeet society, life and clothing as well as portraits of their leaders.

The Blackfeet held onto their territory under constant aggressive pressure from other Indians and white traders until gold was discovered in the 1850s, bringing the railroad, more settlers, missionaries, disease and illicit whiskey trading. Three epidemics of smallpox caused the loss of three-fourths of their population.

They are now on a Reservation to the east of Glacier National Park, which overlooks part of their ancient territory. The headquarters are in Browning, Montana.

Captain Lewis was now in for some harrowing experiences. After shooting a buffalo for his dinner, the captain neglected to reload his gun. Suddenly he saw a bear approaching within twenty feet. The Captain turned to run, the bear pursued him, he jumped into the river and turned upon the advancing bear with his espontoon, pointing at the animal. The bear appeared frightened, turned away and retreated. Experience is the best of teachers. Never again would Captain Meriwether Lewis not reload his gun immediately after firing it.

His next adventure occurred shortly afterwards as he was returning to camp, which was about twelve miles away. What he at first thought was a wolf was in reality *"of the tiger kind,"* possibly a wolverine, a crouching animal about to attack. Lewis raised his rifle, shot, missed, but frightened the animal away. At this he was somewhat disturbed with himself for having missed the shot, but turned and went on. A short time later as he was passing the buffalo herd, three buffalo bulls disengaged themselves and came running full force at him. He turned around and advanced toward them. What nerves of steel! President Jefferson did not misjudge the young man he chose to lead this Expedition. The bulls stopped, gazed at him awhile and then retreated. As if that were not enough adventure, the next morning Lewis looked up at the tree under which he was sleeping and gazed into the eyes of a rattlesnake coiled above him. He killed it and described *"176 scuta on the abdomen, and 17 half-formed scuta on the*

Espontoon

An espontoon is a spear six feet or more in length. Its wooden shaft is an inch and a quarter in diameter and is tipped with a foot-long metal blade. It was still in use in the late eighteenth century as a symbol of authority for infantry officers. It was customary to erect the espontoon outside the tent door as a sign that the officer was "at home". (A lantern known as a "lant horn" could have been hanging from it. This is a pierced tin lantern which contains a "window" made of a thin slice of animal horn). Both Lewis and Clark considered the espontoon a practical implement on the Expedition. They also used it at various times as a weapon, walking staff and rifle support.

tail." What a frontiersman! Who else is recorded as having stared down a pursuing bear, stopped three advancing buffalo, frightened away an attacking wolverine and then slept under the watchful eyes of a rattlesnake? All in one day. Another series of incredible "almosts."

Meanwhile, Captain Clark and the remaining party were advancing upstream in the white pirogue and the six dugout canoes. Traveling was tortuous. Both Sergeants Gass and Ordway agreed *"the most rapid water I ever saw craft taken through"*. Rocks and dangerous rapids impeded their way. Men struggled in icy water, their feet cut and bruised again by sharp and slippery rocks which threw them down. And then there were the rattlesnakes, many rattlesnakes. Clark wrote of incredible fatigue, days that tried mens' souls. He also fretted about Sacajawea, who was growing weaker and more listless.

On June 13, 1805, the little caravan passed the site where the town of Fort Benton is now located..

Fort Benton

Fort Benton was founded by Alexander Culbertson, for whom the town of Culbertson was named, in 1846 as an American Fur Trading Post and claims to be the "birthplace of Montana." It was first named Fort Lewis for Captain Meriwether Lewis and eventually renamed for Senator Thomas Benton. Steamboats were coming up the Missouri by 1850, and in the 1860's Fort Benton was the most important transportation center in the Northwest, supplying not only the U.S. but also Canada. Steamboats docked at Fort Benton. Freight was loaded onto huge wagons pulled by mules and oxen and transported to Idaho, Washington and Alberta. The town ended as a transportation center with the coming of the railway in the 1880's. The area prospers with cattle, sheep and wheat. Fort Benton is unusually creative in preserving its historic past.

On the river front is a sculpture by the late Bob Scriver of Browning, Montana, which depicts Captains Lewis and Clark and Sacajawea. Named "Explorers at the Marias." it is the official Lewis and Clark monument marking the U.S. Bicentennial, 1976.

Also on the river front is a Scriver sculpture of Shep, perhaps the best known of Fort Benton's characters. Shep was a sheepherder's dog that accompanied the body of his master to the railroad station to be shipped East for burial. He stayed there, meeting every train year after year, and became famous when his story was pieced together. Shep's vigil ended when he slipped on the tracks of an incoming train in 1942. He was granted a town funeral complete with "Eulogy on the Dog" and was buried on a bluff above the railroad station. Although Shep appeared to be collie, his statue is reminiscent of Captain Lewis' dog, Seaman.

June 14, 1805, Joseph Fields arrived with a welcome message from Captain Lewis, a confirmation which must have cheered Captain Clark and the struggling men. Captain Lewis had also instructed his co-captain to bring the

This display in the Ag Museum in Fort Benton, Montana, on the banks of the Missouri River in north-central Montana, presents a dynamic view of the buffalo, the American bison. (Photo by Pat Hastings)

The official Montana state statue commemorating the Lewis & Clark Expedition, by the late sculptor Bob Scriver, is located in Fort Benton, Montana. (Photo by Pat Hastings)

boats upriver as far as they could go and establish a camp, which became Upper Portage Camp about two miles below the mouth of Portage Creek, now called Belt Creek. In the journals of Sergeant Gass and Private Whitehouse, a creek coming in from the southeast is called *Strawberry Creek*; Captain Clark called it *Shields Creek* after gunsmith and blacksmith, John Shields. Now it is known as Highwood Creek.

When the two captains met on June 16 at the base of the falls, Lewis had much to tell his good friend of the observations he had made and the adventures he had experienced in the past three days. There were five falls in all and the portage that they understood the Hidatsa to say was *"no more than half a mile"* would be eighteen and a half miles. What news to break upon the exhausted and battered boatmen!

Great Falls, Montana

The city of Great Falls once lay under 600 feet of water of Glacial Lake Great Falls formed by sheets of glacial ice 15,000 years ago. The area was in control of the Blackfeet Indians when the Corps of Discovery camped there and made the grueling portage in 1805. The city itself, however, was built in the 1880's by Paris Gibson, who recognized its strategic location on the confluence of the Missouri and Sun Rivers. Gibson met with James J. Hill of the Great Northern Railway and consequently a railway was built in 1887 which connected Great Falls to the Montana mines to the south. In 1908 the Anaconda Company built its copper reduction plant at Black Eagle, utilizing the electricity generated at Black Eagle Dam.

From then on Great Falls, the "Electric City," became an industrial town and also a major trade center for the farms and ranches in the area. It is also the home of Malmstrom Air Force Base, from which fields of nuclear missiles, weapons of annihilation, which are buried in silos in central Montana, are controlled.

The Charles M. Russell Museum is also located here, a tribute to the cowboy artist who lived and painted here while documenting the early days of Montana, its wildlife, its cowboys, and its Indians.

In 1998 the stunning Lewis and Clark National Historic Trail Interpretive Center opened on the banks of the Missouri River east of the city. The six million dollar center features displays and exhibits which follow the trail of the Expedition from St. Louis to the Pacific and the return.. Special exhibits include replicas of the boats, the clothing, the Indian villages, the portage, the animals plants, landmarks, and other points of interest encountered by the Expedition. The Great Falls Interpretive Center is now the national center for the Lewis and Clark Heritage Foundation.

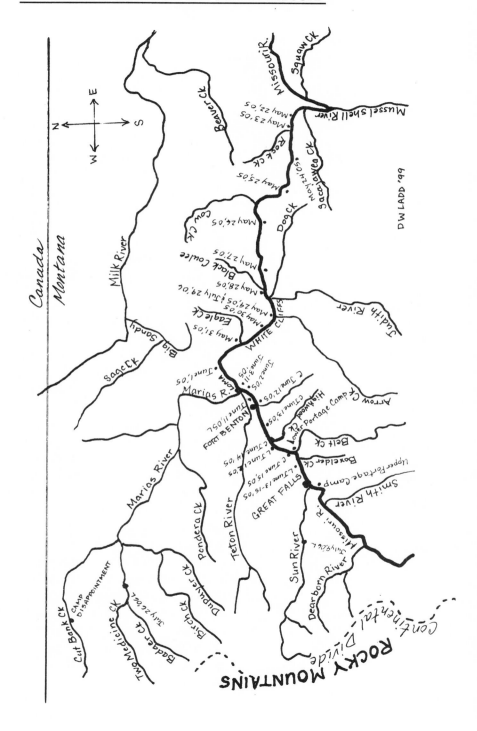

Chapter Four

DOCTORING ON THE TRAIL

After leaving Mandan, the Corps of Discovery faced new challenges, not the least of these were the increased physical activity and diet changes that brought about breakdown to the immune system. Many times over the course of their journey, although physically and emotionally exhausted, circumstances dictated that they pressed themselves to the extreme. As a result dysentery, boils, abscesses were some examples of increasing physical problems.

An example of dysentery, and how resourceful Meriwether Lewis was, is when he was reconnoitering with a small party of his men, trying to decide which river was the Missouri. Lewis had been ill for a few days with dysentery but this time he was in so much pain he was unable to continue. Because they were away from the main group they carried no medicine of any kind with them, and he was miserable. Meriwether remembered his childhood in Virginia, and how his mother, Lucy, a herbalist, had taught him the healing powers of herbs, "simples", as it was known then. From his bed of willow boughs he could see chokecherries in abundance. Captain Lewis had his men gather some of the branches of chokecherries bushes, strip the branches of leaves, break the larger ones into two inch twigs, then boil the twigs. When a strong brew resulted, it was ready for him to try. Meriwether drank a pint of the bitter tea at sunset, and another dose an hour later. He was relieved of pain, broke out in a mild sweat, and had a comfortable night's rest. After taking another pint of the chokecherry tea that morning, he and his fellow travelers walked twenty seven miles before returning to the main camp.

chokecherry

Jean Clary

Dysentery is described in the dictionary as a disease attended with inflamation of the large intestine, gripping pains, and a constant desire to evacuate the bowels. In an article in *Scientific Monthly* of 1925, written by Dr. J. Howard Beard, the usual treatment was a dose of Glauber Salts. In severe cases thirty five drops of laudanum was given. Sometimes, according to the same authority, emesis, meaning a substance to induce vomiting, was employed. Clark gave York a dose of tartar emetic on one occasion that he noted in his journal, "which operated very well and he was much better this evening". In Lewis's account of the same event he noted, he only used the tartar in cases of intermittent fever.

Boils, furuncles and abscesses were not only the result of a diet lacking vegetables and fruit, but also their skin was constantly being broken. Abscesses were called "imposthumes" in the journals, and poultices were the treatment of choice for these. The poultices consisted of whatever material was at hand, boiled, and placed between two cloths, then applied to the affected area .

Wild ginger and wild onion were some of the materials used for these poultices, as well as Peruvian bark, a staple in their medicine chest. The reason poultices were used was to increase suppuration and discharge of the core. Hot packs are used today in medicine with the same purpose in mind, so the boil can be lanced and drained. Doctors in this day and age can rely on antibiotics if conventional medicine fails.

wild onion
from Clary

The Corps of Discovery had worn out their boots before reaching the upper Missouri River, and the moccasins they had to rely on were poor protection against bruises from rocks and stones, and penetration by the accursed cactus. Not only poor protection, but they spent so much of their time in canoes and piroques, their feet were tender, without protective calluses. In July of 1805 Clark reported in his journal that he removed seventeen prickly pear thorns from his feet!

After speaking with health care providers, we can conclude that diarrhea is still a problem, in spite of all our modern medicine and scientific knowledge. Treatment for mild cases is dietary; no dairy foods are on the menu, no high fat foods at all, mostly clear liquids are advised, and lots of them, to prevent dehydration. For severe cases, a visit to the doctor and finding out the cause is advised. We can conclude that in the case of the Lewis and Clark people, poorly cooked food, spoiled meat, and lack of any sanitation would be other reasons for their abdominal problems.

Indian Breadroot
Jean Clary

About the tenth of June, Sacagawea became very ill. Lewis was not in the main camp, so Clark had been doctoring her. He had tried bleeding her, and applying a poultice of Peruvian Bark and laudanum on the pelvic area, the area where she had the most pain.

Bleeding, or blood letting, was a common practice and cure-all at the time, a procedure consisting of piercing a vein and allowing blood to drain out of the body. *"3 best lancets"* are on the list of medical supplies taken on the journey and were most likely used for bleeding in situations like this one involving Sacajawea.

None of these treatments had any positive affect, so Captain Clark was glad to turn her treatment over to Meriwether Lewis. She had a high fever, a faint pulse, her breathing was irregular, and most alarming of all, she began twitching her fingers and arms. Lewis examined Sacagawea more thoroughly, and came to the conclusion that she was no longer menstruating. He gave her "two dozes of bark and opium" which made her a bit better, when her thirst became obvious, he gave her some sulfur water to drink, and her twitching improved. The mineral water must have restored some of her electrolytes, and the poultices helped relieve her discomfort. By evening of that day, Sacagawea was much improved.

She had been very ill for nearly a week by this time. It is probably safe to conclude that Sacagawea had contracted gonorrhea from the time she had spent with the Hidatsas. The following morning, she walked out on the plains, dug and ate great quantities of the White Apple, by that evening she was again very sick. Lewis was angry with her, he had made clear to both her and her husband what foods she should eat, and the white apple was not one of them. He then gave her small amounts of salt peter (a diuretic and diaphoretic, for reducing fevers and gonorrhea) and later that night he gave her some laudanum. She slept well, and was on the road to recovery.

The White Apple

The white apple or Indian Breadfruit, scientific name Psoralea esulenta Pursh, was an important food to the Indian people of eastern Montana. It was called white apple by the French Engages, (Pomme blanche or pomme de prairie), or apple of the prairie. The bulb portion is usually found about four inches below the surface, sometimes deeper. They are good all seasons of the year, but best mid-July to late fall. The bulbs are gathered for winter use, stripped of their rind and strung on small cords and exposed to the sun to dry, or they are placed near the fire to dry by smoke. When used dry, they are pounded between two rocks until they are powdered and then used to thicken soup. The dried white apple will keep several years unless exposed to dampness. Sometimes the dry product is cooked whole with meat. When fresh, they are boiled with meat, or boiled, mashed, and added to marrow grease of the buffalo along with berries, cooked until all is the consistency of hasty pudding or mash. It is also eaten roasted and often raw. Bears have been known to dig it up and eat it as part of their diet. Information about the white apple was gleaned from page 61 of Montana Native Plants and Early Peoples written by Jeff Hart and illustrated by Jacqueline Moore, and Thwaite's Lewis and Clark Journals.

Both syphilis and gonorrhea were endemic among the native Americans, and because of the favors the men of the Corps of Discovery received, both diseases began to surface among them. Syphilis was treated with mercury, calomel or mercurous chloride, and was given orally, both as a laxative and syphilis treatment. Clyster syringes, (used for penile injections and enemas) were in the medicine chest of the Corps. The penile syringes were used for urethral irrigation for gonorrhea. One cringes to think of specifics.

Throughout the journals, both officers treated native Americans for sore eyes. It's true that eye irritation can be caused by wind and dust, also ultraviolet keratitis, precipitatd by the reflection of the sun on the water. Most likely, the severe cases of blindness and sore eyes originated from gonorrhea since its prevalence was so widespread. Dr. Beard states, "Lewis reports the presence of Neisserian infection (gonorrhea) and lues (syphilis) among the many tribes of Indians in the country through which he passed. As syphilis was common among them and developed without treatment, luetic inflamation and degeneration of the eye were undoubtedly factors in the great impairment of sight recorded by Lewis and Clark.

Sexually Transmitted Disease

In the days of Lewis and Clark, the term for sexually transmitted disease was Social Disease. Lewis repeatedly observed the presence of venereal disease and its terrible consequences among the native Americans and subsequently, his men. The word "venereal" is taken from the Greek goddess of love, Venus. The Indian people had no effective way of treatment, and it was pretty much out of control, gonorrhea and syphilis were the main diseases, and mercury was the specific treatment. Mercury itself was not without dangerous side effects.

Information received from Terry Peterson, a Health Officer with Montana State Public Health in Helena, points out that chlamydia is now the STD (sexually transmitted disease) rampant in Montana, and probably nationwide. Until a way was found of isolating and diagnosing chlamydia, gonorrhea and syphilis were most frequently diagnosed. Most probably some of those were chlamydia. Between January first and April twenty eighth of 1999, there were four hundred thirty six cases of chlamydia, sixteen of gonorrhea and one of early latent syphilis. Mr. Peterson reported that syphilis had been nearly wiped out, but like tuberculosis, when we became relaxed and government funding ran out, syphilis again reared its ugly head. He stated that the minute he heard of a case of syphilis, he got in his car, went to the source and ran down every contact person and had them treated. He also stated that the reporting system is flawed, only about twenty five percent of the cases are reported.

There is suspicion that some clinics, instead of reporting venereal disease, will do what is known as "the ro and do shuffle"; they give a cover-all dose of Rocefin and Doxicillin. What Sacajawea may have had, as a result of gonorrhea, was something called adenexia, when the organs become attached to each other, causing cervical tenderness. Other long term problems when gonorrhea becomes systemic (invades the system) are bartholonitis, cystitis, PID, salpingitis, peritonitis, per-hepatitis and /or adhesions. Time was, silver nitrate was used as an eye-drop immediately after an infant was born, to prevent eye problems from gonorrhea. Nowadays erythromycin eye drops are used as an over-all prevention of eye disease.

Smallpox was a disease introduced from Europe and the Indians had no immunity against it. Again, referring to Scientific Monthly, 1925, Jefferson gave Meriwether Lewis a supply of Kine-pox (cow-pox) to be used to inoculate the Indian people to protect them from smallpox. However, Lewis, though not a physician, was familiar with how the Kine-pox worked, i.e. after introduction the skin would redden, bubble up and scab over. Lewis wrote to Jefferson from Cincinnati in 1803, telling him that he had reason to believe the pox was no longer effective and requested that he send more. No notations were observed in the journals to suggest that Lewis received more material. Consequently, the Indians were not inoculated against smallpox. Lewis had received an inoculation while in the army.

Although it is known that the Europeans introduced smallpox to the Indians, syphilis, it seems, developed in the New World from yaws, perhaps 1600 years ago, and Columbus and his crew carried it back to Europe, according to the Archeological Institute of America.

GLOSSARY

Engage'	The French men hired by Lewis and Clark
Bartholonitis	Inflammation of the Bartholin cyst
Cystist	Inflammation of the bladder
PID	Pelvic inflammatory disease
Salpingillis	Inflammation of the fallopian tubes
Peritonitis	Inflammation of the peritoneum
Peri-hepatitis	Inflammation of the liver and peritoneum
Adhesions	Tissues sticking together
Poultice	A soft composition, usually heated and spread on a cloth and applied to an inflamed area of the body.

Chapter Five

PORTAGING THE GREAT FALLS OF THE MISSOURI

When Captain Lewis and his men rejoined the main party downstream, they brought with them six-hundred pounds of dried meat, but they did not bring good news. Captain Lewis estimated the portage route around the falls would be at least sixteen miles, and his inspection of the plains on the north side of the river revealed a land cut by deep ravines. It appeared to Lewis the south side might be the more passable side for the portage corridor, and, if that proved true, it would probably be a faster route, since the Missouri bent southward at the falls. Captain Clark had already sent two men to scout conditions on the south side; however, after conferring with Lewis, he decided to survey the area himself and try to chart a portage route for the Expedition.

Meanwhile, that afternoon, the men began unloading the canoes and establishing camp.

"Capt. C. had already sent two men this morning to examine the country on the S. side of the river; he now passed over with the party to that side and fixed a camp about a mile b[e]low the entrance of a Creek where there was a sufficient quantity of wood for fuel, an article which can be obtained but in few places in the neighbourhood." (June 16, 1805, Lewis)

The camp became the Expedition's Lower Portage Camp from June 16 - June 28 (possibly 30th).

The large creek, falling into the river about a mile upstream from the camp, revealed, upon exploration, a passable inclined path leading from it to the plains above, which the Expedition could use, and it was christened Portage Creek and became the starting point of their route.

Portage Creek is now called Belt Creek. It drains the Little Belt Mountains which are southeast of Great Falls, and flows into the Missouri River just above Morony Dam. Confusingly, Portage Creek was sometimes called Red Creek by the Expedition. One of the sergeants wrote, "We set out passing a red creek which had rose a little and the water was nearly red and bad tasted." (June 28, Sergeant Ordway). Lewis says nearly the same, "Portage Creek had arisen considerably and the water was of a deep crimson color and illy tasted."

There was soft red shale in the bluffs and gullies around the region of falls which probably leached into the water during heavy rainstorms and colored the creeks and parts of the river red. Lewis noticed this on June 27 at White Bear Island. Additionally the sandstone rock of the falls' region is interbedded with iron rich layers, which also could have produced some of the creek's color and peculiar taste. The iron bedding, however, resisted the river's erosion, bringing about the falls, or in Lewis's words, the "sublimely grand specticle" of cascades and rapids.

Ascending Portage Creek was both difficult and dangerous because of the rapids and rocks obstructing the channel. Private Whitehouse wrote about it, "We got our craft up the small River to the falls of it, which was about 8 ft perpendicular, and the water running very rapid down them ... One of our craft turned upside down and the two men that were in her narrowly escaped being drowned, several others of them filled with water." (June 17, 1905) Despite Portage Creek's hazards it was the figurative hole-in-the wall for the Expedition, as the river in the area of the falls was enclosed by high, sheer cliffs of sandstone and shale, some reaching 100 to 200 high. Access to the plains above was nearly impossible. Lewis said, "The bluffs of this creek below and those of the river above its entrance are so steep that it would be almost impracticable to have gotten them (canoes, etc.) on the plain." Portage Creek and its sloping pathway was for the Corps a gateway onto the Plains. Good fortune had smiled on the Expedition.

The Great Falls of the Missouri, Meriwether Lewis' "sublime spectacle" that now serves as the setting of Ryan Dam. (Photo by Dale A. Burk)

Clark and a small team of men set out the following morning on two important missions: to survey, measure, and chart the falls, and to determine a portage route for the Expedition. Lewis remained at camp to supervise the remaining men in preparation-work for the portage, and before Clark's return from his mission around the falls, most of the necessary tasks for the portage had been accomplished.

The unwieldy white pirogue was drawn out of the water and concealed in a thick stand of willow bushes a little below camp. It would be collected on their return trip. Hunters were sent out and the meat dried for use during the portage. Extra food would reduce the need for hunting, adding men and muscle to the transportation effort.

A small crew was set to work preparing wheels for carts. They were to be used to assist the portage party who would not be able to carry every article belonging to the Expedition on their backs. Captain Lewis explains, *"I set six men at work to prepare four sets of truck wheels with couplings, toungs, and bodies, that they might be used without bodies for transporting our canoes or with them in transporting our baggage."* (June 17)

There were few trees in the area near the falls, and large ones were rare. The trees available were primarily thin strips of cottonwood, which followed the water courses, willow and some box elder. Captain Clark commented that *"the land was cut to pieces by ravines, there was little timber, and there was "only one solitary cotton tree in sight of my camp."* (June 25)

At the foot of Portage Creek the men found possibly the only tree in the area wide enough for the cart wheels. It was twenty-two inches in diameter, and when cut crosswise suited their purpose. The mast of the white pirogue served as an axeltree. When the carts were completed, master carpenter Patrick Gass assessed them *"of a very ordinary quality; but it is expected they will answer the purpose."* (July 18)

The baggage was inspected, dried and rearranged. Some of the canoes had been taken up Portage Creek and hauled onto a spot to dry. The men made new moccasins, mended old ones and rearranged their personal gear. Gunpowder canisters and stoppers were waxed, and a cache was prepared for materials not essential for the following journey.

Route

Clark returned June 21 after four days of exploration and surveying. He had established a portage route on the river's south side which covered roughly eighteen miles. Beginning at Portage Creek, it swung away from the River to avoid most of the ravines and gullies, and traveled along the plains which had been marked with stakes by his men. The route ended at the White Bear Islands three miles from the confluence of Medicine [Sun] River and the Missouri:

White Bear Island became their Upper Base Camp from June 22 until July 13.

- - - - -

Lewis, on his earlier survey of the falls and the region around them, had *"visited"* the Medicine River, calling it a *"handsome stream."* It remains beautiful today as it moves through the countryside, cutting a canyon of towering sandstone, colored rocks and waterfalls in its wake. Now, its name is the Sun River. Reputedly, the Blackfeet, who claimed its territory, used the mineral deposits along the river's banks for medicinal purposes, and the river came to be known as the Medicine to the Indians. The area and the river had special significance to the Blackfeet, who were quick to defend their territory. During the time the Expedition was camped on White Bear Island the men hunted along the Medicine River.

Clark's portage route crossed at right angles the great migration route of the buffalo as they arrived in the spring and fall to cross the Missouri. They used a gravel bar just a few hundred yards below the mouth of the Medicine (Sun) River. Those shallows were also used by Indians who thought it the best place to ford the Missouri for miles in either direction. That area now would be located above the 10th Avenue South bridge in Great Falls.

Other Indian tribes used the shallows and the surrounding region for hunting the buffalo. They did not linger, however. Confronting the hostile Blackfeet on their territory was not what they wanted.

- - - - -

Materials

Congress had appropriated $2,500 for the Expedition at Jefferson's request. Lewis spent all of it, plus an additional $4,000 before the journey began. The money was used to buy supplies and equipment. Designing and purchasing the materials needed for the Expedition took months. It was difficult to imagine not only what they would need in the uncharted territory, but how much or how many of an item was needed. There would be no general stores or repair shops beyond the frontier. They had to take with them the necessary materials, and have plans for maintaining them.

Many of the items were double purposed. The lead canisters, which held the gunpowder, could be melted down into bullets when empty. The lightweight iron-framed boat was meant to be used when needed, and collapsed and boxed up again when not. Buttons from their clothing were used for trade or barter with the Indians. There was little waste on the Expedition

Lewis planned to take a minimum of clothing and food. Hunting and natural resources would provide those needs. He did take 193 pounds of portable soup (boiled down beef, eggs and vegetables) which was an emergency food to be used when hunting was poor.

When all the purchased materials were brought together, Lewis estimated the weight at 2,300 pounds, over a ton of materials, not including the boats and canoes.

The materials could be broken down into categories of food, camp supplies, medicine, arms and ammunition, mathematical or scientific supplies, supplies for the men, and trade goods or Indian presents.

The scientific supplies were the most expensive. Care was taken to have them covered in oil skin wraps in specially designed boxes. Some of those items were chronometers, quadrant hydrometer, thermometers, artificial horizons, telescopes, maps, charts and tables, several books on botany, minerology, biology and astronomy.

Over thirty kinds of medicines were taken. One of these Lewis prescribed frequently. They were bilious pills known as "Rush's Thunderclappers." Lewis had ordered fifty dozen. There were also several types of instruments, tourniquets, tinctures, syringes and lancets, among other items.

There was an assortment of tools for every need. There were gunsmith's repair tools and vises, saws, augers, whetstone, drills, files, pliers, chisels, axes and handsaws among others. For the camp there were lanterns, blankets, oil treated tents, yards of flannel and oilcloth, sheets of mosquito curtains, 100 flints and 30 steel for making fires, fishing hooks, fishing line, cooking pots, spoons, candles, awls, field tables, oil skin bags for journals and instruments. Among the food supplies were kegs of pork, bushels of flour, meal and salt, coffee and tea. tems for the men included blankets, soap, shoes, coats, shirts, wool overalls, whiskey and carots of tobacco. For the field there were spy glasses, writing paper, ink, "creyons," powder horns, knives, rifles, guns, gun powder, rifles, muskets, espontoons, pouches and gun slings, bullet molds, brushes and wire, and 400 lbs. of sheet lead to melt down into bullets.

There were 21 bales of Indian presents and trade goods, some of it consisting of colored cloth, 13 pounds. of handkerchiefs, silk ribbon, fish hooks, 130 rolls of tobacco, brass kettles, 144 small scissors, blue beads, white beads, red beads, brass beads, thread, pocket mirrors, scarlet cloth, ruffled shirts, arm bands, medals, hats, shirts, coats, vermillion face point, ear trinkets, among other items

The expedition had a small mountain of equipment and supplies.

On June 21, 1805, the first day of summer, the Expedition was in the final day of preparation for the first portage. Every item of the supplies, every piece of equipment had to be taken around the falls. The men would haul it all, going by foot, back and forth, pushing and pulling over one-half ton of materials over broken, unlevel ground. It took several days and many trips across the plains.

— — — — —

Portage

This morning early Capt. Clark and myself with all the party except Sergt. Ordway, Sharbono, Goodrich, York and the Indian woman, set out to pass the portage with the canoe and baggage to the Whitebear Islands, where we intent that this portage shall end. (June 22, 1805, Lewis)

The "trucks" for the portage were made and repaired with cottonwood, willow and some box elder, all of them soft, brittle wood and not adequate for carrying heavy cargo. There were constant breakdowns. On the first portage, after proceeding approximately eight miles and enduring constant breakdowns, they stopped near a little creek to repair the *"axeltree and the tongues and howns"* of the cart's wheels. They also "dined" there. Because the little creek was lined with sweet willow, with which they repaired the truck, they named it Willow Run. (It was sometimes called Willow Creek. Now it is Box Elder.) It became a convenient resting spot during the portage. The men cooked and ate there, it was sometimes a regrouping area when storms caught them on the plains, and near the end of the portage it was a campsite.

The journey from Willow Run to their destination at White Bear Camp was roughly eleven miles without trees or a source of water. That was a problem for the crew during the entire portage. Private Whitehouse, on reaching the Upper Camp at White Bear Island on June 25 was overheated and thirsty. He drank *"harty of water"* and became ill immediately. Clark bled him (a medical procedure often used in that era) and he recovered by the following day. On another occasion a sudden heavy storm which was short lived but created puddles almost ankle high and was greeted as if manna by the men. They drank *"hearty out of the puddles"* and revitalized proceeded on through the mud to camp.

The plains were fairly level except for several gullies, two hills, and a rough steep ascent of one quarter of a mile. Getting the cargo up the ascents and through the gullies was a grueling effort. The floor of the plains added its own agony. It was carpeted with prickly pear cactus, a source of continuing pain and annoyance, as it penetrated the feet of the men through their thin moccasins. The day following the first portage Clark described the experience. *"...to state the fatigues of this party would take up more of the journal..."* than I have time to write, *"...the men has to haul with all their strength, wate, and art, maney times every man all catching the grass and knobs and stones with their hands to give them more force in drawing the canoes and loads ... at every halt those not employed in reparing the course are asleep in a moment, many limping from the soreness of their feet and some become fant for a few moments." (June 23)*

The evening of the first portage the weary crew finally arrived, long after dark, at White Island Camp. The wagon collapsed one-half mile short of camp. The faded sun meant no repair work could be done. The truck and canoe were abandoned until morning and the men took as much baggage as they could carry on their backs. Arriving at camp, they discovered the wolves had devoured most of the food Capt. Clark had stored for them. Lewis had earlier said, *"These fellows [wolves] are ever at hand and ready to partake ... and there is no means of putting the meat out of their reach in these plains."* *(June 14)* As the numbed crew, dead with fatigue, rolled into their blankets that night, they *"determined to employ every man, cooks and all, on the portage after that day."*

Clark shortened the route a bit the following day, and returning to Lower Portage Camp the men *"repaired their mockersons,"* sewing on double soles.

Captain Lewis and a small party remained at White Bear Island Upper Camp to receive the incoming baggage and refresh the portage crew, and, of great importance for the next part of their journey, to assemble the Iron Boat, which was to take the place of the two cached pirogues, and prepare it for launching.

At Lower Portage Camp, on July 24, the portage crew, now with doubled soled moccasins, set out on the second portage, hauling the heavily laden carts

The prickly pear was an ever-present, literal thorn-in-the-flesh problem during the arduous portaging effort, and it was to plague Expedition members all the way up the Missouri. For example, on July 24, 1805, writing near where Three Forks, Montana, is located today, Captain Lewis wrote "Our pests still invade and obstruct us all occasions, these are the Musquetoes eye knats and prickly pear." (Photo by Pat Hastings)

across the plains to White Bear Islands. Before completing the portage task the men would trod over the plains several more times.

— — — — —

The portage was punishing. Although the temperature was never much above 70°, the strenuous labor forced them out of most of their clothes. Sudden squalls caught them unaware and pelted them with bruising hailstones and cold lashing rain while they were nearly naked. Furious rainstorms saturated the prairie, turning the soil into thick paste, immobilizing the trucks and making walking hopelessly difficult. Even though the men put double soles on the moccasins, the sharp spines of the cactus continued to menace their feet, along with the ruts and stones. The men constantly patched and made new moccasins. They wore out quickly under the hard conditions. *"One pair of good mockinsons will not last more than about 2 days."* (Ordway)

Violent thunderstorms, even more violent winds, lightning and hail pelted the Expedition members during the portage, as well at other locations along the upper Missouri. (Photo by Dale A. Burk)

Rainstorms caused ravines to swell and rush toward the Missouri, carrying along rocks and debris. Captain Clark, with Charbonneau, Sacajewea and baby Pomp, were caught in one of those violent storms. Clark wrote, *"After a torrent of rain and hail fell, more violent than ever I saw before, the rain fell like a voley of water from the heavens."* They found refuge under some overhanging rocks in a dry ravine and settled in to wait out the storm. Hearing a rumbling sound they turned to find a torrent of water, a short distance away, hurtling down the ravine's path. Immediately they began to climb out. The water was fast rising to Clark's knees and was to his waist as he began the climb. Sacajewea with Pomp, and Charbonneau were in front of him. The water was fifteen feet high when they finally scrambled out of the ravine.

In their rush to escape the deluge, several items were left behind. Clark left his compass and other items, Charbonneau a gun, tomahawk, horn and Lewis's wiping rod. Sacajewea watched the water sweep away Pomp's clothing and his cradleboard as she held tightly on to him.

The following day the men found Clark's compass in the mud near the mouth of the ravine. It was the only article found. The area of the ravine where they were the day before was filled with huge rocks.

Many factors contribute to Montana's weather. Most of the heavy precipitation comes from "westerlies" coming from the Pacific region and colliding with warmer or cooler air as it slides down or swirls over the mountains and region. The abrupt ending of the mountains meeting the spreading plains, along with shifting air currents, and the advance and retreat of arctic air are all some of the factors in making Montana's unique weather.

Strong downslope winds drive across the plains east of the divide. Both Captains while at the falls made references to the wind in their journals:

• *"wind as usual"*

• *"the wind blew violently"*

• *"We experienced a most dreadful wind"*

• *"The wind blew violently this evening, as it did yesterday, and as it does frequently in this open country"*

A bright side to the wind-saga came from the portage crew.

"it may be here worthy of remark that the sales were hoisted in the Canoes as the men were drawing them and the wind was a great relief to them being sufficently strong to move the canoes on the Trucks, this is Saling on Dry land in every sence of the word." (June 25, Clark)

– – – – –

But No One Complains

The falls presented a real problem for the Expedition. They blocked further movement of the boats. The Corps had to find an answer to the water's barrier, or the Voyage of Discovery would be a failure and all their previous effort on the expedition would become meaningless. They needed a way around the impeding barrier blocking them from movement to the Mountains and the Shoshone horses. The Corps' answer to the barrier was concerted and cooperative effort.

The portage was part of the answer to the barrier confronting them. It was the brutal part, with its storms, spiny pathways, breakdowns and incredible fatigue. But the men of the Expedition were the real answer. Their determination, effort, and unwavering resolve made the difference and was the real answer to the barrier.

The Captains, knowing the journey would be tough, had selected resourceful men for it. They chose men who were familiar with frontier life and the backwoods. Journeyman type skills were important, carpenters, gunsmiths and metal workers, as well as translators, boatmen and hunters. They preferred recruits who were young, unmarried and physically fit.

The men had come into the Corps as a collection of rugged individualists, plus a few who were rough and wild. The Captains did not choose politically-referred men, dilettantes, or gentleman's sons. Over the months of regulated camp life and through shared experiences along the way – the death of their comrade (Sergeant Floyd), the standoff with the Teton Sioux, the winter among the Mandans, their camp life together and daily river toil – the men had become an engaged unit. They were now strongly committed to the mission assigned them, and to each other, and when they met the punishing test at the falls they showed their mettle.

• *"We all believe that we are about to enter on the most perilous and dificuelt part of our Voyage, yet I see no one repining; all appear ready to meet those dificuelties which wait us with resolution and becomeing fortitude."* (June 20, Clark)

• *"Maney limping from the soreness of their feet some become fant for a few moments but no one complains, all go chearfully on."* (June 23, Clark)

– – – – –

The portage, which began June 22, was completed July 2. *"about 2 P.M. the party returned with the baggage, all well pleased that they had completed the laborious task of portage."* (July 2, Lewis) Lower Portage Camp was abandoned and the Expedition was all together again, camped at White Bear Island Upper Camp with all the baggage and canoes. The Corps, first in part and then in its entirety, camped on one of the White Bear Islands from June 22 to July 13, 1805. The islands were aptly named. Grizzlies abounded on the three islands. DeVoto says they "infested" them. The bears were fond of and inhabited the thick willow brush which grew abundantly throughout the islands. They were located about three miles from the joining of the Missouri and Medicine Rivers and today's city of Great Falls.

While camped there, just about every member of the Expedition had an encounter with the "white bear." Several of the men, including Cpt. Lewis, escaped only by running into the river, prompting Lewis to issue a new command to the Corps. *"I do not think it prudent to send one man alone on a errand of any kind." (June 28)* For protection and hunting, the Expedition used rifles that were flint-locked, muzzle loading, and one shot. They lacked shocking power for the large animal and the bullets, which were low velocity, didn't bring the bear down unless the shot was lucky. After being mortally wounded, the bear would seem impervious to the shots for a long and dangerous period of time. Capt. Lewis reflected that the hand of providence had been wonderfully in their favor with respect to the bears or some of them would long since have fallen sacrifice to their ferocity.

Describing White Bear Island, he wrote, *"The river is about 800 yards wide opposite to us above these islands and has a very gentle current the bottoms are ha[n]dsome level and extensive ... it is a pretty little grove in which our camp is situated." (June 25)*

At White Bear Island Upper Camp there was a concentrated effort by everyone to ready the iron boat. As soon as it was completed the Corps could proceed on to the mountains and the Pacific. Everyone at camp at some time in some way and at some point in time worked on the boat. However, they all took time for some festivity and relaxation on a special day.

Music

July 4, Independence Day, was celebrated by everyone. Late that afternoon they drank the last of the *"Sperits."* [They would have no more whiskey (unless ill) until September 14, 1806, when they bought some on the Missouri, near St. Louis and home.] There was a sumptuous feast to celebrate the birth of the nation. Lewis called it *"a very comfortable dinner of bacon, beans, [suet] dumplings and buffalo beaf."* The fiddle was played, and they danced very merrily until nine o'clock.

There were two festivities while at the falls. The other was not a celebration as on July 4, but an occasion for refreshing and rejuvenation after a prolonged period of difficult work, and in the face of much more to come.

"The party that returned this evening to the lower camp reached it in time to take one canoe on the plain and prepare their baggage for an early start in the morning after which such as were able to shake a foot amused themselves in dancing on the green to the music of the violin which Cruzatte plays extremely well." (June 25, Lewis)

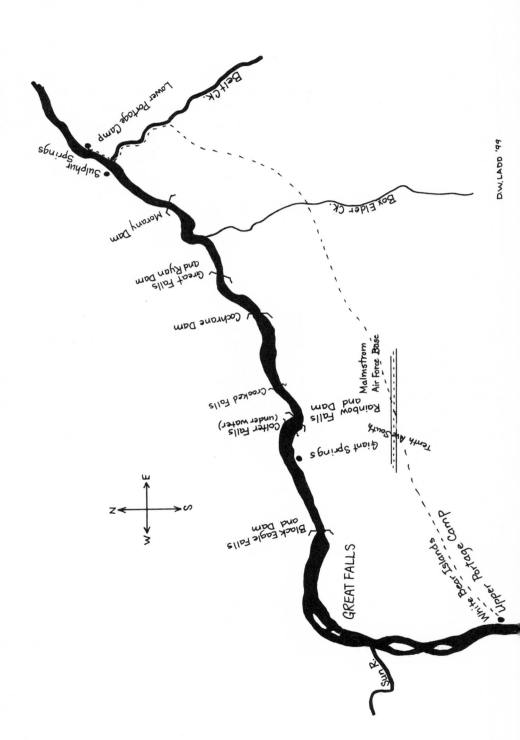

D.W. LADD '99

There was not much opportunity for amusement or entertainment for the Expedition, but when it happened Pierre Cruzette and his violin seemed always in the middle of it. Holidays and special events were celebrated by singing and dancing in accompaniment to his violin.

On New Year's Day, 1805, at Fort Mandan, the Corps was invited by the Indians to visit and dance. They carried with them a fiddle, a tamborine and a sounden horn. Some believe a few of the men brought tin whistles to the Expedition with them from home. If so, they would have taken them to the dance also. They were small, cheap, portable noisemakers popular at that time. The sounden horn was not a musical instrument, but a signal horn which could produce only one note. It would also be a noisemaker at festivities (or blown to maintain the rhythm or beat of a tune, much as a percussion instrument).

The men danced and sang for their own entertainment. We don't know the songs the men sang and danced to, they were not mentioned. We do know Cruzatte was part French, which makes it probable he knew some old French tunes. In addition there were popular songs of the time he might have known, holiday songs and maybe a hymn or two. Whatever the songs, the men clearly enjoyed the spirit of festivity they created.

The Expedition's constant entertainment appears to have been music. It was mentioned throughout the journey. Cruzatte's fiddle was a catalyst for forgetting, for a little while, tomorrow's challanges, the next load of baggage, the next grizzly encounter, back home and their loved ones. It both relaxed and enlivened the men while providing sociability, opportunity for good laughs, and camaraderie. A bow to music and Cruzatte.

"...the fiddle was played and they danced very merrily until 9 in the evening when a heavy shower of rain put an end to that part of the amusement tho' they continued their mirth with Songs and festive jokes and were extreemly merry untill late at night." (July 4, Lewis)

– – – – –

Map

While everyone was working on the Iron Boat Capt. Clark was preparing a map.

"Capt. C[lark] completed a draught of the river from Fort Mandan to this place which we intend depositing at this place in order to guard against accedents." (July 4, Lewis)

Clark's map of the river, west of the Mississippi from St. Louis to the Mandan was already on the way to President Jefferson. Ten men from the Expedition were escorting the map and other materials to the President. More material was to come from the Expedition as they journeyed, but the Captains decided not to proceed with that plan, believing they needed every man they had. The unexpected encounter with five water falls instead of one, leading to a prolonged transport and not the Hidatsa's promised portage of one-half day, had proved that. Misinformation had cost them time and great difficulty. Further difficulties or possible hostilities on the journey would be met more safely with a large contingent. The Captains made the decision not to separate more men from the Expedition.

The Cache

A cache (kash) was a hiding place used to conceal or store articles. Explorers, pioneers, frontiersmen and trappers used them often when in the wilderness. The agricultural Missouri River Valley Indians used them for storing their dried corn and vegetables. The Corps of Discovery made several caches on their journey which were used to deposit items for safekeeping and to store items not needed for the journey ahead. They then recovered the items on their return trip. The hiding place was later located by landmarks.

To prepare a cache, a circle of soil or sod was removed which was about two feet in diameter. Digging continued straight down another foot or so. The hole was then gradually widened as it was dug to a depth of six or seven feet. When completed the hole's shape resembled a cola or water bottle.

The floor of the cache was covered with several inches of dry sticks, which were then covered with dry grass. The items to be stored were wrapped and placed in the pit so as to not touch the hole's walls. When everything was in the cache, the articles were covered with hides and the hole filled with soil and carefully covered with sod. The cache, if well made, should give no outward trace of its existence and appear as if the ground had never been disturbed.

The materials meant for the President gathered by Lewis and Clark from Mandan to the falls consisting of maps, charts and other items were cached at the falls for safe-keeping. The following spring, however, Captain Lewis on opening the cache found many of the items damaged by water, but *"the chart of the Missouri fortunately escaped damage."* (July 13, 1806)

Part of the legacy of the Lewis and Clark Expedition was the series of maps they produced. They drafted a range of cartographic materials documenting their journey through the western territory. Every mile of travel was plotted on charts and maps. Tables of courses and distances covering the day's travel fill the journals.

Clark's map of the Missouri's Great Falls or as he called it the "Draught of the Falls and Portage," is an example of his craftsmanship and drafting skills. It contained sketches of the various falls and springs with descriptions, the heights or "pitches" for each of the falls, the course of the eighteen mile portage route, the location and sketches of islands, current flow details, and a lengthy chart of courses and distances. It is a classic.

Lewis knew of Clark's skill when he sought him to take place in the Expedition. Although not formally trained, his ability for map making became apparent in the army. Clark drafted most of the maps of the Expedition. The two men undoubtedly shared information. They assembled all their data and evaluated it during the long winters at Forts Mandan and Clatsop, Lewis usually choosing to write about it. Clark charted and mapped it.

The Expedition carried many surveying instruments. Most were crude by today's standards. However, with those crude instruments Clark produced some very significant maps.

The maps from the Expedition were important for determining a more accurate perception of the newly purchased Lousiana Territory. Additionally, many geographical concepts were clarified by Lewis and Clark's charting of the Territory. They found:

•The geographies of the two coasts were not identical.

•The mountains of the west proved much more complex than those of the east.

•The Missouri River's drainage was not fan shaped; nor did the river divide into two branches above the Mandan.

•The Missouri was the major river west of the Mandan and did not head in the southwest.

•Finally there was no direct waterway to the Pacific.

Also, they learned about an important geographical landmark on the Upper Missouri. As the river flowed onto the plains, leaving the mountains, it descended 360 feet over a distance of fourteen miles, creating a great falls at the 47th parallel.

– – – – –

Both Captains spoke of a phenomenon occurring in the falls' area for which there was no explanation. It was a noise which, according to Clark, was *"a rumbling like a Cannon at a great distance...heard to the west of us."* Lewis described it also, *"since our arrival...we have repeatedly heard a noise coming from the mountains...to the north of west. ..It is loud and resembles precisely the sound of a six-pound piece of ordnance at a distance of three miles."* (July 4) Lewis had believed the noise to be thunder, but later changed his mind.

He noted the noise occurred on calm cloudless days as well as stormy days. Sometimes many discharges would sound and at other times only a single discharge or rumble would be heard. It would not occur at a specific time of day, but at any hour of the day or night.

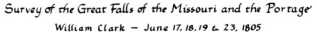

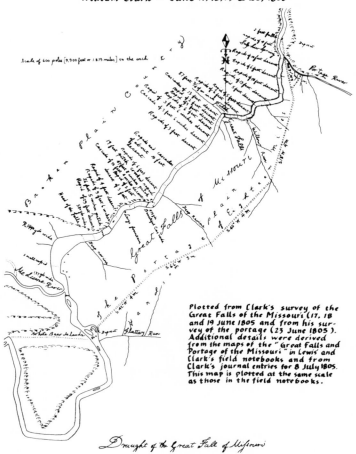

Dr. Robert Bergantino of Butte, Montana, plotted this illustration of the Great Falls of the Missouri of the Portage from Captain William Clark's survey done in July of 1805. It is a portion of a large 22x29-inch poster of the "Survey of the Great Falls of the Missouri and the Portage" sponsored by the Portage Route Chapter of the Lewis and Clark Trail Heritage Foundation as part of its fund-raising efforts. It is exquisitely done and is suitable for framing. Copies are available by writing the Portage Chapter at Box 2424, Great Falls, Montana 59403.

Others heard the noise and tried to explain it. The boom of avalanches was one theory. Some thought there might be geysers in the region whose hot gases exploded before they began to spout. The boatmen believed it was the bursting of rich mines of silver confined within the bosom of the mountains. None of those conjectures or others proved to be accurate.

The Hidatsa frequently mentioned that the mountains made a noise like thunder. The Pawnee and Ricara Indians heard the same explosions in the Black Mountains west of their territory, and similar noises are heard around the Gates of the Mountains. The historian Olin Wheeler called the noise "a weird child of nature." Many other historians and writers have paid no attention to the mention of the noise, believing it picturesque or legend. Writer and historian Elliott Coues says, however, "Every old miner and mountaineer in Montana and Idaho has heard just such noises."

Lewis and Clark's *"rumbling cannon"* or *"discharge"* is still an acoustical phenomenon for which no answer as yet has been given.

This Bob Scriver statue located at the Visitor's Center in Great Falls, Montana, titled "Explorers At The Portage," depicts Captains Meriwether Lewis and William Clark with York (kneeling) and Lewis' Newfoundland dog Seaman. (Photo by Pat Hastings)

Iron Boat

The Iron Boat consumed a great amount of time and energy and experimentation. The pirogues, which it was replacing, were heavy and unwieldy, but the iron boat would be light enough when assembled and sided to be easily carried by a few men. It was thirty-six feet long and buoyant enough to hold and carry over a thousand pounds or more. Captain Lewis thought, *"The boat in every other rispect (except the want of a sealant) completely answers my most sanguine expectations; she is not yet dry and eight men can carry her with the greatest ease; she is strong and will carry at least 8,000 lbs. with her suit of hands." (July 5)*

The idea for this unique boat was conceived by President Jefferson with Captain Lewis. Lewis designed the boat and supervised its construction at Harpers Ferry. It had been carried unassembled from St. Louis to White Bear Island.

The project was finally completed on July 9. The boat was assembled and covered with twenty-eight elk and four buffalo skins, caulked and ready to be launched. Lewis had complained *"my constant attention was necessary to evry part of the work,"* because the absence of available materials necessary for the boat called for experimenting with what was at hand. The men indefatigably rendered one-hundred pounds of tallow for making a binder; attempted to make tar from driftwood; searched for a bark wood for its siding and crossbars; dressed, shaved and sewed skins for the covering; mixed charcoal and tallow into glue, stoked fires to dry it, etc.

In the end, Lewis's boat, the "Experiment," as it was called, did not work. The lack of pitch used for the binding material to seal the boat's seams, was the fundamental reason. There were no pine trees in the region to provide pitch and Lewis's concoction of crushed charcoal, tallow and beeswax did not adhere strongly or permanently. Contributing causes were: the sewing awl was too large and crude, creating enlarged holes in the boat's leather covering; and the thongs used were not large enough to fill the holes; finally Lewis's preferred elk-shaved skins did not hold the sealing compound. (The buffalo skins, partly shaved, did.)

The mistakes could have been amended and set right, but there was not time. The Expedition would be at risk if they didn't move on soon to find the Shoshone and their horses.

Lewis, hugely disappointed, accepted the failure and ordered his boat cached. The irony was that they were two days from pine country where resin was abundant.

"...this circumstance mortified me not a little ... I therefore relinquished all further hope of my favorite boat and ordered her to be sunk in the water that the skins might become soft in order the better

to take her in pieces and deposited the iron frame at this place as it could probably be of no further service to us." – *M. Lewis, July 9*

The following morning (June 10) Clark and a work crew set out under the guidance of the White Bear hunters, who had kept in mind a stand of fairly large cottonwood trees a few miles southwest of camp. The trees were to be made into two dug out canoes to replace the failed iron boat.

Lewis remained at White Bear Island Camp to oversee the cache of his boat, the "truck" wheels, papers, maps and non-essential materials. He would also oversee the transfer of the baggage by boats to Clark's Canoe Camp where the men were readying the long, hollowed-out new canoes. It took five days to complete them. The canoe work-crew contended with axe handles which broke continually; on a single day the men had to whittle thirteen new ones. They also endured mosquitoes, which were "very troublesome all day and all night."

"The Musquetoes and knats are more troublesome here if possible than they were at the Wite bear Islands. I sent a man to the canoes for my musquetoe bier which I had neglected to bring with me; as it is impossible to sleep a moment without being defended against the attacks of these most tormenting of all insects;" (July 13, Lewis)

Clark continued the procedure of building up a store of meat. This time it was meant for the next leg of the journey. Lewis and Clark had been warned by the Indians at Mandan that there would be no buffalo shortly after leaving the falls. They were both drying the meat and making pemmican as a hedge against "fasting." While on the plains the Expedition had not been hungry. They consumed, every twenty-four hours, four deer; or and elk and a deer, or one buffalo, for thirty-two people. The diminishing buffalo meant an unhappy farewell to one of Lewis's culinary delights, the *"boudin blanc,"* a *"white pudding"* made by the interpreter and cook Charbonneau. There was another member of the party who would also lose a job with the diminished buffalo. That was Seaman, Lewis's alert Newfoundland. He held the buffalo and grizzlies and other animals at bay around the camp. Capt. Lewis said of him, *"My dog seems to be in a constant state of alarm with these bear keeps barking all night." (June 27)* *"They (white bears) constantly infest our camp during the night, though they have not attacked us, as our dog which patrols all night gives us notice of their approach." (June 28)* Seaman had done the same job with buffalo when at the Lower Portage Camp.

On July 13, White Bear Island Camp was broken down, and the final load of baggage was sent down the river. Lewis started overland to Camp Canoe with Sacajewea, her baby "Pomp," and Baptiste LaPage, who was ill. The overland travelers while on the way passed an abandoned, large (two-hundred foot) circular Indian lodge, which Lewis believed was used for councils, ceremonies or feasts. The markings of eighty lodges surrounding the large lodge and the remains of a large fire in it were evidence of recent Indian activity. The Corps, since leaving the Mandan in April, had not seen any Indians, but along the way they continued to find evidence, such as the circular structure and other markings, which told them Indians were in the vicinity.

On the morning after arriving at Canoe Camp (July 14), Captain Lewis climbed onto an *"emenence"* affording a *"commanding view of the country,"* took bearings and made some interesting observations. The bearings he took noted the point at which the Missouri entered the mountains; the termination of the first and second chain of the Rocky Mountains; and the most distant point of the third chain. Then, of most interest, this observation, *"The Southern extremities of these ranges not visible and believe they continue probably to Mexico."* This was a hint of the complexity of the mountain range before him, and its vast proportions. It also spoke to the geographers' misconceptions of the North American continent. The density and difficulty of the mountains were not yet apparent, but those bearings were a nudge to his consciousness of an awesome range, or at least one more grand than imagined. It would soon become plain that the mountains before them were not as simple and uncomplicated as President Jefferson, geographers and map makers had previously believed.

– – – – –

The two new canoes were completed, and along with the others were laden with baggage and extra loads of dried meat and grease for the journey. The portage around the falls, which had given the men the most arduous labor they would endure during the twenty-eight month journey, plus the *"mortifying"* failure of Lewis's iron-boat experiment, was behind them. They were now on the river again and headed into new territory. Lewis, as was often the case, walked along the shore as they started off. The mountains awaited them. Thirty-two men, a baby, one woman, eight canoes and a black Newfoundland on a gentle current. The portage and the long month at the Great Falls were over.

"At 10 A. M. we once more saw ourselves fairly underway much to my joy and I believe that of every individual who compose the party." July 15 , 1805 M. Lewis

Chapter Six

PIONEERS IN NATURE

Thomas Jefferson made it very clear to Meriwether Lewis that the Expedition would include a scientific aspect as well as objectives in geography, commerce and diplomacy. The President considered himself an amateur biologist and paleontologist. "Nature," Jefferson once said, "intended me for the tranquil pursuits of science, by rendering them my supreme delight."* *¹*

"These pursuits, of which he spoke, embraced all natural objects and agencies from the grandest to the most common: wind currents and temperature fluctuation, the advent of the first spring flowers, minerals and medicinal springs, mountains, lakes and interlocking streams, the aboriginal American and his customs, migrating birds, petrified bones of extinct animals."* *²*   Therefore, it is not surprising that he would include within his extensive instructions to Lewis a request for information on *"the animals of the (Western) country generally & especially those not known in the U.S."* *³* Without a wide-ranging technical background, Jefferson would have been unable to write the set of instructions that he gave to Lewis and Clark.

But Jefferson had a great knowledge and command of the sciences, especially biology, geography, meteorology and ethnology, and an insatiable interest which began in his youth. When only twenty-one he began botanical and phenological observations in his *Garden Book* which described his garden plants when they bloomed, lost flowers, their colors, etc. Soon his knowledge included local herbs, shrubs and trees. In *Notes on Virginia* he listed one hundred and thirty plants common to his state, dividing them into four groups: medicinal, edible, ornamental, and "useful for fabrication". In each instance he included the scientific and common names, as he was well versed in Latin. For more that fifty years he kept weather records and was probably the best informed meteorologist in the United States, being intensely fascinated with the correlation of weather data with periodic biological occurrences such as migration of nesting birds and the flowering and fruiting of plants.

He possessed a vast knowledge of surveying and navigation and was able to use such instruments as the quadrant, sextant and the transit. He was interested in maps and map-making, having come by this interest legitimately, as his father,

Prairie Dogs OWL '99

Peter Jefferson, and Joshua Fry had made the first map of Virginia in 1751. With regards to Indians, Jefferson enjoyed amassing a collection of their "vocabularies". He was also a pioneer in paleontology and assembled a large collection of fossils in the East Room of the White House. "The instructions which Jefferson put into the hands of Lewis and Clark clearly reflected his appetites, his thinking, and his persistant preoccupation with scientific matters. They carried with them the prestige of the President of the United States."*.⁴

During his two years in the White House, with Jefferson as his mentor, Lewis served an important apprenticeship in many of the sciences. But to accumulate additional scientific education and to be able to carry out Jefferson's instructions, Lewis was sent to various authorities to "bone-up".

In Lancaster, Pennsylvania, he spent time with Andrew Ellicot, an astronomer and mathematician, to acquire the skill of using instruments to measure latitude and longitude; Robert Patterson, a mathematician, in Philadelphia, still furthered this endeavor. Jefferson also took pleasure in sending Lewis to Dr. Benjamin Smith Barton, professor of botany at the University of Pennsylvania. Barton taught Lewis how to preserve plant, animal and bird specimens, and how to label them, including place and date of collection. Instruction included an expanded range of biological knowledge – a list of over two-hundred terms for describing new plants and animals. Lewis developed a remarkable awareness of scientific terminology. The last authority Lewis turned to in his "studies" was Dr. Casper Wistar, the chairman of anatomy at the University of Pennsylvania who had published the first American textbook on anatomy. He gave advice regarding fossils and suggested Lewis keep an eye out for them on his journey.

In his final preparations Lewis selected his traveling library. This included Barton's *Elements of Botany*, a book on mineralogy, a two-volume edition of *Linnaeus* (on the Latin classification of plants), a four-volume dictionary, and three nautical astronomy books. He also had a borrowed book from Barton on the history of Louisiana. Can you imagine lugging a stack of twelve volumes across the West and back by dugout and horseback? This is surely an example of real loyalty and dedication to the goal of carrying out a mission.

Thus, armed with his instructions for the Expedition, Lewis logged in his journal, not only daily events and observations, but noted or recorded vast amounts regarding plants and wildlife of all kinds. In just the category of animals alone, he referred to some two-hundred and fifty species – twenty-six descriptions running a full page or more. The three animals given the most attention were the grizzly bear, the buffalo, and the beaver, in that order. Through his studies he extended the known range of many plants and animals, and was the first white man to observe and describe many species "new to science". Some species he compared to those he already knew, but also noted wildlife not present in his travel: for example, bees. One instrument he carried for measuring his samples was a tape with inches and feet marked on it. This was stored in a circular leather box.

Because the Expedition journals focused upon careful scientific observation, they are extremely valuable, as today we try to understand the real character of nature beyond the Mississippi River before it was altered by the settlement of the West. While the Corps of Discovery passed through the region of the upper Missouri River, Lewis noted countless plants, bird and animals. The following will include highlights of a few of each, and the remaining will be listed in their groupings.

ANIMALS

BEAVER

Since one of the objectives of the Expedition was to ascertain the possibility of diverting the fur trade with the western Indians from the British companies, Lewis and Clark were careful to record their observations on the distribution and abundance of beaver.

The beaver in North America was important in the fur trade long before it was established as a distinct species. A specimen, collected in the Hudson Bay area, was named *Castor canadensis* by Kuhl in 1820, but prior to that time it was apparently considered to be the same as the Old World, *Castor fiber*. Beavers are of the Family *Castoridea* and Genus *Castor*. The species which the Expedition observed along the Missouri River is called *Castor canadensis missouriensis* – the scientific name not given until 1919 by V. Bailey.[*5]

It is believed fur traders were active in the area of present-day Minnesota as early as the late 1600's. French traders founded St. Louis in 1764, and for a century it was one of the great centers of the fur trade. By the time the Lewis and Clark Expedition started up the Missouri, that river was already known to the trappers and traders as far northwest as today's Montana border.

The beaver is the largest rodent north of Panama, many adults weighing over sixty pounds. The body is thick-set and compact, legs short, ears small, hind feet large, and the five toes webbed. The tail is broad, flat, nearly hairless and covered with large scales. The fur is unusually dense with the upper parts a rich glossy brown (the shade varying seasonally and geographically), and the underparts brown to tawny. The black tail is like a powerful sculling oar, making him a successful and expert swimmer. And his tail, along with his hind feet, enables him to sit bolt upright while working to cut down trees. They have strongly developed incisors for gnawing. There are two in each jaw which have a somewhat curved shape. Trees and shrubs are felled for dam and lodge building and for food. Beavers are aquatic mammals but most always inhabit streams. A dam of sticks, mud and rocks is constructed to restrict water flow, thus creating ponds upstream of the dam – some many acres in area. Beavers also construct and live in dome-shaped lodges made of sticks and mud. The lodges are built near the shore with the living room above the water level. There are one or more sub-

Beaver
Jean Clary

aqueous passages. In small streams where the water is too shallow to conceal the passageway, the beavers build dams to increase its depth. However, in especially large rivers, like the Missouri, beavers do not build lodges but instead burrow into the banks. The entrances are about eight feet above the water's edge and the chambers accommodate a number of animals that live there. Beavers eat bark and cambium from plants and trees like willows, alders, birches, aspens and cottonwoods.

The great importance of beaver arose from the commercial value of its fur, which is one of the finest that nature produces. As the streams of the West originally swarmed with these animals in numbers that rivaled the buffalo herds of the plains, it is easy to understand the gold mine of wealth awaiting the trader and trapper. The greatest harvest of beaver and other fur bearers began on the headwaters of the Missouri in 1822; but because of the extreme trapping activity, by 1838 beaver were radically reduced in numbers. However, trapping of beaver continued into the early 1900s when the average price was $4.00 per pound of fur, and since the beaver pelt weighs up to two pounds, one pelt was worth from four to ten dollars.

Trappers became very expert in their knowledge regarding the beaver's habits and the best methods of taking him. The universal method to snag him was with the steel trap. The strong trap weighing about five pounds and attached to a five foot chain is set in three to four inches of water close to the bank. Immediately overhead a little twig is set so that one end is a few inches above the water. On the point of the twig is put the bait, beaver castorum, the odor of which has a great attraction for the beavers. To reach the bait he raises his mouth towards it and brings his feet directly under it. Then, stepping upon the trap, it springs shut and he is caught. After an ineffectual struggle, he sinks to the bottom and drowns. The beaver is skinned near the place of capture. Only the skin, tail and the castorum glands are taken to the trapper's camp. Oddly enough, the castorum used as the beaver's bait actually supplied the means of alluring its race to near destruction.* [6]

The Lewis and Clark Expedition first encountered beaver and signs of beaver in July, 1804, around present-day Leavenworth, Kansas, and again near Council Bluffs, Iowa. But after leaving Fort Mandan, beaver were bountiful wherever cottonwood and willow trees were plentiful enough to insure adequate food supplies. Along the Missouri, the party trapped beaver at almost every campsite. They were awed by the numbers of beaver they saw – swimming, feeding on tree bark, and watching them from the banks. Lewis noticed how much larger, fatter and darker the fur was than previously observed. Near the

Yellowstone River Lewis commented upon having seen a quantity of timber cut down by the beaver – one tree being three feet in diameter; Clark noted seeing beaver at every bend!

On May 6th, Lewis wrote, *"two beaver were taken in traps this morning and one since shot by one of the party. saw numbers of there anamals peeping at us as we passed, out of their wholes which they form of a cilindrical shape by burrowing in the face of the abbrupt banks of the river."*[*7] The party particularly enjoyed feasting on the tail of the beaver. Lewis claimed, *"the flesh of the beaver is esteemed a delicacy among us; I think the tale a most delicious morsal, when boiled it resembles the fresh tongues and sounds of the codfish, and is usually sufficiently large to afford a plentifull meal for two men."*[*8]

Abundance of beaver continued above the junction of Three Forks, and vast numbers of beaver dams on the Jefferson River made travel increasingly arduous for the men pulling the canoes along. Beaver continued to be encountered until the party trudged up from the Prairie Creek drainage to Lemhi Pass in mid-August. Later, in descending the Yellowstone River in 1806, Captain Clark was the first white man to record the great abundance of beaver native to the valley of this river.

Cottonwood tree cut down by beaver near Loma, Montana. (Photo by Pat Hastings)

BLACK TAILED PRAIRIE DOG

The prairie dog, *Cynomys ludovicianus ludovicianus*, was an animal new to science, described for the first time by the Lewis and Clark Expedition. He is a stocky little rodent; his head and body measures ten to sixteen inches, and the tail is three to four inches in length. He has a broad head, a yellowish brown body and a black-tipped tail. To better view his surroundings, he sits up on his haunches, and gets his name from his barking alarm signal. Prairie dogs live in burrows – an elaborate network of tunnels extending more that twelve feet below the surface. The sprawling underground cities are called dog towns, where they live in colonies and are very social. Long ago the size of some towns were of enormous acreage; but today those of any large size are few, except in remote and protected areas.

Lewis and Clark first encountered this little squirrel on September 7, 1804, in (today's) Boyd County, Nebraska, where they found a large colony of the animals. This village, describes Clark *"covd about 4 acres of ground on a gradual decent of a hill and Contains great numbers of holes on top of which those little animals Set erect make a Whisteling noise and whin all armed Step into their hole."* [9] Lewis wanted some specimens, but, the creatures being very wary, Private John Shields was able to shoot only one. So the decision was made to resort to digging. Just imagine, while one man stood guard over the boats, the remainder of the Corps spent the entire day in a massive effort to capture some ground rats, as Clark called them. *"We attempted to dig to the beds of one of those animals, after diging 6 feet found by running a pole down that we were not half way to his Lodge."* Also, water was carried from the river and poured in the passageways. Into one hole they poured five barrels without filling it. It wasn't until nightfall that one prairie dog was, at last, flushed out and captured alive!

During both the outbound and return trips the explorers described the location and size of some of the most noticeable prairie dog villages along the Missouri. Lewis called this little animal the Barking squirrel. It was Sgt Ordway who referred to it as a "prairie dog," the term we use today.

While west of the Musselshell River, Lewis wrote on May 31, 1805, of his observation that the barking squirrels never visiting the brook or river for water, some of their villages being a distance of five to six miles from water. He was astonished how this animal could live without it. We now know the phenomenon Lewis observed is true of a few other animals, too; they can live their entire lives on a diet of nothing but dry plant food in which the water content does not exceed 5 to 10%.

Not until Lewis was at Traveler's Rest in today's Lolo, Montana, on July 1, 1806, that he took the time to write a lengthy and detailed description of the prairie dog. He begins, *"The little animal found in the plains of the Missouri*

Display of mounted black-tailed prairie dogs at the Ullm Pishkun Visitor's Center at Ulm, Montana. (Photo by Pat Hastings)

which I have called the barking squirrel weighs from 3 to 3 ◄ pounds, it's form is that of the squirrel. it's colour is an uniform light brick red grey, the red rather predominating. " He continues to thoroughly describe the animal's entire body, its length of one foot five inches including the four inch tail, its burrowing behavior, and how it rests above the ground erect on hind feet and rump and *"will generally set and bark at you as you approach them. Their note being much that of the little toy dogs. "* He notes how they live a considerable distance from water, yet are never seen at any distance from their burrows, feed on grass and weeds, and hibernate in the winter, *"when frost comes it shuts up it's burrow and continues until spring. " [10]*

Whatever became of the shipment of specimens, artifacts and live animals (including one prairie dog) that left Fort Mandan on the keelboat on April 7, 1805? Well, it arrived at St Louis on May 20th and was sent to President Jefferson. However, he did not find an opportunity to inspect the collection until October 4th, six months later. He wrote Charles Willson Peale, artist, taxidermist and proprietor of the prestigious Peale's Museum at Independence Hall in Philadelphia, that after sorting out various horns and Indian treasures for himself, he would send the remainder to him which included various skins and skeletons and 1 living burrowing squirrel of the prairies and 1 living magpie. [11]   On April 5, 1806, Peale wrote Jefferson that the little animal was still alive and he would do a description and drawing when it became more animated, as the spring got warmer. Unfortunately, no further mention was made of Lewis's little barking squirrel.

Charles Willson Peale

Charles Willson Peale (1741-1827) Born in Chestertown , Maryland, he studied art in Boston and London. After returning to the United States from England he quickly established a reputation as a portrait painter. In 1791 he painted the oil portrait of Thomas Jefferson; and it was he who, in 1807, painted the famous and most popular oil portrait of Meriwether Lewis, and William Clark in 1810. Peale founded the Peale's Museum which housed a vast collection of natural history based upon the Linnaean classification. This was the first museum with emphasis on teaching scholars as well as the general public. He had taught himself the art of taxidermy and was the originator of habitat arrangement – a placing of mounted specimens in front of backgrounds painted to create an illusion of an actual natural environment.

It is estimated that at one time five billion black-tailed prairie dogs inhabited the American West – now only ten million. They ranged over huge areas of prairie, 100-200 million acres, but have now been reduced to less that 1% of that area over ten states. The remaining colonies are increasingly small and isolated from each other. Where continuous colonies once covered hundreds of square miles, now most surviving colonies are less than 50 acres. The fragmentation of a prairie dog habitat means that once a colony is exterminated, it is increasingly unlikely to be re-colonized from neighboring colonies. Each exterminated colony represents the loss of a bridge to survival for the species. Conversion of habitat into agriculture lands probably had the biggest impact historically, but subdivision and urban sprawl throughout the eastern front of the Rocky Mountains certainly has taken its toll. Ranchers and some government agencies continue to poison prairie dog colonies in the mistaken belief that prairie dogs compete with livestock and that livestock will break their legs stepping into dog burrows.

Many species of wildlife also utilize or depend on prairie dogs for food and prairie dog burrows for shelter. The black-footed ferret, the most endangered mammal in North America, is endangered because of the reduction in prairie dogs on which they are 100 percent dependent. The Fish and Wildlife Service is about to list the Mountain Plover as a threatened species. In most areas plovers are found only on prairie dog colonies. Without prairie dogs some species will go extinct and many other wildlife species such as swift foxes, golden eagles, and feruginous hawks will become less abundant. Protection of prairie dogs is key to the survival of the entire prairie ecosystem. To protect this ecosystem, the National Wildlife Federation has recently submitted a petition to list the black-tailed prairie dog as a threatened species under the Endangered Species Act. In response to this petition, the Fish and Wildlife Service recognized a need to do a review of the plight of the prairie dog.

Some other small animals new to science which were described in the upper Missouri River area are: the coyote, white-tailed jack rabbit, the bushy-tailed wood rat (pack rat), thirteen-striped ground squirrel, yellow-bellied marmot, and the kit fox.

GRAY WOLF

Lewis and Clark were also the first naturalists to describe the wolf of the plains. However, the description was overlooked for eighteen years, until Thomas Say classified it based on specimens gathered by Major Long's expedition of 1819-20. He named the gray wolf, *Canis lupus nobilis.* The head and body of this large dog-like animal measures forty to fifty-two inches, and the tail from thirteen to nineteen inches. The fur is usually gray but varies from silvery white to black. The wolf has a complex social organization. The pack, usually numbering four to seven individuals, is a society of parents, young and close relatives that follow a rigid hierarchy. Wolves are mainly game hunters, preying on deer and other large mammals, but will also attack smaller mammal and birds. The wolf is in the Order *Carnivora;* animals of this grouping exhibit unique features relating to their eating habits which distinguish them from other orders of mammals. They survive by eating other animals, locate prey before the prey sees, hears or smells them, move with great speed, are able to kill and digest an animal efficiently, and are smarter than the animal being caught.

In the early 1800's, wolves were numerous on the lower Missouri River and abundant over the plains of the Upper Missouri basin, being most common where game was most plentiful. They were an important element in the balance of ecology. They eliminated the weak and diseased animals ranging from buffalo to rodents, helping to prevent overpopulation within species. But with the settlement of the West, livestock claimed the plains; wolves and human activities were in direct conflict until eventually, only a few thousand wolves remained.

On May 5, 1805, when the Expedition was above the Yellowstone River on the Missouri, Lewis wrote in his journal, *"The large wolf found here is not as large as those of the Atlantic states. They are lower and thicker made, shorter leged . – their color, which is not effected by the season, is gray or blackish brown and every intermediate shade from that to cream colored white; these wolves resort to the woodlands and are also found in the plains, but never take refuge in the ground or burrow so far as I have been able to inform myself. We scarcely see a gang of buffaloe without a parsel of those faithfull shepherds on their skirts in readiness to take care of the maimed wounded. The large wolf never barks, but howls as those of the atlantic states do."* [12]

The party was always in competition with the wolves for their meat supply, finding it necessary to hang the meat out of reach of the wolves, a precaution indispensable to its safekeeping even for a night. When retrieving buffalo meat from one hunt, the men informed Lewis that the wolves had devoured the greater part of the meat.

The explorers generally found the wolves to be only moderately wary and even rather docile. The one exception was an August night in 1806 when a wolf bit Sergeant Pryor through his hand while he was sleeping. And when the wolf then attempted to grasp Windsor, Shannon shot the wolf.

The British fur traders of both the Hudson Bay Company and the North west Company had been maintaining fur trading posts on Rainy Lake, Lake Winnepeg, the Assiniboin River and the Red River of the North for several years prior to 1804. The Mandan and Hidatsa Indian tribes of present-day North Dakota were carrying on a non-vigorous fur trade with the British companies. And Manuel Lisa and a few other adventuresome traders from St. Louis were also operating on the Missouri as far north as the Mandan Village. However, wolves constituted only a minor portion of the total fur catch considering all species. The boom period of the upper Missouri River basin and Rocky Mountain fur trade arrived twenty years later.

During the 1700's the gray wolves roamed North America. However, their turning point came when man shifted from being a hunter to being a farmer. Stock animals were easy prey. Therefore, "bounties" were instituted, payment of a cash fee for each dead wolf. Bounty hunting is not new. In the Old World wolf hunting has been going on for over 2,000 years. By such efforts, the wolf became extinct in Europe in 1900. In 1884, Montana instituted bounties. Indeed, the spread of bounties across North America paralleled the westward spread of civilization. And with the development of the steel leghold trap in the mid-1800's, wolf trapping really "took off." Nationwide, there was large scale extermination in the late 1800's and early 1900's, which led the way to the wolf's near extinction.

However, in 1973 Congress enacted the Endangered Species Act, mandating recovery planning for endangered and threatened species. The gray wolf was listed as threatened.

By 1980 the U.S. Fish and Wildlife Service had formulated a recovery plan for the gray wolf in the Northern Rocky Mountains; this plan was revised in 1987. And in 1965-66, a reintroduction of wolves from Alberta, Canada, took place in Yellowstone National Park and in the Frank Church Wilderness in Idaho. These were designated as "experimental non-essential populations." By the spring of 1999, the wolf recovery program showed population numbers in Yellowstone alone had risen to 160 wolves. Nevertheless, because of recent federal court rulings, the program is in limbo, leaving the future of these wolves uncertain. As Steve Fritts, Northern Rocky Mountain wolf coordinator, has said, "The key to wolf population recovery in the northwestern United States lies in human tolerance – a relatively new perspective in our society." [13]

BIGHORN SHEEP

On May 25, 1805, the Expedition was on the Missouri River above the mouth of the Musselshell River where large numbers of bighorns were observed. Lewis wrote, *"As we ascended the river today I saw several gangs of big horned Animals on the face of the steep bluffs & clifts on the Star side . . ."* [14] then he gave a lengthy description of the bighorn sheep in remarkable detail. These animals, later known as Audubon's Bighorn Sheep, were in a country characterized by towering sandstone and shale cliffs, deep coulees, and rugged hills. Let us, for a moment, review some background of the taxonomic history of this curious quadruped, the size of a deer with circular horns.

During the fall of 1800, Duncan McGillivary, a clerk in the service of the North West Fur Company, was with explorer David Thompson near Banff, Alberta. While hunting he came upon a small herd of a new species of animal, and realizing this could be an important discovery, he sent one of the animals to the Royal Society of London, where it arrived in 1803. Immediately it was named and described by many who were prominent in the field of zoology. A Dr. George Shaw was to get his name published first; so on February 4, 1804, the bighorn species became *Ovis canadensis Shaw*, Bighorn Sheep of North America. A year later bighorns were encountered in the breaks of the Missouri River by Lewis and Clark and again in 1806, and also by Audubon in 1843. It was C. Hart Merriam, the father of mammalian classification, who, in 1901, named this eastern Montana bighorn population a subspecies: *Ovis canadensis auduboni Merriam. Ovis canadensis* is formed of several subspecies which includes the extinct Audubon sheep. They range from the Peace River in Canada to northern Mexico, occurring in all the Rocky Mountain states. The subspecies *Ovis canadensis canadensis*, the Rocky Mountain Bighorns, is the largest group, the most northern in range, and the most abundant of the bighorns.

Bighorn sheep are in the Order *Artiodactyla* which includes sheep and goats, the even-toed ungulates. The size of an adult bighorn is five to six feet from head to rump and is two and a half to three and a half feet high at the shoulder. The ram's horns are massive and spiraling, measuring rarely to four feet, while the ewe's are much smaller and slightly curved. The fur is brown or grayish-brown with a whitish rump. These sheep inhabit rugged, sparsely wooded mountain slopes. They are gregarious and primarily live on grass and forbs, herbaceous plants that are not grass, but in winter may rely on willows and other woody plants.

Even though it had been reported that white man had seen bighorns in the

New World before the Lewis and Clark Expedition, Lewis first learned of this animal on October 1, 1804, from a French trader, Jean Valle, whom they came upon near the mouth of the Cheyenne River near present day Pierre, South Dakota. He told of *"A kind of anamale with large circular horns this animale is nearly the Size of an Elk that lived in the Black Hills to the west."*[15]

When the Expedition overwintered at Fort Mandan in 1804-05, they learned from the Indians that the bighorn animals, they called Ar-Sar-ta, resided in the breaks further upriver. They showed Lewis some horns of one. The following spring these same horns accompanied the weighty shipment of Indian objects and plant and animal specimens to be sent back to St. Louis in the keelboat. Lewis and Clark were later to learn that the natives made great use of the bighorn animal. They found that the Teton Sioux used the horn as a large two-quart spoon or cup; the Shoshone used many bighorn skins for clothing and made bows from the horns; the Indians of the Pacific Northwest also used this animal's skin extensively for clothing.

At last the Expedition was to get its first glimpse of a bighorn; it was near the mouth of the Yellowstone River on April 26, 1805. At Lewis's request, Joseph Fields had made a short exploratory trip up the Yellowstone. Upon returning he reported that he saw several of the bighorned animals in the course of his walk; but they were so shy that he could not get a shot at them; he found a large horn of one of these animals which he brought with him, wrote Clark.[16]

Also, on the 29th of May the party arrived at the mouth of the Judith River where Lewis reported seeing a great abundance of Agralia or bighorned animals in the high country. He was now in the very heart of bighorn country and was *"a fascinated observer of these graceful creatures."*[17]

The party was to find bighorn sheep inhabiting the bluffs and cliffs of the Missouri and its tributaries whenever such habitat occurred, from the mouth of the Yellowstone to the Beaverhead Mountains. In an area of cliffs above Three-forks, Clark remarked, *"I killed a Ibix on which the whole party dined."*[18]

On the party's return trip in 1806, the bighorns were again noted. Captain Clark and his group saw some in the Bitterroot Valley and again along the Yellowstone River. Lewis and his party encountered them again after returning to the Missouri from his Marias excursion. While camping at the mouth of the Slaughter River, Lewis wrote, *"On our way today we killed 9 bighorns of which I preserved the skins and skeletons of 2 females and one male; the flesh of this animal is extremely delicate, tender and well flavoured ; they are now in fine order."*[19]   Three days later Gass wrote, *"We embarked early in a wet disagreeable morning . . . and at noon halted to dine at some old Indian lodges. Captain Lewis being afraid the dampness of the weather, that the skins he had procured of these big horned animals would spoil, thought it advisable to stay here this afternoon and dry them by a fire in these old*

This full-body mount of an Audubon sheep is on display at the Montana State University-Northern in Havre, Montana. It was shot in the 1890s by Hans Feldt on Eight Mile Ridge south of Big Sandy. (Photo by Pat Hastings)

The sleekly-bodied Audubon bighorn sheep present along the Missouri River in north-central Montana at the time of the Lewis & Clark Expedition is gone. This full-body mount specimen of the Audubon bighorn sheep displayed at the Valley County Pioneer Museum in Glasgow, Montana, was killed in the Missouri River Breaks in the early 1900s. (Photo Courtesy The Print Shop, Glasgow, Montana)

lodges." [20]   This incident exemplifies the diligence of Lewis to bring his specimens back in the best possible quality.

Audubon's bighorns were still abundant in the Missouri River breaks in the mid-1800's, a fact noted by passengers aboard steamboats traveling up and down the Missouri. But sadly, in less than one hundred years after Lewis and Clark's first observations, sheep in this region were nearly extinct. The various factors responsible for the extinction are complex. Surely man played the chief role. Competition from livestock was an important element, with about six-hundred thousand cattle and a half-million domestic sheep grazing in Montana during the 1880's. There were no modern livestock management practices to minimize the impact. This early grazing brought profound changes in the vegetation of rangeland and altered the quality of these areas as potential wildlife habitat and contributed to their decline. By 1909 over a million acres were homesteaded; people flooded to eastern Montana. These effects on wildlife, including bighorn sheep, were severe. Bighorns were over-hunted and also contracted diseases from domestic sheep (i.e., Pasteurella pneumonia). This was an era of limited game regulations and enforcement; the science of wildlife management had not yet been developed. According to record, the last known Audubon was killed in the Missouri Breaks in 1916.

It has long been assumed that the Rocky Mountain bighorns and the Audubon bighorns were separate subspecies. In the 1940's a man named I. M. Cowan, in his pioneering attempts, wrote a taxonomy of North American Bighorn sheep. But due to using small samples and lacking methods of statistical study, his support for many of his subspecies of sheep were later unfounded. However, recent in-depth scientific studies have been done and reported on in 1996 by Dr. Rob Roy Ramey, II, at the University of Colorado at Boulder, Colorado, and Dr. John D. Wehansen at the University of California, Bishop, California. They used statistical methods to examine the geographic variations in the skull and horn characteristics of bighorn sheep as well as using DNA testing. After lengthy research, these men concluded that the Audubon's bighorn should not be a separate subspecies from the Rocky Mountain bighorn sheep (*O. c. canadensis*). Additionally, the northern California bighorns from Washington state and British Columbia (*O. c. californiana*, should also be grouped with the Audubon and Rocky Mountain bighorns. Although horn measurements exhibited the greatest overall variation in their studies, it is now recognized that much of those differences within the supposed subspecies are from variations in the animal's nutrition and environment; the regions of habitat have great variation.

Yes, recent studies have shown that the Rocky Mountain and Audubon bighorns are of the same subspecies. But as author Duncan Gilchrist of Corvallis, a Montana expert on hunting bighorn sheep, suggests, for the sake of nostalgia, we still enjoy referring to the big horned animals encountered by the

Corps of Discovery as Audubon Sheep.

Today there are a small number of full Audubon mounts on public exhibit. They were shot by hunters in the early 1900's. Examples include one located at the Northern Montana College in Havre, Montana, one at the Valley County Pioneer Museum in Glasgow, Montana, one at the Montana Bar in Miles City, and one shoulder mount at the Foundation for Northern American Wild Sheep in Cody, Wyoming. Although the mounts are frail, we are fortunate to have these preservations of our Montana history still with us.

BISON

During the seventeenth century, American Bison ranged as far east as the Allegheny Mountains, but with the settlement of the States, they had been driven back well beyond the Mississippi River. On August 23, 1804, the Corps of Discovery was below present-day Vermillion, South Dakota, when they saw and killed their first buffalo. This provided their first meal of roast bison meat. Sergeant Ordway wrote in his journal, *"Jo Fields came to the Boat informed us that he had killed a Bull Buffalow, Capt. Lewis & myself & 10 more of the party went out Bucherd & brought it to the Boat. I saw the beds & Signs of a great many more Buffalow but this was the first I ever Saw & was great a curiosity to me."* [21]

Technically, the American Bison, *Bison bison*, is not a true buffalo. (buffalo live in Asia and Africa.) But early white settlers and explorers coined the term "buffalo" for these animals, which is used interchangeably today. Bison

belong to the cattle family. Like their close relatives, domestic cattle and sheep, they chew their cud and are cloven-hoofed. Both sexes have but a single set of hollow, curved horns. The bulls are immense, often weighing a ton or more and standing five or six feet at the shoulders. The huge head and great hump, covered with a dark brown, wooly hair, contrast sharply with the small hips. The cows are smaller and less striking. Despite their great size and bulkiness, buffalo can wheel and charge quickly. They have amazing mobility, speed and agility.

After the Corps' first bison meal, this large animal was common to abundant all the way to the Gates of the Mountains. An exception was the close proximity to the Mandan villages where hunting had reduced the numbers of game. But a few day's travel from Fort Mandan again brought great herds of buffalo, antelope, elk and deer. Traveling upstream, they met putrefying bodies of dead buffalo floating in the current, lodged in river edge driftwood or stranded on the banks. Many predators fed on these carcasses. This sight was a result of the spring river ice breakup. In great numbers, bison would fall through the ice and drown. One such location where rotten, stinking buffalo were heaped up, many wolves were feeding on the putrid meat one so gorged that Lewis approached and killed it with his espontoon. Lewis named the nearby stream Slaughter Creek, which is now called Arrow Creek. A popular canoe campsite currently at this location is called Slaughter River Campground.

At the mouth of the Marias River on June 3rd, Lewis observed that, in every direction was one vast plain in which innumerable herds of buffalo could be seen. Approaching the Great Falls provided views of immense herds feeding and also coming to water at the river.

While traveling across the plains, buffalo provided a bounty of fresh meat for the Corps; but remembering the Mandan's warning that there would be no buffalo when entering the mountains, Lewis kept his hunters busy at White Bear Island drying large quantities of meat. Shannon alone jerked six hundred pounds in a couple of days. Drouillard jerked eight hundred pounds. Buffalo grease was processed and packed into bags; Charbonneau alone produced three kegs.

The hide of the buffalo also played a significant role in the success of the Expedition. This dressed leather had been used for making moccasins. Ordway claimed that while crossing the plains, one pair would not last more than two days. Looking ahead, a year later when Clark and his party arrived at the Yellowstone River, one of the hunters shot a buffalo especially to obtain leather for making moccasins for the sore-footed horses. According to Clark, the improvised booties were *"to releve them very much in passing over the stoney plains."*[*22]

Another critically important use of the hide was in the making of a bull boat. This boat was a large round leather covered tub made of one buffalo skin, and when green is drawn tight over a frame of willow sticks and fastened with thongs to the brim to form a perfect basin. Twice during the Corp's return in 1806, members constructed bull boats to serve critically important purposes. When Captain Lewis returned to White Bear Island on July 6th, he needed to cross the river to find and open the cache left the year before. The men shot buffalo for the hides and made two boats – one boat of one hide, and the second *"of two skins on a plan of our own."** [23]

The second occasion was later that month. Captain Clark had dispatched

---

Bullboats

Bullboats were used by the Mandan and other Upper Missouri village Indians (the Arikara and Hidatsa). They were light weight boats and easily carried. The women used them for carting wood and other items across the Missouri.

Bull Boats *Jean Clary*

The boats were made of three materials; sticks about one and one-half inches thick, the skin of a bull buffalo, and thongs for binding everything together. The boat was constructed by tying the sticks together to produce two loops each with a circumference of about seven feet for the boat's top and bottom. Once the top and bottom loops were attached to the ribbed, three foot long, stick-framed siding, the buffalo skin was stretched around it and secured using the remaining thongs. The effort produced a basin-like vessel which could hold six to eight men and their gear. The boat handled well, and was efficient and secure.

Expedition members used bullboats twice. Lewis and his small party (July 11, 1806) built and used them to cross the Missouri from the mouth of the Medicine River to White Bear Islands and the falls to retrieve caches left there. Sergeant Pryor and his men built two of the boats (August 8, 1806) to descend the Yellowstone after the Crow Indians quietly got away with their horses. Pryor later said the little boats were better on the river than the Expedition's dugout canoes.

Sergeant Pryor and three others to deliver the horses to the Mandan Indians. But when the animals were stolen by the Crow Indians, the men had to figure alternative travel so as to catch up with Clark who was downriver. At today's Pompey's Pillar they killed two buffalo and skillfully made two bull boats, each seven feet three inches in diameter and sixteen inches deep. In a twelve day float trip they arrived in Clark's camp surprising everyone!

Until 1800 over sixty million bison roamed North America, with the greatest concentrations on the plains and prairies from the Rocky Mountains to the Mississippi River and from Great Slave Lake in Canada to Texas. The bison provided most of life's necessities for Indians in this region. Then, as the stream of settlers moved westward, the slaughter of bison began. Some historians say it was the U. S. Army's strategy to destroy the buffalo and with it the Indian's pantry, which seemed the best way to subdue the tribes. But the creation of a profitable market for the hides hastened the killing. Profit was also made from grinding their bones for fertilizer. By 1889 less than 1,100 bison remained in the United States and Canada.

Fortunately, during the period of destruction, a few concerned people were protecting small captive herds in Texas, Montana, New Hampshire, and South Dakota. Then in the early1900's, a group of conservationists organized the American Bison Society. This group, together with the New York Zoological Society, began advocating federal herds in addition to the one herd already established in Yellowstone National Park. One such herd was established in 1908 at Moiese, Montana, where the National Bison Range is now located. It is administered by the United States Fish and Wildlife Service. What a wonderful place to visit today, to see the grand animals that once roamed our land.

GRIZZLY BEAR

Lewis and Clark were not the first white men to report the occurrence of the grizzly bear in western North America. By the late 1700's it had been seen by other explorers, notably Alexander Mackenzie while on the Peace River in Canada. But no one, until the Expedition, had supplied its anatomical detail. It was the French trader, Jean Valle, who in 1804 first told Lewis about several remarkable animals he had seen up the Cheyenne River, including a big bear known as the white bear.

On October 20, 1804, across the river from present Bismarck, North Dakota, Private Cruzatte was the first to encounter a grizzly bear. He wounded him, but being alarmed at the formidable appearance of the bear, he left his tomahawk and gun to run for safety in a small ravine; he returned later to retrieve his dropped items. Clark's diary recorded, *"Our hunters killed 10 deer and a goat today and wounded a white bear, I saw several fresh tracts of those animals which is 3 times as large as a man's track."* * [24]

The grizzly bear, *Ursus arctos horribilis*, measures head and body six to ten feet and is three to three and a half feet high at the shoulder. It weighs from two hundred and forty to nine hundred pounds. The fur is yellow to dark brown even black, and the tips of the hair is whitish or grizzled from whence comes its name. There is a hump on the shoulder and the tail is hidden in the fur. Its habitat once extended from the mountains to the plains of North America, but with the depletion of its prey base and man's settlement of the West, it is now found primarily in the mountain forests. The grizzly lacks natural enemies and does not always conceal itself when disturbed, but rears up on its hind legs to get a better view of the situation. It can run as fast as a horse for short distances. Although this bear is capable of killing moose or deer, it generally feeds on small animals like rodents, and fish, carrion, and on plant material. It is dangerous to man only when surprised, cornered, wounded or with cubs.

At last, on April 29, 1805, near the mouth of the Yellowstone River, the explorers killed their first grizzly; thereafter, this species was encountered frequently on the upper Missouri, all the way to the Three Forks. (From Three Forks to the Pacific Ocean none were reported.) Lewis had no trouble distinguishing the grizzly, which he sometimes termed a brown or yellow bear, from the black bear (*Ursus americanus*). The former was larger, its talons longer, the fur was finer and thicker, did not climb trees, and was not *"passive as the common black bear." "It is a much more ferocious and formidable animal, and will frequently pursue the hunter when wounded. It is astonishing to see the wounds they will bear before they can be put to death."*[*25] Several hunters, including Lewis, had narrow escapes from them.

At the Great Falls of the Missouri the bears had become so troublesome that Lewis did not think it prudent to send one man alone on an errand if he was to pass through the brush. Bears lurked beyond the camp each night, Seaman kept guard and warned of any visitations; the men slept beside their guns.

COLOR SECTION

(Editor's Note – This section of "Lewis and Clark On The Upper Missouri" is intended to give an overview, color paintings and photographs, of both the historical and natural perspectives of the Expedition's travels through the upper Missouri River country. We are indebted to both the artists and the photographers for their work.)

CAPTAIN CLARK OVERLOOKING HELENA VALLEY, JULY 19, 1805, by Robert F. Morgan of Helena, Montana. 44½ x 35¼, oil on canvas. This scene shows Captain William Clark, Joseph Fields, John Potts and York on a hill-point overlooking the Helena Valley, with Prickly Pear Creek in the bottom. (Photo by Dale A. Burk)

MISSOURI RIVER IN MONTANA. The famous "Eye of the Needle" formation in the White Cliffs area of the upper Missouri River, downstream from Fort Benton, Montana, had stood for eons as one of the most amazing views along the wild Missouri River in Montana. It was vandalized by unknown persons in 1998. (Photo by Pat Hastings)

QUILT – LEWIS & CLARK ON THE UPPER MISSOURI, *by Patricia B. Hastings of Stevensville, Montana. 50x60-inch wall hanging quilt highlighted with black Ultra-suede silhouettes to depict aspects of the Expedition's experiences on the upper Missouri. Inspired by the artist's involvement with the Discovery Writers as a co-author of this book and the earlier "Lewis & Clark In The Bitterroot," for which she also designed a special quilt, and authored a quilt-making book, on that theme. (Photo Courtesy of Dale A. Burk)*

CAPTAIN LEWIS AND PARTY AT FIELD'S GULCH, MORNING JULY 20, 1805, by Robert F. Morgan of Helena, Montana. 60 x 40 inches, oil on canvas. This incredible painting of the Expedition breaking camp at Field's Gulch, near the Gates of the Mountains on the Missouri River, on the morning of July 20, 1805, was chosen for the cover of our book. We believe it to be one of the finest paintings on the Expedition ever done. (Photo Courtesy of Dale A. Burk)

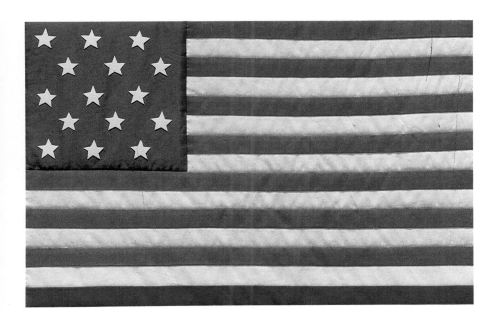

THE AMERICAN FLAG. *This is the design of American flag that accompanied the Expedition, which was in use by the country from 1895 to 1818. It contained fifteen strips and stars. The Expedition carried at least one large flag, a number of flags of a medium size, and at least 19 of a smaller size. Above the Great Falls of the Missouri, the party being anxious to encounter some of Sacajawea's people, flags flew from the canoes. A few days before arriving at the three forks of the Missouri, Whitehouse recorded in his journal, "We hoisted our flag on board our Canoes and proceeded on." This photo represents a close-up of one of the blocks depicted in the quilt of Lewis and Clark on the Upper Missouri designed by one of the Discovery Writers, Patricia B. Hastings of Stevensville, Montana. (Photo Courtesy of Dale A. Burk)*

WHITE CLIFFS OF THE MISSOURI, by Monte Dolack of Missoula, Montana. 15x35⅞acrylic. (From the collection of Bob Giest)

THE PRICKLY PEAR. *This cactus was an ever-present problem for Expedition members on their travels in the upper Missouri country. In fact, Meriwether Lewis called it one of the three "pests" of the journey, the others being mosquitoes and eye gnats. On July 15, 1805, he wrote of the prickly pear that it "...is now in full blume and forms one of the beauties as well as the greatest pests of the plains." (Photo by Jeanne O'Neill)*

WHITE BEARS AND WHITE CLIFFS, *by Robert F. Morgan of Helena, Montana. Oil on canvas, 1988. Hailed by critics as one of the finest artistic depictions ever of the Expedition's arduous journey up the Missouri River in what is now Montana, this major work is on display at the Montana State Historical Museum in Helena, Montana. (Courtesy of the Montana State Historical Society)*

WHEN THE LAND BELONGED TO GOD, by Charles M. Russell. Oil, 1914. This scene of a migrating herd of buffalo on the Missouri River is one of Russell's most famous paintings. (Courtesy of the Montana State Historical Society)

LEWIS AND CLARK AT THREE FORKS, by Edgar S. Paxson. This stylized depiction has become one of the most widely-viewed paintings of the Expedition. (Courtesy of the Montana State Historical Society)

LEWIS AT BLACK EAGLE FALLS, *by Edgar S. Paxson. Oil, 1912. It hangs in the Montana State Capitol Building in Helena, Montana. (Courtesy of the Montana State Historical Society)*

PINION JAY, by Joe Thornbrugh of Victor, Montana. 14x17-inch acrylic on ragboard. Meriwether Lewis first described this bird on August 1, 1805, in the Jefferson River Valley. "I also saw near the top of the mountain among some scattering pine a blue bird about the size of the common robbin," he put in his journal. Thornbrugh created this painting specifically for this book. (Photo Courtesy of Dale A. Burk)

THE BEAVER'S HEAD ROCK. *This famous landmark along the Beaverhead River (called Jefferson River by the Expedition) in southwestern Montana. According to the journals, Sacajawea "recognized the point of a high plain to our right which she informed us was not very distant from the summer retreat of her nation, on a river beyond the mountains which runs to the west, this hill she says her nation calls the beaver's head from a conceived re(se)mblance of its' figure to the head of that animal." Its name was ultimately given to the county in which the beaver's head rock is located, Beaverhead County, Montana, and to a national forest in that part of Montana, the Beaverhead National Forest. The photos present two views of the famous rock. (Photos by Pat Hastings)*

ALONG THE TRAIL: LEWIS' WOODPECKER, by Joe Thornbrugh
of Victor, Montana. 18x15-inch acrylic on ragboard. Painted especially
for this publication and the book "Lewis and Clark In The Bitterroot."
This stunningly beautiful bird was first seen and recorded on July 20,
1805, in the area near where Helena, Montana, is located today. (Photo
Courtesy of Dale A. Burk)

CLARK'S NUTCRACKER, *by Elmer Sprunger of Bigfork, Montana. 8x10-inch oil on canvas, painted especially for this publication and the book "Lewis and Clark In The Bitterroot." "I first met this bird above the three forks of the Missouri and saw them on the hights of the Rockey Mountains...." Meriwether Lewis wrote in his journal. (Photo Courtesy of Dale A. Burk)*

AT LEMHI, by Robert F. Morgan of Helena, Montana. Oil on canvas, 1988. This scene depicts Lewis and Clark at the Continental Divide between the Beaverhead River drainage (present-day Montana) and that of the Lemhi River (present-day Idaho). This, literally, was the crown of the continent for the Expedition. (Courtesy Montana State Historical Society)

More than once members of the party had to dive into the river to escape a charging bear. But on one instance, a willow tree was used for safety. On July 15, 1806, Lewis sent McNeal to ride down and check on the cache prepared the year before, below the Falls. Before nightfall McNeal returned with his musket broken off at the breach and related his tale of earlier coming suddenly upon a white bear in the thick brush. In panic, the horse threw off McNeal and he landed under the bear. The animal stood on his hind feet for battle, giving McNeal time to recover from his fall and strike the bear over the head with the gun, breaking it off at the breach. The stunned bear fell to the ground and began to scratch his head with his feet! McNeal quickly escaped by climbing a nearby willow tree where he was treed for three hours before being able to come down, retrieve his horse and return to camp.

In 1982, Montana's school children worked on a project to choose a state animal. Seventy four different animals, native to Montana, were nominated. Thus began an elaborate campaign and election process. Arguments favoring the grizzly were: Montana is the only one of the lower forty-eight states that has a grizzly population, plus its historic significance: Lewis and Clark made numerous references to the bear and episodes regarding them in their journals. Upon the final vote, the grizzly bear won two to one over runner-up elk. Therefore, on April 7, 1983, Governor Ted Schwinden signed the bill designating the grizzly as the official animal of the State of Montana.

During the 1960's and 70's the lower forty eight states listed the grizzly bear as a threatened species. ("Threatened" means that a species is <u>becoming</u>

COYOTE   D. LADO '99

Mountain lion.

"endangered". "Endangered means that there is a threat of the species <u>is in danger of becoming</u> extinct.) Under the Endangered Species Act, the United States Fish and Wildlife Service is required to do something to assure viable populations of the threatened species. They have set up population objectives for grizzly bears in six ecosystems in the northwest United States: Yellowstone (National Park), North Continental Divide (Glacier Park and Bob Marshall Wilderness), Bitterroot, Cabinet (Yaak area), Selkirk (North Washington), and North Cascades. Most of their activity in these zones involves monitoring the population number, documenting encounters, and managing (controlling human interaction).

Today the two principal grizzly populations in Montana are the Yellowstone and the North Continental Divide eco-systems. The United States Fish and Wildlife Service has determined goals for viable populations in these areas. In Yellowstone, the goals have been achieved; therefore, there is a move to de-list them from threatened. The Glacier/Bob Marshal populations are doing well by holding-their-own.

– – – – –

Some other animals seen and reported by Expedition members while on the Upper Missouri watershed were: otters, coyotes, red fox, mountain lion, pronghorn antelope, whitetail deer, mule deer, and elk. A few moose, too, were spotted in May of 1805 near the Mile River by Ordway and Whitehouse.

BIRDS

Of the many birds encountered in the Upper Missouri River basin, Lewis mentions in his journals over a dozen which were new to science. Let's look at some examples.

Meriwether Lewis is credited with being the first white man to describe the pinyon jay, although it was not given a scientific name, *Gymnorhinus cyanocephalus,* until 1841 by Maximilian. On August 1, 1805, Lewis discovered this bird along the Jefferson River near present-day Cardwell, Montana. *"I also saw near the top of the mountain among some scattering pine a blue bird about the size of the common robbin. its' action and form is somewhat that of the jay bird and never rests long in any one position but constantly flying and hoping from sprey to sprey. I shot at one of them but missed it. Their note is loud and frequently repeated both flying and when at rest and is char ah, char'r-ah, char-ah, as nearly as letters can express it."* [26]

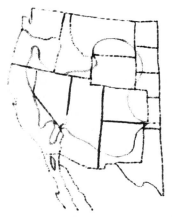

Range of the pinyon jay.

The pinyon jay is in the Family *Corvidae,* which includes crows, ravens, magpies and nutcrackers. This bird measures nine to eleven inches and is locally common in pinyon pines, junipers and into areas of sagebrush. It looks like a small dull-blue crow, but nearer the size of a robin with a long sharp bill. It lacks the crest of the Steller's jay and differs from the scrub jay with a shorter tail and uniform steel-blue coloration. Pinyon jays are gregarious, often gathering in large noisy flocks and walk about like small crows. Their voice is a high mewing call in flight and when perched, jay-like notes and chattering. The range of this jay is the inland area of the western states. (See illustration.)

Lewis reported on April 17, 1805 that, *"Clark saw a Curlou today."* [27] And a month later in the vicinity of Great Falls he wrote, *"Saw . . . quantities of little birds and the large brown curloo ; the latter is now setting; it lays its eggs . . . on the ground without any preparation of a nest."* [28] Lewis was familiar with curlews. In that period of American history, huge numbers of the Eskimo curlew of Alaska migrated over the eastern half of the United States. Over time, however, hunters took such sport in shooting these birds, that by 1890, they had become nearly extinct. The Eskimo curlew is smaller than the one Lewis saw near the falls.

The long-billed curlew, *Numerius americanus americanus,* belongs to

Long-billed curlew.

the Family *Scolopacidae* – wading birds, including sandpipers and phalaropes. The curlew, largest of North American shorebirds, measures twenty to twenty-six inches, plus a very long sickle-shaped bill up to eight and a half inches long. It is mottled buff-brown with cinnamon wing linings visible in flight. In the summer it lives on the high plains and prairies of Montana, and parts of Utah, Idaho, Nevada, Washington, and Oregon, feeding on insects, berries and seeds. It winters along the Pacific coast on marshes, muddy flats, beaches and grasslands. Curlews migrate in large noisy flocks. Their voice is a loud cur-lee with a rising inflection, or a rapid whistled kli-li-li. Its numbers are declining. Not only has it been over-hunted, but it has suffered a loss of habitat, as the plains have been turned into cropland.

One songbird Lewis discovered during the portage at Great Falls was the western meadowlark. *"There is a kind of larke here that much resembles the bird called the old field lark, with a yellow brest and a black spot on the croop; tho' this differs from ours in the form of the tail which is pointed being formed of feathers of unequal length; the beak is somewhat longer and more curved, and the note differs considerably; however, in size, action and colours there is no perceptable difference; or at least none that strikes the eye."* * [29]

Meadowlarks are in the Family *Icteridae* which includes blackbirds, orioles, bobolinks, grackles and cowbirds. The old field lark Lewis mentions is the eastern meadowlark, *Sternella magna*. When John James Audubon rediscovered the western meadowlark in 1843, the scientific name he gave to it reflected the many years between sightings. He called it *Sternella neglecta* which means neglected meadowlark!

This chunky, starling-shaped brown bird measuring nine inches in length, has a conspicuous patch of white on each side of its short, wide tail, and has a bright yellow breast crossed by a black V. The yellow extends slightly farther into the face than the eastern meadowlark, and its body is also browner. Walking, the bird flicks its tail open and shut. Another interesting behavior is how it obtains its food by using specially powerful muscles for opening the bill. Probing for insects and worms, it inserts the closed mandibles into the earth and then forces them open.*[30] The unique flight habit consists of several short, rapid wing beats alternating with brief periods of sailing. The song is variable, with seven to ten flute like notes, gurgling and double-noted, unlike the clear whistles of the eastern meadow lark. And the call is a low-throaty "chuck." In a hidden spot on the ground, the roofed-over nest holds three to seven white eggs speckled brown. Western meadowlarks range in southwest Canada and throughout the western United States in grasslands, cultivated fields, meadows and prairies.

Besides Montana, five other states have picked the western meadowlark as their state bird: Kansas, Nebraska, North Dakota, Oregon and Wyoming. In 1930 Montana's school children were polled to select the bird that most represented their state. The response overwhelmingly favored the western meadowlark. Therefore, the 1931 Legislature declared the western meadowlark the official bird of Montana.*[31]

On the day after the explorers passed through the Gates of the Mountains, near present-day Helena, Lewis made a new discovery. *"I saw a black woodpecker (or crow) today about the size of the lark woodpecker as black as a crow. I endevoured to get a shot at it but could not. It is a distinct species of woodpecker; it has a long tail and fly a good deal like the jay bird."*[32]

Today this bird is known to all as the Lewis' woodpecker, *Melanerpes lewis,* and is in the Family *Picidae* which includes woodpeckers, flickers and sapsuckers. But it wasn't until the next spring that he got a close look at the dark woodpecker that flies with the rowing wingbeat of a crow. The party was camped with the Nez Perce tribe at Camp Chopunnish in today's Idaho, when on May 27, 1806, Lewis finally held this bird for close inspection, and reported, *"we killed and preserved several of them."*[33] His five hundred word recounting included, *"the throat is of a fine crimson red, the belly and breast is a curious mixture of white and blood red, wings and tail are of a sooty black, top of the head black . . . with a glossy tint of green in a certain exposure, and so forth."*[34]

The Lewis' woodpecker measures from ten and one-half to eleven and one-

Blue grouse.

half inches long. It is a large black-backed woodpecker with an extensive pinkish red belly (the only North American woodpecker so colored). It has a wide gray collar and a dark red face patch. The pink underparts and wide black wings are the best field marks; the sexes are similar. It frequents open stands of pine and scattered trees beside streams. A favorite haunt is the charred remnant of a burned-over forest. This bird eats insects by snapping them up in the air, but also eats freely on the ground – ants, grasshoppers, crickets, and beetles. Its voice is usually silent, but occasionally there is a harsh but soft curr or chee-ur . In

Male Sage Grouse – courting ritual.

some respects it is un-woodpecker-like, as it tends to light crosswise on a limb rather than right side up on the truck, does very little hammering on the tree, and seldom, if ever, digs its own nest, moving instead into one made by another woodpecker.

As of the summer of 1999, there are still occasional sightings of the Lewis' woodpecker, but it has become scarce. The serious decline is largely due to loss of nest holes to starlings, a Eurasian species which was introduced into this country in 1890 and boldly proliferated nationwide at the expense of other cavity nesters, like bluebirds and woodpeckers.

Upon returning from the West, Lewis turned to his friend, Alexander Wilson, for drawings of his preserved birds. Wilson obliged by sketching, describing and naming several of the specimens including Lewis's woodpecker which he called, *Picus torquatus.* (Scientific names are periodically corrected as the naming protocol becomes more sophisticated, along with more knowledge of the taxonomic process. Therefore, this woodpecker soon was renamed *Asyndesmus lewis,* and still again, much later, to the current name, *Melanerpes lewis).* Even though Wilson initially had no formal training in drawing or technical writing, he succeeded in completing seven of nine volumes of his American Ornithology with help from his friends such as George Ord. This was the first inclusive study of birds in the United States. (Ord was a naturalist who, in 1812, founded the Academy of Natural Sciences of Philadelphia).

Some other new birds which Lewis noted on this leg of the journey are: the great horned owl, northern flicker, western willet, Brewer's blackbird, white-rumped shrike, McCown's longspur, western goldfinch, western mourning dove, and the Richardson's blue grouse..

FISH

Meriwether Lewis anticipated that fish would be an important food source for sustaining his Expedition. We know that the baggage included at least *"4 Groce fishing Hooks assorted"*[*][35] Although bought in Philadelphia, it is likely that they were imported from England where iron hooks were forged near Redditch. These hooks were useful not only to the Corps, but became trade items with native Indians whose hooks would probably have been fashioned from bone or antler.

The typical hook and line outfit would have been a long pole or sapling with a braided line of horsehair to which the hook was attached; handlines were also used. As the Corps proceeded on, they improvised other methods such as weirs and traps which were highly effective. On several occasions in August of 1805, the Journals report literally hundreds of fish being caught as they dredged holes in the upper Beaverhead River or Horse Prairie Creek with large drags of willow brush.

The party used a variety of bait. In the entry for June 11, 1805, while on the lower reaches of the Tansey River (today's Teton River, a tributary of the Marias River), Lewis reports that Silas Goodrich, the party's best angler, caught *"several douzen fish of two different species on meat and grasshoppers."* These fish were sauger and goldeye, the first time these species had been catalogued. The following day on the Missouri River Lewis *"amused myself catching those white fish mentioned yesterday, they are here in great abundance. I caught upwards of a douzen in a few minutes; they bit most freely at the melt of a deer which Goodrich had brought with him for the purpose of fishing".* [36] "Melt" is another word for spleen.

Lewis and Clark can be credited with the discovery of many species of fish found in the Northwest. But it is the cutthroat trout that we will focus upon; it was encountered by the Corps while fishing at the Great Falls. On June 13, 1805, Goodrich caught a number of these fish for a sumptuous meal. They ranged in size from sixteen to twenty-three inches in length. Lewis wrote, they *"precisely resemble our mountain or speckled trout in form and the position of their fins, but the specks on these are of a deep black instead of the red or gould colour of those common to the U' States. these are furnished long sharp teeth on the pallet and tongue and have generally a small dash of red on each side behind the front ventral fins; the flesh is of a pale yellowish red or when in good order of a rose red."* [37] Lewis was comparing this new trout to the brook trout he had enjoyed fishing for in the mountains of Virginia. The description of the red dashes is conclusive evidence that this was our cutthroat, the fish which has since become Montana's state fish.

In 1836 naturalist John Richardson gave this fish its scientific name, *Salmo clarki,* as a tribute to Captain Clark. About twenty years later Charles Girard, the Philadelphia naturalist, was inspecting some subsequent specimens collected at Great Falls and named the cutthroat trout *Salar lewisii,* giving Lewis recognition. Nevertheless, the accepted name became *Salmo clarki.* [38] Originally the genus name *Salmo,* included all species of North American trout, Atlantic salmon and Eurasian species of trout as well as a trout in Siberia called the Kamchatka. However, systematists recently concluded that North American trout have a greater affinity with Pacific salmon, which are the genus *Oncorhynchus*, and they have given these native cutthroat trout this new name. (Old World species, including brown trout which have been introduced in North America, remain *Salmo* [39]

There are fourteen subspecies of cutthroat trout, *Oncorhynchus clarki*, in western North America. Two are in Montana and are commonly known as "blackspotted cutthroat trout". These two subspecies are *O. clarki lewisi* and *O. clarki bouvieri*. The former is the westslope cutthroat trout which inhabits streams on both sides of the Continental Divide. On the east side they are distributed mostly in Montana in the Missouri Basin downstream to about thirty-seven miles below Great Falls and in the headwaters of the Judith, Milk and Marias Rivers. On the west side of the Divide this subspecies occurs in the upper Kootenai River, the Clark Fork drainage in Montana and Idaho downstream to the falls on the Pend O'reille River and in other river basins in Idaho, Washington and Oregon. One may wonder how these cutthroat trout can inhabit both sides of the Divide. According to Fred Allendorf, professor of biological sciences at the University of Montana, this occurs through a phenomenon called Headwater Capture. During certain geological or flood events, the bodies of water located on the crest of the divide flow either way, thus making an avenue for fish to cross from one drainage to the other. The other subspecies, the Yellowstone cutthroat trout, *clarki bouvieri,* is native to the Yellowstone River drainage. The appearance of these two fish is very similar except that the latter exhibits fewer, larger and rounder black spots.

For over two decades the so-called black-spotted cutthroat trout has been the state fish of Montana. On February 10, 1977, Governor Thomas Judge signed the law designating the black-spotted cutthroat trout as Montana's official state fish. In choosing the state fish, two candidates for the honor were proposed – the black-spotted cutthroat trout and the Montana grayling, but others were also accepted. Proponents set six criteria: 1) Native to Montana, 2) Not already adopted by another state, 3) Well accepted by people, 4) A game fish, 5) Distinctive in appearance, 6) In more than one area of the state. In support of the cutthroat trout, it was thought that such a fish would meet all the requirements and add to Montana's image as a fisherman's paradise of clean, sparkling waters, combined with the historical significance of its connection to the Lewis and Clark Expedition. Of the thousand votes received, the black-spotted cutthroat trout got five hundred and twenty, easily outdistancing the grayling's two hundred votes, prompting the Legislature to designate the black-spotted cutthroat trout as the official Montana state fish. The name thus honors both of Montana's cutthroat species.

Westslope cutthroat trout begin to mature at age three and usually spawn at age four and five. They spawn from March to July at water temperatures near ten degrees Celsius, predominantly in small tributaries. The fry emerge from their gravel beds between June 20 and July 14, moving downstream with the peaks of stream flow. These offspring may remain one to four years in their natal stream. The distribution and abundance of the more mature Westslope cutthroats has been strongly associated with pools; streams with numerous pools support the highest densities of fish.

Although closely related, cutthroat trout and rainbow trout have remained reproductively distinct where they originated in the same geographic area. However, where non-native rainbow trout have been introduced, hybridization with cutthroat trout is wide-spread. Additionally, Yellowstone cutthroat trout have also been widely introduced into the range of the westslope cutthroat, particularly in routine stocking of high mountain lakes. Hybridization between these subspecies is common and again appears to be a problem throughout most of the range of the westslope cutthroat trout.*[40]

Distribution and abundance of this fish is declining. It is now believed that they persist in only twenty seven percent of their historical range in Montana and are genetically unaltered in only two and a half percent. Some factors leading to this decline are: construction of dams, irrigation diversions, or other migratory barriers such as culverts. Overfishing and competition also restrict distribution to a smaller portion of the original range. But the three basic causes of decline are: competition with and predation by non-native species, genetic introgression (hybridizing), overfishing and habitat loss. Disturbance of stream banks and riparian areas, construction of roads and removal of upland vegetation have been associated with alteration of stream flow, increased erosion and sediment loading and increased water temperatures. The strongest populations remain largely in roadless and wilderness areas or national parks.

Westslope cutthroat trout are considered a sensitive subspecies by Regions One and Four of the U.S. Forest Service and the Bureau of Land Management, and considered a species of special concern by the Idaho Department of Fish and Game. Both states have set harvest regulations. But the good news is that both states have established captive broodstocks free of introgression of rainbow or Yellowstone trout. In both states Westslope cutthroat populations are being restored in waters where they were once eliminated or crossed with non-native trout.*[41]

REPTILES

As the party approached the Great Falls base camp area on June 15, Captain Clark described the arduous chore of pulling the boats upstream and of the *"great numbers of dangerous places, and the fatigue which we have to encounter untill night hauling the cord and boats, walking on sharp rocks and round sliperey stones which alternately cut their feet and throw them down, not with standing all this dificuelty they go with cheerfulness, aded to those dificuelties the rattle snakes are inumerable & require great caution to prevent being bitten."*[42] This new reptile was the prairie rattlesnake, *Crotalus viridis viridis*, which inhabits the rocky ledges of the Missouri River banks. Lewis had seen this snake earlier near the mouth of the Yellowstone River. In his journal description he says, this snake is smaller than those common to the middle Atlantic states, being about 2 feet 6 inches long, *"that it exhibited 176 scuta on the abdomen and seventeen on the tail, and is of a yellowish brown colour on the back and sides, variagated with one row of oval spots of a dark brown colour lying transversely over the back from neck to the tail."*[43]

There were frequent encounters with this reptile. For example, on August 10th near present-day Clark Canyon Dam, Montana, Lewis tells about the number of rattlesnakes around the cliffs where the party stopped. *"We called them rattlesnake clifts. – this serpent is the same before described with oval spots of yellowish brown."*[44]

Another snake new to science was one described on July 23, 1805, called the western hog-nose snake, *Heterodon nasicus nasicus*. Lewis wrote, *"I saw a black snake today about 2 feet long - the belly of which was as black as any other part, or as jet itself. It had 128 scuta on the belly, 63 on the tail."*[45]

INSECTS

Of all the insects the Corps encountered on their journey, mosquitoes were the most mentioned. The journalists often complained of mosquitoes, *Aedes vexans* , *"as verry troublesome"* – certainly an understatement. Lewis had anticipated dealing with mosquitoes, and with this foresight had purchased in Philadelphia *"Muscatoe Curtains"* along with *"8ps Cat Gut for Mosquito Curtains"*, and two hundred pounds of tallow mixed with fifty pounds of hog's lard for an insect repellent.*[46]

The party incorporated a variety of defenses in dealing with this winged tormentor. The first was in applying the grease. (It had long been known that Native Indians used oil or grease as an armor against mosquitoes.) Although seldom mentioned in the journals, on June 18, 1804, Clark described the men greasing themselves with the tallow.

Use of the mosquito netting (biers) was a fundamental necessity and main line of defense between the men and the hordes of blood-sucking, sleep destroying insects. Sergeant Ordway on June 19, 1804, records that that night the men *"Got Musquetoes bears (biers) from Capt. Lewis to sleep in."*[47] A year later Lewis wrote that the *"men are all fortunately supplied with mosquetoe biers otherwise it would be impossible for them to exist under the fatigues which they encounter without their natural rest which they could not obtain for those tormenting insects if divested of their biers."*[48]

Two summers later, with their equipment wearing out, Clark and his party stayed only one night at the mouth of the Yellowstone River. The urgency to push further down the river to a new site was due to the unendurable mosquitoes, particularly to the men *"who have no bears (biers) to keep them off at night, and nothing to Screen them but their blankets which are worn and have maney holes."*[49] Conditions at the next campsite must have been no better; the men had another sleepless night. Nearby Clark saw some Bighorn sheep on a bluff; he approached the hill below to take a shot. *"The musquetors were so numerous that I could not Shute with any certainty . . ."*[50]

Campfires were another line of defense for the men and even their horses. Standing in the smoke provided a respite from mosquito vexations. On July 3, 1806, Clark records, *"we were obliged to kindle large fires for our horses . . . insects torture them in such manner until they placed themselves in the smoke of the fires . . . "* [51] Later that month Sergeant Ordway wrote, *"the musquetoes and Small flyes verry troublesome we made fires of buffaloe dry dung to make Smoaks etc."* [52]

Using the wind to advantage was another line of defense. The search was always on for campsites open to breezes. These were often found on sand bars, high bottoms thinly timbered, and bleak, exposed areas. As an example, on August 8, 1806, Clark wrote, *"our best retreat from those insects is on the Sand bars in the river and even those Situations are only clear of them when the Wind should happen to blow . . . "* [53]

As if the trials of the Expedition were not enough, the Corps were compelled to battle the age-old drama of man verses the mosquito – using the same defenses campers still use today, except, maybe, the type of bug repellent!

A variety of grasshoppers inhabit the plains, and their presence was recorded in the journals. While observing the abundance of a certain sparrow-sized bird resembling a lark (the McCown's Longspur), Lewis speculated on how the grasshopper population could be their food source. *"There are meriads of small grasshoppers in these plains which no doubt furnish the principal aliment (food) of this numerous progeny of the feathered creation."* [54] And Clark noted in mid July of 1806, while near present-day Columbus, *"It may be proper to observe that the emence Sworms of Grasshoppers have destroyed every sprig of Grass for maney miles on this side of the river, and appear to be progressing upwards."* [55]

Lewis mentioned the honey bee only because of its absence. He noted, *"the bee martin or Kingbird is common to this country, tho' there are not bees . . . nor have we met with a honey bee since we passed the entrance of the Osage River".* [56] Historically, the honey bee, Apis mellifera, is not native to the United States; it was brought here by the early colonists. As their descendants moved west, the bee followed in their wake.

PLANTS

In crossing the North American continent, Lewis and Clark passed through a remarkable variety and number of climatic plant communities. At the start they traveled through great deciduous forests. Then they came to the high plains, grasslands devoid of trees except cottonwoods and willows restricted to river banks. Then, as they traversed the Rocky Mountains, they passed through green coniferous forests which continued until they dropped into the arid, treeless country beyond. Finally they entered another green world on the Pacific Coast, the most important coniferous timberland in our country with the largest trees the explorers had ever seen. Lewis methodically kept track of this flora diversity throughout the expedition. Let us focus upon a few of the plants along the upper Missouri which created a special impression.

The first mention of the prickly pear is noted on September 19, 1804. It is a place they called Prickly Pear Creek, near present-day Big Bend, North Dakota, where great quantities of prickly pear cactus grew on the plains.

The genus name of prickly pear cactus is *Opuntia*. The Corps encountered two species: one is *Opuntia fragilis* in which the stem segments are oval to cylindric and are easily detached; the other is *Opuntia polyacantha,* of which the segments are flattened, are much wider than thick, and not easily detached.

It wasn't until the later part of the following June that the prickly pear made its first great impact upon the Corps. During the portage at Great Falls, the men made numerous trips pulling the wagons over ground that was thickly covered by a prickly blanket. The spiny plants contributed immeasurably to the endless hours of extremely difficult labor. It was nearly impossible to avoid the spines that penetrated the men's thin-soled moccasins. Even after reinforcing their soles with buffalo rawhide, there was still no protection from spines entering from the side. In the evening the men suffered the awful painful process of pulling cactus spines out of their feet. Even Seaman sustained the ravages of the prickly pear.

Lewis considered the prickly pear to be one of *"our trio of pests"* – the other two were gnats and mosquitoes. On July 15, he wrote, *"The Prickley Pear is now in full bloom and forms one of the beauties as well as the greatest pests of the plains".*[*57] While nearing Three Forks, Clark's feet were a raw bleeding mass of flesh assaulted by prickly pears. He wrote, *"I opened the bruises & blisters of my feet which caused them to be painfull."*[*58]

Another "new" troublesome plant was the greasewood, *Sarcobatus vermiculatus*. It is a thorny, fleshy leaved shrub which grows commonly in alkaline soils of the West. Lewis called it *"the pulpy-leaved thorn"*, one of the many dry-land plants which inhabited the benchlands boarding the Missouri River as the party approached the Marias River.

Yet another "new" pesty plant was found below Three Forks. This is commonly known as needle and thread grass, *Slipa comata,* a form of a grass with barbed seeds. Lewis exclaimed, *"these barbed seeds penetrate our mockersons and leather legings and give up Great pain untill they are removed."*[*59] Even Seaman suffered, biting and scratching, *"as if in a rack of pain"*.

There was one plant species Lewis noted which he thought might be useful if cultivated. It grew in the river bottoms and resembled the common flax with which he was familiar. *"The bark of the stem is thick (and) strong and appears as if it would make excellent flax."* [60]   When botanist Frederick Pursh formally described it in 1814, he honored Lewis and named it Lewis's wild flax, *Linum lewisii*.

Prickly pear catcus   D. LADD '99

Moving up the Beaverhead River, Lewis noticed how the uplands, and drier areas adjacent to bottomlands, were dominated by the plains prickly pear, needle and thread grass, sedge, greasewood, and the big sagebrush, *Artemisia tridentata*. As he gained elevation, so did the appearance of sagebrush. Big sagebrush, which grows one to twelve feet tall, has silver-gray to whitish foliage – the leaves two-thirds to one inch long, narrow and generally three-toothed or more at the tip. The other, common to Montana, is silver sagebrush, *Artemisia canadensis,* a silver-gray to yellowish shrub one to three feet tall. The leaves are two-thirds to three inches long and narrow.

Additional plants "new to science" which Lewis noted for this region are: golden currant, sticky currant, western blue flag, silvery lupine, large monkey flower, white margined spurge, Saskatoon serviceberry, and the chokecherry.

Meriwether Lewis noted at least three trees which were "new to science": the Rocky Mountain maple, *Acer glabrum*, the western paper birch, *Betula accidentalis*, and the narrow-leafed cottonwood, *Populus angustifolia*. But it is the cottonwood tree which will be highlighted here. As Paul Russell Cutright puts it in his book, *Lewis & Clark: Pioneering Naturalists*, "Of all the western trees, the cottonwood contributed more to the success of the Expedition than any other. Lewis and Clark were men of great talent and resourcefulness, masters of ingenuity and improvision. Though we think it probable that they would have successfully crossed the continent without the cottonwood, don't ask us how!"

Upon reaching the Teton River between the Marias River and the Great Falls on June 12th, Clark discovered many cottonwood trees with narrow leaves resembling those of the wild cherry tree. And a few days later Lewis wrote, *"The narrow leafed cottonwood grows here in common with the other species of the same tree with a broad leaf or that which constituted the major part of the timber of the Missouri from its junction with the Mississippi to this place. The narrow-leafed cottonwood differs from the other in the shape of its leaf, height, and greater thickness of it's bark".* [61] The "broad leaf" tree he speaks of is the plains cottonwood, *Populus deltoides,* a large tree, 60 to 90 feet tall, and the trunk growing to six feet in diameter. It has a broad open crown with stout, erect,

Big sagebrush,
Artemisia tridentata.
(Photo by Pat Hastings)

spreading branches. The leaves are broadly triangular, three to six inches long and usually slightly longer than broad. The bark is gray and smooth on young trees, but thick and ash-gray and furrowed on older trees. Like all cottonwoods, it grows where there is abundance of soil moisture. The narrow-leafed cottonwood, *Populus angustifolia*, is a medium sized tree of fifty to seventy feet. Its leaves are two to six inches long and 3/4 to 1 ½" wide. The bark is smooth, unbroken and pale green on young trees, and light gray-brown and brown on older trees.* [62]

When the Corps arrived at the junction of the Missouri and Knife Rivers, a winter fort was built near the Mandan villages. With Sergeant Gass in charge, construction began with the only suitable timber available, the plains cottonwood trees. Also made of cottonwood were tables, shelves, beds, benches and other wooden items. This tree, too, supplied the firewood required for cooking, and also heating the rooms during that bitterly cold winter. Sergeant Ordway commented on a particular attribute of the tree, *"We find the cottonwood timber will split Tolerable well"*.* [63]

As the spring of 1805 neared, Sergeant Gass was again assigned a woodworking project – this time to construct dugout canoes. With his crew of fifteen men, he cut cottonwood trees found a few miles above Fort Mandan. In three weeks they built six dugouts, each large enough to hold a crew, food, and their gear. Without these water-craft for transportation, the Expedition could hardly have continued. As the keelboat was to be sent back to St Louis, they would be left with only the two piroques.

Weeks after the Expedition left the fort, cottonwoods were appreciated for their esthetic value. Lewis noted near the Judith River, *"these appearances (of cottonwoods) were quite reviving after the drairy country through which we have been passing."* In addition, their groves soon provided shade from the relentless hot sun, and protected the party during the prairie downpours.

When Lewis and Clark arrived at a campsite below the Great Falls, they determined that the only way to portage the six heavy dugouts around the falls was to build two wagons. Sergeant Gass was in charge *"to p(r)epare four sets of truck wheel with couplings, toungs and bodies."** [64] To make the wheels, slices were cut from a 22-inch diameter cottonwood tree. Then, at White Bear Island, when the construction of the famous "iron-boat" failed (which was to replace the two piroques), two more dugouts had to be made. Captain Clark,

Cottonwood Tree
Jean Clary

Sergeant Pryor and a crew went on a search for two big trees. When they finally reached a grove of trees, they found only two cottonwoods big enough. One was hollow at the end, and they were both "windshaken". Nevertheless, the axemen shaped two canoes, 25' and 33' long. The cottonwood had once again saved the day!

A year later, on July 15, 1806, when Captain Clark and his party arrived at the Yellowstone River near present-day Columbus, Montana, they halted three days to build dugouts for their river travel. The cottonwood trees here were not large enough to make single boats, so they made two dugouts and lashed them together. Each measured 28 feet long and 16 to 24 inches deep. This craft could carry the party and their baggage and would be stable enough for the swift and sometimes shallow Yellowstone River. Again the cottonwood tree made a valuable contribution.

Today, more than two hundred dried and preserved plant specimens which the explorers brought back, are kept at the Academy of Natural Sciences of Philadelphia. Botanical and zoological samples collected from Wood River to the Mandan Villages were returned downriver in the spring of 1805 via the keelboat. All material gathered from Fort Mandan to the Great Falls were buried in a cache at White Bear Island in July of that year. In another cache in Shoshone Cove, near present-day Clark Canyon Dam, Lewis put *"specemines of plants, minerals, seeds & which, I have collected between this place and the falls of the Missouri".*[65] But to Lewis's profound dismay, upon opening the cache at the falls site the following summer, he found, *"my bearskins entirely destroyed by water, the river having risen so high that the water had penitrated. All my specimens of plants also lost."*[66] When Clark opened the cache at Shoshone Cove, he thought everything was safe – although a little damp. Nevertheless, of all the plant material stored here, only one, the golden current, arrived in Philadelphia. Possibly the others mildewed and had to be discarded.

Therefore, the remaining specimens carried home would have been collected from the Lemhi Pass to Fort Clatsop, and also those obtained during the following spring on the homeward trek to St. Louis. To break it down, Lewis collected and brought back one hundred and thirty-five plant specimens from the Columbia watershed, and sixty five from the Missouri watershed.[67] The seeds, roots and cuttings collected by the Captains were given to several individuals, including their relatives and friends. The only surviving zoological specimen, the Lewis woodpecker, is presently at the Museum of Comparative Zoology at Harvard University in Cambridge Massachusetts.

For years after the Corps' return, naturalists worked to give names to the new species. Indeed, if Lewis had lived to write the account of the Expedition, including a book devoted only to natural history, he, instead of many others, would today be recognized and honored as the discoverer and describer of most, if not all, of the species he found new to science.

Giant Springs State Park

Giant Springs, described by Captain Clark, June 18, 1805, as "...the largest fountain or spring I ever saw, and no doubt if it is not the largest in America known." and by Sergeant Ordway as "it is clear as crystal I could have Seen to the bottom of the fountain to pick up a pin" originates in the Little Belt Mountains southeast of Great Falls, Montana, churns up 134,000 gallons of water per minute, maintains a constant 54 degree F. temperature, is carbon-dated approximately 3,000 years old. It is one of the largest freshwater springs in the world. From Giant Springs the Roe River, average length 201 feet, flows into the Missouri. The Roe River is listed in the Guinness Book of Records as "The World's Shortest River."

Upper Missouri River Dams

HAUSER DAM: Located on the Missouri River, seventeen miles northeast of Helena and five miles upstream from the Gates of the Mountains scenic canyon, Hauser Dam generates 16,500Kw. It dates from 1907 but was washed out by a flood in 1908. Samuel T. Hauser, who built the plant, was nearly driven into bankruptcy after the 1908 flood and was forced to sell, not only Hauser Dam, but Canyon Ferry, and the partially- built Holter Dam. This ended Sam Hauser's dream that Hauser dam would be the state's largest on the Missouri and was to have demonstrated, along with Hauser's earlier installation at Canyon Ferry, hydroelectric power's great potential for supplying growing industrial centers efficiently. Montana Power acquired the rights in 1912 and completed Hauser dam. The reservoir, Hauser Lake, supports recreation including picnicking, camping, hiking, fishing, and boating.

HOLTER DAM: Located on the Missouri River about forty-three miles northeast of Helena. Although construction began in 1908, Holter Dam was not completed until 1918 by Montana Power Co. Holter Lake supports picnicking, camping, hiking, fishing, boating, displays, visitor center, and commercial boat tours of Gates of the Mountains, which lie behind the dam.

CANYON FERRY DAM: the largest of the three lakes on this portion of the Missouri River includes twenty-five miles of lake and nearly eighty miles of shoreline. Early-day travelers found this to be a suitable place to ferry across the river as it flowed through the canyon. The dam was built in 1950 by the Bureau of Reclamation and is managed by the BLM. The Lake boasts twenty-five state parks, abounds in fish and is a favorite recreation area for camping boating and surfing. Below the lake the river is a favorite attraction to bald eagles who gather in late fall to feast on the spawning kokanee salmon, where in 1805 Captain Lewis observed that the bald eagles were more abundant than at any other part of the country.

Chapter Seven

DUE SOUTH ON A WESTWARD JOURNEY

Canoe Camp to Three Forks

Determined to complete their mission, the Corps of Discovery leave Canoe Camp on the morning of July 15, 1805, in six old and two newly hand-hewn canoes. As they head upstream on a course due south, they are immediately put to the test. The swift flowing river presents a series of tight U-shaped switchbacks. Navigating these successfully, without the aid of either Captain, the unskilled river men that left Wood's Camp on May 14, 1804, are now adept boatsmen. This southerly course should take them to the source of the Missouri River – fulfilling one of the tasks assigned to the Expedition by President Thomas Jefferson.

Despite having to cache or discard their superfluous treasures and carry only those items necessary to the success of the mission. Captain Lewis writes that he believes every individual in the party finds it a joy to be underway once again. The Expedition is running one and a-half months behind schedule. With hope of soon encountering the Shoshone and acquiring the needed guides, horses and information to take them over the mountains to the Pacific, everyone is on constant look out for the Indians. If the party could cache the canoes and travel overland, it would allow them to make up valuable time and possible avoid being impeded by heavy mountain snow.

Fear of a diminishing food supply once they enter the mountains, canoes are heavily ladened with buffalo meat and tallow. The captains along with "two invalids", LaPage and Potts unable to row because of injuries, choose to lighten the load by walking the shoreline. Traversing several miles of sun baked buffalo tracks and dodging large clumps of low-growing prickly pear cactus, the overlanders have fallen behind the main party. The cactus are now in full bloom as are the sunflowers. Captain Lewis acknowledges the beauty of each. He describes the Indians use of sunflower seed for bread and a soup base. To save time and energy, they abandon their shoreline walk and cross the peninsulas formed by river bends. Captain Clark, the Expedition cartographer, finds this convoluted section almost impossible to map.

Approximately twenty miles from Canoe Camp, they discover the mouth

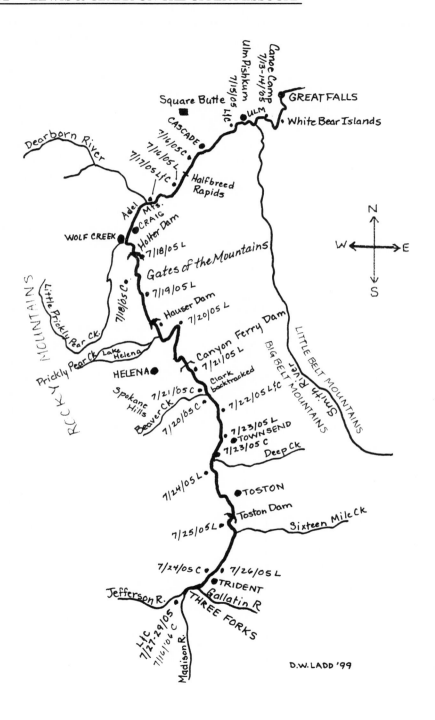

D.W. LADD '99

of a beautiful stream descending from between two mountain ranges to the southeast and name it Smith's River in honor of Robert Smith, Secretary of the Navy. [1]

It is here that Seaman, Captain Lewis' Newfoundland dog once again proves himself a valuable member of the Corps. Drouillard shoots and wounds a deer, which runs to the river. Seaman catches and drags it to shore. Finding a grove of trees on the west bank, they dine on fresh venison and camp for the night, upstream from present day Ulm. Their campsite is located in an area of rolling prairies broken only by an occasional volcanic lacolith. This grass covered rangeland is prime grazing for huge herds of buffalo. Shadowed by a prominent flat topped geologic formation twelve miles due west and rising one thousand feet above the surrounding prairie, the captains, thinking it looks inaccessible, name it Fort Mountain, present day Square Butte. [2] Noting this, they are apparently unaware of an ancient buffalo jump located four miles northwest of the confluence of Smith's River.

Buffalo Jumps

The Ulm Pishkun used by the Blackfoot Indians for thousands of years is one of the largest in the United States. Thirty feet high and extending approximately one mile in length, this jump was used to slaughter large numbers of buffalo before the Indians acquired horses and guns. One or more braves, dressed in buffalo hides, lured the herd toward the edge of the cliff, through a corridor of stones and hiding tribesmen. As the animals approached the rim, tribesmen emerged from behind, driving them over to their death – from the fall or at the hands of other bands camped near the base of the precipice. An on the spot processing plant, the pishkun (Blackfoot word meaning deep blood kettle) lived up to its name. Women, children and men participated in skinning hides and stripping the carcasses. Every possible part of the animal was used as they prepared jerky, cooked down fat and harvested sinew, intestines, bones and horns. If not used for food, it would be made into clothing, shelter, weapons or tools.

With no reference in the journal to another pishkun, the Madison Buffalo Jump, located near Three Forks, which is thought to be four thousand years old and used most recently by the Blackfoot, Salish and Shoshone tribes, it seems logical to assume members of the Expedition had no knowledge of these two sites. Familiar with pishkuns and the essential role they played in the Indian culture, Captain Lewis, upon seeing a huge deposit of buffalo bones along the Missouri on May 29, 1805, gave a detailed description of a site and its function.

Today these two prehistoric pishkuns are a part of the Montana State Park system offering interpretative information as well as a series of trails leading to the kill sites where fragments of primitive tools and buffalo bones can be found in deep layers of bone meal.

July16, 1805 At daybreak, Sgt. Ordway is sent to retrieve an axe he carelessly misplaced. While the journals give little insight into the regimen of a military expedition, this incident gives credence to the continued military discipline of the Corps. After a breakfast of buffalo entrails cooked in the Indian tradition (boiled with all contents and no prior washing), Captain Lewis, Drouillard, LaPage and Potts set out overland, leaving Captain Clark to command the fleet of canoes. Constantly looking for fresh sign of Indians and wild game, the small party of four discover forty willow huts with evidence to indicate the huts had been occupied within the last ten days by a number of Indians having many horses. Suspecting this might have been the Shoshone, their hopes of an encounter are renewed.

The Ulm Pishkun

Pishkun is a Blackfeet word meaning "deep blood kettle" referring to a great abundance. The Ulm Pishkun is a steep cliff over which the Indians drove buffalo, hence a "buffalo jump." Lewis wrote a detailed description of a pishkun in his journal, May 29, 1805. For over 1,500 years the cliffs of the Ulm Pishkun have been a gathering place for ancient peoples who hunted buffalo before the introduction of the horse.

The Ulm Pishkun was designated a state park by the Montana Legislature in 1971, and a new visitor center has been built beneath the cliffs as a "gathering place for all peoples to learn, to teach, to see the area in a new way and to celebrate the diversity of life on the Northern Plains." (Ulm Pishkun State Park). The visitor center, which is managed by the Montana Department of Fish Wildlife and Parks, is located ten miles southwest of Great Falls and six and one-half miles off Interstate 15 and is dedicated to bringing the intriguing story of this place alive.

Ahead of the main party, the scouts reach an area where the river narrows to approximately seventy yards in width. Stopping to take celestial observations and wait the arrival of the main party, they discover an old Indian trail along the shore passing under cliffs that arise abruptly from the water. As is procedure for mapping and plotting courses, Captain Lewis ascends a four hundred foot rock from where he has a magnificent view downstream of the area through which they have just passed. He sees large herds of buffalo – probably the last they will see on their trip westward. He names this lookout, Tower Rock. Waiting to help the main party ascend the rapids, around Tower Rock, they camp near a spot they call Pine Island. [5] Lewis realizes he has left his insect netting in

DW LADD '99

" *TRIO OF PESTS* "

the canoe. Totally frustrated, he writes, *"the Mosquotoes are extremely troublesome this evening and I had left my bier, of course suffered considerably and promised in my wrath that I never will be guilty of a similar piece of negligence while on this voyage."*

Convinced the Expedition is in some way foreordained to endure the "Trio of Pest", Captain Lewis has an ongoing list from which he chooses the areas three most prevalent annoyances. This list includes lice, eye gnats, mosquitos, fleas and prickly pear cactus. In spite of nuisances such as the recent setback and the ever present "trio", the Captain, in a high degree of scientific awareness, notes in great detail his natural surroundings. His childhood years with his mother, a medical herbist, and the two years he was President Jefferson's private secretary and student, has prepared him well. As evidenced throughout his journals, his discovery and delineation of species gives credence to his abilities to learn quickly and retain information. His description of the purple, black and yellow currants, the serviceberry and a 'fuzzy' red berry[4] found near Tower Rock and that of other plants and animals leaves many modern day scientists marveling at his knowledge and perception.

Meanwhile, back on the river, Captain Clark records seeing the poles of a large encampment consisting of a leather lodge measuring sixty feet in diameter, eighty leather teepees and forty or more smaller lodges. There are many indications this encampment was constructed in the fall of 1804.[5] These signs again spark hope of contacting the Shoshone.

After spending the night on the right bank near an island, and getting an early start, Clark and the main party join the scouts by 8 a.m. Following President Jefferson's directives to map the Missouri, Clark takes some observations. Plans are finalized and preparations made to navigate the swift, churning rapids. For fear of capsizing, every individual unessential to maneuvering the canoes upstream walks the rocky shoreline. Captain Lewis has the instruments taken overland as an extra precaution. With difficulty, the party passes the steep overhanging cliffs, and reaches calmer water.

The river continues to narrow. Ascending an area having little timber on the banks and only a sparse growth of pine on the mountain slopes, the Corps of Discovery enters a walled canyon of *"dark black grannit"*.[6] The entire party camps on the right, near present day Dearborn.

July 18, 1805. As morning breaks, the sunlight reveals a beautiful sight.

The steep rock ledges along the river bank are the home and playground of large bands of mountain goats and bighorn sheep. Watching the animals perform spectacular feats of balance, Captain Lewis writes *"...they walked about and bounded from rock to rock with no apparent unconcern where it app[e]ared to me that no quadruped could have stood and from which had they made one false step the[y] must have been precipitated at least 500 ft.... they are perfectly secure from the pursuit of the wolf, bear or even man himself."*

The Rocky Mountain Front
The Missouri River from Great Falls to Three Forks is one of the most scenic routes in the northwest. This Rocky Mountain front marks the boundary where open plains melt into the majestic mountains covered with spruce, fir and pine extending from lofty heights to the banks of the Missouri River. Enormous walls of overthrust rock rise to meet a big blue sky. Colorful outcrops, steep limestone cliffs interspersed with granite intrusions, suddenly give way to broad, fertile, alluvial valleys. An ecosystem teeming with wildlife and wild flowers complete this magnificent picture.

Traveling upstream for approximately two and a half miles, they pass the mouth of a large, clear, rapid stream entering from the west. To honor Henry Dearborn, Secretary of War, the captains name it Dearborn's River. [7]

Eager to acquire the much needed horses from the Shoshone, it is decided that Captain Clark and a small scouting party should travel overland on the west side of the river. They are to take every precaution not to frighten any Indians that may be in the vicinity. Realizing four men pose a greater threat than one, Captain Clark walks ahead of Joseph Fields, Potts and York. All experienced woodsmen, they are instructed not to discharge their weapons until they are sure there are no Indians in the area for fear the sound of a shot might push the elusive Shoshone further into the mountains. The Captain leaves bits and pieces of paper and fabric with signs of peaceful intent in case the Shoshone should pick up their trail. Progress is slow. Clark writes *"the Countrey is mountainious and rockey except the Valey...."* Passing over a mountain, he finds a well-traveled Indian road which he follows. Ascending another mountain, he discovers two streams with large beaver populations – probably Little Rock Creek and Little Prickly Pear Creek. After traveling about twenty miles, the foursome camp on a small stream, possibly opposite present day Ming Bar and the confluences of Elk Horn Creek.

Likewise, Captain Lewis is cautious. He has the men hoist American flags on all the canoes as a gesture of peace. Approximately sixteen miles above their camp, the main party passes the mouth of a stream entering from the right. They call this confluence Ordway's Creek, present-day Little Prickly Pear Creek, after Sergeant Ordway, a member of the Expedition. The shoreline is lined with blooming blue flax. Believing this variety to be excellent and superior to any grown in the United States, the captain hopes to collect some ripened seeds on the return trip.

Close to eighty-five miles above the falls and the last influx of muddy water,[8] this clear, swift mountain stream snakes the Corps of Discovery through alternating walled canyons and broad open valleys. Captains Lewis and Clark, Sergeants Gass and Ordway, along with Private Whitehouse, continue to fill the journals with information pertinent to this newly purchased frontier – clearly noting the natural diversity that contrast the eastern and western cottonwood species. Aspen, spruce, fir, pine and narrowleaf cottonwood timber the mountain slopes and line the river bottoms.

A Short Cut?

There has been much speculation as to why the Expedition took the Missouri River south instead of heading west from Great Falls along the buffalo trail leading through the mountains to the Columbia River system. Some say they were committed to Charbonneau, the mid-aged husband of Sacajawea, and to her reunion with her people, the Shoshone. Others propose that Sacajawea was the guide and that she purposefully lead them south to her homeland. Whatever the speculation, the fact remains that President Jefferson commissioned the Corps of Discovery to find the source of the Missouri. Without horses for overland transport of supplies and equipment, the shortcut was an impossibility.

Traveling twenty miles, they camp on the left bank, upstream from present day Holter Dam, in a grove of cottonwood trees where they dine on elk and deer before retiring under their indispensable insect netting.

July 19, 1805 A fine clear morning, Lewis hunts the shoreline, killing two antelope while the main party continue upstream. They move through a canyon enclosed by mountains on both sides, where the air hangs hot and heavy. The party find themselves almost suffocating. Ironically, they get occasional glimpses of distant snow-capped peaks to the southwest through breaks in the canyon walls. Enduring a thunderstorm accompanied by hail, the exhausted party enters an area known as the Gates of the Mountains. The Captain writes, *"this evening we entered much the most remarkable clifts that we have yet seen. these clifts rise from the waters edge on either side perpendicularly to the hight of [about] 1200 feet. every object here wears a dark and gloomy aspect. the tow[er]ing and projecting rockes in many places seem ready to tumble on us. the river appears to have the distance of 5-3/4 Miles and where it makes it's exist below has th[r]own on either side vast collumns of rocks mountains high.*

Captain Lewis wrote on July 19, 1805, "from the singular appearance of this place I called it the gates of the rocky Mountains." Today it is the setting of upper Holter Lake and boat tours are held there regularly. (Photos by Jeanne O'Neill)

the river appears to have woarn a passage just the width of it's channel or 150 yds it is deep from side to side nor is ther in the 1st 3 Miles of this distance a spot except one of a few yards in extent on which a man could rest the soal of his foot. several fine springs burst out at the waters edge from the interstices of the rocks. it happens fortunately that altho' the current is strong it is not so much so but what is may be overcome with the oars for there is hear no possibility of using either the cord or Setting pole. it was late in the evening before I entered this place and was obliged to continue my rout untill sometime after dark before I found a place sufficiently large to encamp my small party; at lenght such an one occurred on the lardside where we found plenty of lightwood and pi[t]ch pine....from the singular appearance of this place I called it the gates of the rocky mountains." The campsite mentioned above is near present day Upper Holter Lake.

Meanwhile, the overlanders miss this spectacular site as they circumvent the Gates of the Mountains. With the discovery of more willow huts and, for the first time, trees stripped of their bark[9] comes anxiety and the pressure to keep pushing. They must find the Shoshone soon! Tired and hungry, the party stop for

Our cover painting by Robert F. Morgan of Helena, Montana, shows the Expedition breaking camp at Field's Gulch near the Gates of the Mountains the morning of July 20, 1805. Morgan's painting depicts 29 members of the Corps of Discovery getting ready to proceed on up the river. (Photo Courtesy of Dale A. Burk)

An interesting geological formation located in the canyon downstream from the Gates of the Mountains northeast of present-day Helena, Montana. (Photo Courtesy of Billie Linkletter)

lunch. There is no wood to build a fire. As a substitute, Captain Clark uses dried buffalo dung. After a dinner of elk, they continue along an old Indian road leading to a place overlooking a large valley. Captain Clark records, *"passed a butifull Creek on the Std. Side this evening which meanders thro' a butifull Vallie of great extent,..."* [10] He named this creek Pryor's Creek, present day Prickly Pear Creek, after Sgt. Pryor. The last leg of the trip carries them over hills and mountains thickly covered with sharp flint fragments and prickly pear. [11] Captain Lewis records, The prickly pear cactus *"have now become so abundant in the open uplands that it impossible to avoid them and their thorns so keen and stif that they pearce a double thickness of dressed deers skins with ease."* [12] Having crossed two mountains and traveled a distance of more than thirty miles, the party reaches the river. Fatigued, with feet torn, bruised and infested with briers, they make camp (northeast of Helena, approximately one mile above the mouth of present day Spokane Creek). Lewis writes, *"Capt. Clark informed me that he extracted 17 of these bryers from his feet this evening after he encamped by the light of the fire."*

Negotiating hairpin curves again, Sergeant Gass records July 20, 1805, *"The river is very crooked in general, and here is a great bend to the southeast; and in the afternoon it turned so far that our course was north of east."*

Gates of the Mountains

<u>*GATES OF THE MOUNTAINS*</u>: *was named by Captain Meriwether Lewis when on July 19, 1805 ,while traveling upriver the Missouri he and his crew came to a spectacular canyon, a deep gorge cut by the River through through limestone rock. Lewis described "the most remarkable clifts that he had as yet seen." and called it the gates of the rocky mountains."   When Holter Dam was flooded it lessened the rush of the water through the "Gates" which appear to close and open as one approaches. The Gates of the Mountains Wilderness is home to bighorn sheep, eagles, osprey, mountain goats and other wild animals. Indian pictographs are proof of the Native American presence here long before the white men saw and recorded them. Meriwether Landing and Coulter Campsite are reminders of the members of the Expedition under Lewis stopped here. Captain Clark never saw these spectacular "gates." although Sergeant Ordway and his detachment passed through it in 1806 when they left the Three Forks to travel downstream to the Great Falls.*

Bucking strong currents, the main party reaches an area where the mountains give way to a large valley with extensive plains ten to twelve miles wide. Set between parallel mountain ranges running east to west, it is watered by a clear mountain stream and timbered only along the shore by narrow leaf cottonwood, pine and aspen.   The men and Sacajawea continue to enjoy the bounty of ripe berries. Lewis, the hunter gatherer, preserves seeds from each variety. Of the black currant, he writes *"this currant is really a charming fruit and I am confident would be prefered at our markets to any currant now cultivated in the U. States."* They pass a large creek on the right which they name Pott's Creek after John Potts.[13] Around 10 a.m., the party sees the smoke of a prairie fire several miles south. Spotted also by the scouts, they suspect it has been set by Indians as a warning of approaching danger. Advancing slowly up the river, they discover elk meat, a hide and an accompanying note from Captain Clark stating his intent to proceed past another mountain and wait their arrival. Experiencing rain and high winds, the main party goes ashore on a steep bank near a spring in the vicinity of present day York[14] where Lewis records, *"the prickly pear are so abundant that we could scarcely find room to lye."* As the day ends, the captain spots *"a black woodpecker as black as a crow"* and similar to one he had seen a few days earlier. Recognizing it to be a *"distinct species"*, he describes it as having *"...a long tail and flys a good deal like the jay bird."* [15]

Camping on the river above the mouth of White Paint Creek, present day Beaver Creek, the sore-footed scouts backtrack to the main party. While nursing their sore feet and waiting the arrival of the canoes, they scout the area around their camp. Discovering no fresh sign of Indians and feeling safe to fire their guns, they kill three deer.

The Mann Gulch Fire

THE MANN GULCH FIRE: Tragedy awaited the fifteen smokejumpers who parachuted into Mann Gulch the afternoon of August 5, 1949. The U. S. Forest Services crew was dispatched from Missoula to fight a routine lightning-caused fire burning on a ridge between Meriwether and Mann Gulches in the Helena National Forest. They were joined by the guard at Meriwether who had called in the fire.

After setting up camp and gathering up their gear the men headed down the gulch toward the fire which was starting to heat up. At 5:45 p.m. the fire climbed toward them, cutting off access to the river. Black smoke and gases exploded with the force of a massive flame-thrower. Eleven men died on the slope as they attempted to scramble to safety. Three survived. Memorials to these firefighters are erected at Meriwether; white crosses mark the spot where each body was found. Recently marble plaques have been placed next to the crosses as a lasting reminder of all the women and men who have served as wildland firefighters, especially those who have paid the ultimate price. The late Norman Maclean memorialized the Mann Gulch tragedy in his book Young Men and Fire.

A few miles upstream, the main party is surrounded by molting swans, the first they have seen for days. Seaman cannot resist his natural instincts to catch them. The fact that they are featherless and can't fly is bound to take some of the sport out of his pursuit. The old ones are too tough for consumption, so Seaman's two-legged friends eat only the young. The surrounding prairies and river bottom provide a natural sanctuary for the sandhill cranes, their chicks, the *"Yellow leged plover.....fesants"* [16] and many other small birds. Preferring red meat over fish, the captains rarely mention seeing fish in the streams. (*Today, the upper Missouri River and its watershed is known world-wide as a premier trout fishery. Fishermen literally trip over each other to fish these cool transparent streams for browns, cutthroat and rainbow*). As evening approaches, they move into an open plain about ten miles wide and stretching south as far as the eye can see. It is bordered by parallel mountain ranges and forested with scattered timber extending from below snow-capped peaks to the valley floor. Here the river, surprisingly swift, deltas out and is riddled with islands. The land is fertile and supports lush vegetation. As pretty as it is, all this beauty becomes distorted with fatigue as was evidenced in Captain Lewis' description of the Gates of the Mountains. They find a left-side campsite in a beautiful valley upstream from present-day Canyon Ferry. Mosquitos and gnats continue to be troublesome. Masters of construction, beavers add to the problem. They constantly build dams across the branched and meandering Missouri and its tributaries, causing water to pool. Without drainage, these stagnant pools form excellent incubators for

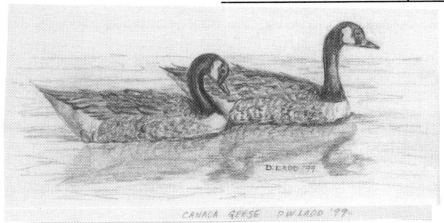

CANADA GEESE   D.W.LADD '99

mosquito larvae. July is the height of the hatch!

Since Captain Lewis first viewed the Rocky Mountains from a high point near Cow Creek on May 26, 1805, the Corps of Discovery possesses geographic information of which the President has no knowledge. Contrary to the United States maps and the skin maps of the Mandans, which depict the Rocky Mountains as a single chain of mountains interspersed with large gaps, the Expedition sees first hand the reality of what lies before them. These mountains with all their beauty are a dreaded series of obstacles. Travel has been difficult since first entering them. They have been on a southeasterly course since passing the confluence of Ordway's Creek, July 18, 1805.

THE PACIFIC IS WEST! The water is too deep to pole and the banks too high to tow. Rowing and sheer determination are the means to overcoming its pounding resistance. With no more whiskey or favorite cuts of buffalo meat, the fatigued men of the Expedition, draw more and more on the inner strength that enables them to reach goals beyond their self-limiting expectations. Every hard-earned mile is a milestone. The rowdy young men who gave Sergeant Ordway and the Captains a difficult time in the spring and summer of 1804 are now disciplined, goal-oriented, bonded men of character. They are the Corps of Discovery inching their way to the ocean.

July 22, 1805 Working through a maze of large and small islands, the main party push upstream while Captain Lewis, bent on charting the course of the Missouri, seeks an overlook from where he can discern and map the main channel. Task accomplished, he continues to walk ahead and soon discovers a high island covered with small, pleasant-tasting onions. Waiting to have breakfast with the main party, he gathers a half bushel. Pleased with the good flavor and high yield, after dinner, the Captain collects ripened seed to carry back to the United States while others gather more onions. They call this Onion Island. Pursuing his overland course, he passes the mouth of a large confluence fed by three sizeable streams on the west side (present-day Beaver Creek). He stops again to wait for the main party. To pass the time, he places a thermometer in the shade. After eating dinner, he walks on leaving it behind. Realizing what he has done, he sends Sergeant Ordway (famous for his ability to retrieve forgotten objects) back for it. It reads 80 a.o. – second warmest day of the summer.

A pleasant surprise for all, Sacajawea begins to recognize this area as the place where the Shoshone come for "white paint". She assures the party that her people live on this river and the three forks is not too distant. Captain Lewis writes, *"this peice of information has cheered the sperits of the party who now begin to console themselves with the anticipation of shortly seeing the head of the missouri yet unknown to the civilized world."* Passing the entrance of a large creek, Lewis breaks his pattern of naming major confluences after statesmen and members of the Expedition to name this stream White Earth Creek [17] for the white paint the Indians find in its banks. Continuing to see large numbers of birds, the Captain obtains a small curlew specimen different from any yet

A scouting trip took Captain William Clark and three others, Joseph Fields, John Potts and York to this point above present-day Prickly Pear Creek overlooking the Helena Valley in Montana. This painting by Robert of Morgan of Helena, whose home is located near this site, is titled "Captain Clark Overlooking Helena Valley, July 19, 1805." (Photo Courtesy of Dale A. Burk)

described. He had first seen the bird near Smith's River but was unable to collect a specimen. The main party arrives at the scout's camp late in the afternoon. Taking the hunters and meat on board, they proceed a short distance to an island where they camp on the left approximately eighteen miles upstream from their campsite of July 21st, near present-day Winston.

The men are exhausted. Their feet are now worse than ever. Clark writes, *"I opened the bruises and blisters of my feet which caused them to be painful."* Captain Clark, who usually supervises the navigation while Captain Lewis scouts the shoreline has become obsessed with the need to find the Shoshone. Desire has turned to desperation. He is pushing himself and the scouting party both physically and mentally. Realizing he is in no condition to be walking, Captain Lewis volunteers to relieve him but *"finding him anxious...I readily consented to remain with the canoes..."*

July 23, 1805 With the urgency and weight of time a growing burden, Clark sets out early with a party of four men, one of which is Charbonneau. After traveling about six miles, they meet Drouillard who is waiting on the shore after being separated overnight. Leaving him behind, they continue their search. The hunters kill several animals which they leave on the bank for the main party. Discovering an old Indian trail, they walk about twenty-five miles. Seeing

---

Lewis and Clark County

LEWIS AND CLARK COUNTY is the only county in the United States named after both explorers, and is one of nine original counties established in Montana, 1865. First named " Edgerton" after Montana Territorial Governor Sidney E. Edgerton, the name was later changed to Lewis and Clarke. Eventually, the "e" was dropped. In 1890-1900, parts of Deer Lodge and Meagher counties were annexed to Lewis and Clark, and in 1941 part of Cascade County was annexed to Lewis and Clark and a part of Lewis and Clark county was annexed to Cascade County the same year. The state capitol, Helena, first called Last Chance City, is also the county seat, and the county courthouse once served as the state capitol. Lewis and Clark County boasts a population of 52,785 residents, a ratio of 15.3 people per square mile, in an area of 3,461 acres.

---

antelope, deer and large numbers of elk, but no recent sign of Indians, they make camp along the river, approximately six miles upstream from present-day Townsend.

By mid-morning, the main party finds Drouillard waiting with five deer he had killed the day before. Taking both on board, they work their way through miles of islands. Here the river flows rapidly over a bed of smooth stones and its banks are lined periodically by bluffs of red and yellow clay. Sacajawea tells the party that her people use the red clay for paint. Passing a large creek on the left the Captain names it Whitehouse Creek after Joseph Whitehouse.[18] Continuing upstream, gathering more onions, discovering a type of garlic too strong for use and noting the abundant growth of thistle and flax, Lewis finds the ripened flax seed he had hoped to collect on July 18, 1805. Some articles in the canoes have gotten wet. Stopping early to dry them, the prudent captain has the party hoist the flags once again in case Indians are watching. Now the river is shallow enough to use setting poles, the same poles with iron metal tips used a year ago to push the keelboat and pirogues from Wood's Camp to Fort Mandan. In water too shallow for oars, this method usually works well. However, with a bed of rounded, slippery rocks the men are having difficulty. On close examination, the Captain discovers many tips are missing. Using another of his many attributes,

---

Lewis & Clark Leave Legacy In Montana

IN MONTANA:

According to University of Montana Professor Harry Fritz, the Lewis and Clark Expedition spent more time in Montana than in any other state.

•Camped here more often.

•Lived in constant danger.

•Made most significant discoveries here.

•Encountered greatest dangers .

•Discovered mountains were insuperable barrier to water transport. (Fifty-three mountain ranges in Montana alone)

•Montana was geographic and scientific center of the Expedition.

•Thirty-one indigenous Montana flora described in journals.

•Bitterroot Flower, Lewis rediva,, named for Captain Lewis.

•Lived off the land.

•Met Indians, both helpful and hostile.

•Left their stamp on the state:

Rivers – Milk, Musselshell, Judith, Marias, Smith, Dearborn, Clark Fork, Beaverhead, Jefferson, Madison, Gallatin, Clark's Fork of the Yellowstone.

Locations – Gates of the Mountain, Lewis and Clark County, Lewis & Clark National Forest, Beaverhead National Forest,County, and Mountain Range, Lewis and Clark Caverns, Clark Canyon Reservoir, etc.

Nearly every member had a stream or location named for them, Pryor Creek and Pryor Mountains, Clark's Fork of the Yellowstone, Sacajawea River, Pompey's Pillar, etc.

• "Lewis and Clark recorded Montana. They entered a land unknown in any particular to the rest of the civilized world, explored it, explained it. They put Montana on the map." – Harry Fritz

he fashions new ones from gigs and heavy wire. They work! With a better foothold, they advance upstream through open plains, taking on meat left by the scouts and completing their course of twenty-four miles.

Nine days have passed since the Corps pushed off from Canoe Camp. Skirting the eastern front has brought no consolation. Jagged snow-capped peaks form a deep, continual barrier blocking the Expedition from its westward goal. Just when the men are having trouble mustering enough energy to get one foot in front of the other or lifting that pole and setting it one more time, the evening sun throws sprawling mountain shadows like great hovering vultures. With gripping fatigue comes the looming, gnawing questions: How much longer must we battle this river? Where are the Shoshone? Will they be friend or foe? Is there adequate

Horned Lark
Jan Clary

Last Chance Gulch, Montana

HELENA; As Captain Clark and his advance party left the river and followed an Indian road overland in search of the Shoshone, they unknowingly trod over gold fields that would be discovered fifty-nine years later. In 1864, four miners, subsequently to be known as the Four Georgians, returned from the Marias country discouraged at finding no gold. They decided on one last chance on a stream they had previously panned but which had shown colors. On July 14, 1864, they prospered in a gulch called Last Chance on a stream, which would eventually be called Prickly Pear Creek. The Last Chance gold rush was on, and the city of Helena, now Montana's state capitol, was born. By 1888 Helena was the richest city, per capita, in the United States and boasted 750 millionaires. Lewis and Clark County in Montana is the only county in the United States named for both captains.

food in those mountains to sustain thirty-one men, a woman, a baby and a dog? Will we make it through before the dead of winter? Feeling the piercing grip of fatigue and discouragement, they halt to camp on an island at the upper end of present-day Canyon Ferry Lake, near Townsend.

July 24, 1805. Getting their usual early start, they pole through strong currents, small rapids and red and black streaked banks lined with willows, red dozier dogwood and wild rose. The Captain begins to worry about possible obstructions of falls further upstream. Sacajawea, hoping to comfort, tells him there are none and that the river continues much the same. In spite of her attempts, he worries. Maneuvering past fallen trees brought down by swift currents and a large beaver population, they continue to see many birds, deer, antelope and snakes. The captain, eager to see if the snakes are poisonous, examines the teeth and finds *"...them innocent."* [19] Lewis writes *"the men complain of being much fortiegued...I occasionaly encourage them by assisting in the labour...and have learned to push a tolerable good pole in their fraize (phrase)."*

Townsend, Montana

TOWNSEND: the county seat of Broadwater County, Montana, did not just "grow-up" as most Montana towns but was platted and planned in anticipation of the arrival of the railroad. It was named for Mrs. Charles B. Wright, whose maiden name was Townsend and whose husband, Charles Wright, was president of the Northern Pacific, 1874-1879. A post office opened in 1883, and the Townsend House, a ten thousand dollar hotel was built. Townsend became a crossroads for transportation. The Missouri River enters Canyon Ferry Lake just north of Townsend which has now become a recreational center.

Sensitive to the welfare of his command, his willingness to struggle bonds the Corps. He continues to record *"our trio of pests still invade and obstruct us on all occasions, these are the Musquetoes eye knats and prickley pears, equal to any three curses that ever poor Egypt laiboured under, except the Mahometant yoke."* Thankful for insect nets and having reached the end of their nineteen mile course, they camp on the right, about mid-way between present-day Townsend and Toston.

Clark's party, following an Indian road, spots a fine horse grazing in a nearby meadow. Unfortunately, it proves to be unapproachable. Passing five streams and finding no fresh sign of Indians for thirty miles, they camp on the river and dine on venison. [20]

July 25, 1805. The scouting party gets an early start and quickly arrives at the three forks of the Missouri. While having breakfast of left-over deer ribs, they discover a recently burned prairie and horse tracks about five days old. [21] After quickly exploring the area, Captain Clark, believing the southwest fork will take them closest to the headwaters of the Columbia, leaves a note of intent and proceeds upstream with Charbonneau, Joseph Field and Frazier. Nearing the end of their twenty-mile course, Charbonneau's ankle gives out. Camping on the right bank of the west fork, present-day Jefferson River, the Captain records *"....in this quarter emence number of beaver & orter maney thousand enhavit the river & Creeks near the 3 forks..."*

The main party, about two days behind the scouts, continues through an area very similiar to that traveled for the last two days. Members of the party kill two geese after which Captain Lewis forbids them to waste the time or ammunition for so little meat. Seeing large herds of antelope, and a brown bear, they journey through plains until late afternoon when they enter an area where mountains bank the river. The silence is broken by rushing water and roaring rapids. As the canoes cut the strong current, they pass high rocky cliffs where the river grows swifter and the rock along the left bank exude freestone water. Captain Lewis records, *"two rapids near the large spring we passed this evening were the worst we have seen since that we passed on entering the rocky Mountain; they were obstructed with sharp pointed rocks, ranges of which extended quite across the river."* Successfully navigating the rapids, they enter a plain and soon pass the mouth of a large creek on the right, fed by five streams (present-day Crow Creek). Naming it Gass' Creek after Sergeant Patrick Gass, they find a campsite under high bluffs on the right thought to be covered by backwater of present-day Toston Dam.

Toston, Montana

TOSTON: located on the banks of the Missouri where the Expedition traveled in July, 1806, was named for Thomas Toston, an early homesteader and first postmaster, who operated the Toston Ferry. Mining, smelting, stock racing, a racetrack, and land development formed part of Toston's history.

July 26, 1805. Using poles and tow ropes, the main party travels through a serene area of bare mountains and shorelines timbered with cedar and spruce. After advancing three and three-quarter miles, they pass a large creek to the left on which the Captain bestows the name Howard's Creek after Thomas Howard, (present-day Sixteen Mile Creek). Entering an open valley several miles wide, Lewis discovers *"...another speces of the prickly pear of a globular form..."* and describes in detail the seed of needlegrass. The seeds of the later are wicked and pose quite a problem for overlanders. They pierce the leggings and moccasins and reek havoc with poor Seaman who, according to Captain Lewis, *"...is constantly binting and scratching himself as if in a rack of pain."* Enduring the pain of both cactus and needlegrass, an overlander finds an Indian bow made of cedar, similar in construction to those made by the Mandans. Picking up a note from Captain Clark along with a deer hide, the party travels sixteen and a half miles before camping on the left near present-day Eagle Rock.

Several miles upstream from the Three Forks, Captain Clark, Reuben Fields and Frazier leave Charbonneau with Joseph Fields while they journey twelve miles west to the top of a mountain from which they have a wonderful view of the three confluent streams forming the Missouri. Seeing no recent signs of Indians, they descend the mountain along an old Indian trail. Their plan is to rendezvous with Charbonneau and Joseph Fields, explore the middle fork (present-day Madison River), and rejoin the main party at the mouth of the southwest fork. Hot, tired and thirsty, they find a cold water spring. Adhering to proper procedure of wetting the hands, head and feet before drinking, Clark drinks too much, too fast. Quickly, he feels the ill effects. Feet and muscles throbbing, they continue downstream, reaching their old camp and companions for a dinner of fawn. Too sick to eat, the Captain takes a small ration, rests a short time and travels with his party to a large island. Attempting to ford waist-deep water, Charbonneau, who can't swim, is overcome by the swift current. Sure to drown without help, he is rescued by the ill captain who has just struggled to the opposite shore. Later in the day, they encounter two grizzly bears. The Captain writes, *"We killed 2 bear which was imediately in our way, both pore..."* They camp on Philosophy River, (present-day Willow Creek), where the Captain endures a night of chills and high fever.

July 27, 1805 Captain Lewis records, *"We set out at an early hour and proceeded on but slowly the current still so rapid that the men are in a continual state of their utmost exertion to get on, and they begin to weaken fast from this continual state of violent exertion."* Traveling almost one and three-fourth miles, they pass steep limestone cliffs with sediment lines running perpendicular to the water. These rocks appear to be standing on end. Spotting large herds of bighorn sheep on the cliffs above, they round a bend and enter a valley (ninety to one hundred miles wide and surrounded by high mountain peaks). Immediately to their left, a swift stream enters the Missouri.[22] It is the first of a trio forming the headwaters. Bringing the canoes to the left bank, they stop for breakfast. Captain Lewis, eager to see what lies before him, walks up the east fork a short distance where he ascends a high limestone cliff. Overlooking a huge valley, he writes, *"...I commanded a most perfect view of the neighboring country."* Charting the area, he then descends the cliff to join the party for breakfast. After eating, they proceed less than a mile to the second confluence entering from the southwest[23] and a third from the south.[24] Having followed the course of this river for almost three-thousand miles, they are delighted to have reached the headwaters of the Missouri! At the mouth of the second confluence, they find Clark's note attached to a pole. The note informs Captain Lewis of their intentions to proceed up the southwest fork in search of the Shoshone. If the trip proves successful, Captain Clark expects the main party to follow the same course. If unsuccessful, the scouting party will return to this location. Of the three forks, Lewis agrees with Clark that the southwest fork follows closest to their charted course. Captain Lewis records, *"beleiving this to be an essential point in the geography of this western part of the Continent I determined to remain....untill I obtained the necessary data for fixing its latitude Longitude &c."* Approximately one and a quarter miles up the southwest fork, the main party spots a nice left-side meadow where they camp. Given a chance to rest, the tired and weary men leisurely air the baggage, hunt, soak and prepare hides – fashioning them into leggings and moccasins while Lewis continues to explore. Finding little differences in the confluent streams other than width and velocity, he notes the general direction and character of each as well as the fauna and flora along their banks. Rich in resources, especially wildlife, the hunters keep the cooks well-supplied with meat.

Headwaters State Park

Compared to most historical sites, the three forks has changed very little since 1805 when the Corps of Discovery first saw it. Railroad tracks, powerlines, highways, sparse ranch buildings, remnants of an old mining settlement and the town of Three Forks compose the major changes. This five-hundred-sixty acre park, located approximately four miles north of Interstate 90, provides historical and geographical information, campsites, picnic areas, river accesses for fishermen and floaters plus a chance to view, firsthand, many of the plants and animals described in the journals.

A favorite hunting and meeting ground for the Blackfeet, Crow and Shoshone Indians for centuries, the headwaters area was a battlefield for warring tribes. Besides serving as a campsite of the Expedition in 1805, the point where Clark's party split on their return in 1806 and the spot where Sacajawea was taken captive in 1800, it was also the burial site of several fur trappers who were ambushed and killed in the early 1800's. Two of these trappers, Drouillard and Potts, were former members of the Lewis and Clark Expedition.

Captain Clark, July 27, 1805, *"I was verry unwell all last night with a high fever & akeing in all my bones. My fever &c. continus, deturmind to prosue my intended rout to the Middle fork., accordingly Set out in great pain across a Prarie 8 miles to the Middle [fork]..."* Seeing many beaver and otter but no sign of Indians, they return mid-afternoon to the mouth of the southwest fork where they rejoin the main party. Lewis persuades Clark to ingest five of Dr.

This is what is called "Lewis' Lookout" above the Gallatin River near the Three Forks of the Missouri River. On July 27, 1805, Captain Meriwether Lewis wrote, "...I walked up the SE fork about ½ mile and ascended the point of a high limestone clift from whence I commanded a most perfect view of the neighboring country. (Photo by Pat Hastings)

Rush's pills and to bathe his feet and legs in warm water. His crash course in medicine under Dr. Benjamin Rush in 1803 proves valuable once again. Given the condition of his co-commander, Captain Lewis tells the men they will stay in the three fork area for at least two days.

The melancholy Lewis worries and writes, *"we begin to feel considerable anxiety with rispect to the Snake Indians. if we do not find them or some other nation who have horses I fear the successfull issue of our voyage will be very doubtfull or at all events much more difficult in its accomplishment. we are now several hundred miles within the bosom of this wild and mountainous country, where game may rationally be expected shortly to become scarce and subsistence precarious without any information with rispect to the country not knowing how far these mountains continue, or wher to direct our course to pass them to advantage for intersept a navigable branch of the Columbia, or even were we on such an one the probability is that we should not find any timber within these mountains large enough for canoes if we judge from the portion of them through which we have passed. however I still hope for the best, and intend taking tramp myself in a few days to find these yellow gentlemen if possible. my two principal consolations are that from our present position it is impossible that the S.W. fork can head with the waters of any other river but the Columbia, and that if any Indians can subsist in the form of a nation in these mountains with the means they have of acquiring food we can also subsist."*

Captain Lewis, July 28, 1805, *"My friend Capt Clark was very sick all last night but feels himself somewhat better this morning since his medicine has opperated."* After sending two men out to explore the southeast fork and several others to hunt, the Captains confer and *"corrisponded in opinion with rispect to the impropriety of calling either of these streams the Missouri and accordingly agreed to name them after the President of the United States and the Secretaries of the Treasury and state....In pursuance of this resolution we called the S.W.fork, that which we meant to asent, Jefferson's River in honor of that illustrious personage Thomas Jefferson. (the author of our enterprise) the Middle fork we called Madison's River in honor of James Madison, and the S.E. Fork we called Gallitin's River in honor of Albert Gallitin....the beds of all these streams are formed of smooth pebble and gravel, and their waters perfectly transparent; in short they are three noble streams."*

Three Forks, Montana

THREE FORKS, MONTANA; located in Gallatin Valley near the three forks of the Missouri was a logical site for a fur trading post. Although several attempts were made to establish such a post, the Blackfeet Indians, in defense of their lands, succeeded in destroying them. Pierre Menard wrote to his brother-in-law, Pierre Choteau, Esq., that their trappers had been set upon by the Blackfeet...traps and horses were stolen and two men were killed...Unless we can have peace with these (Indians) or unless they can be destroyed it is idle to think of maintaining an establishment at this point (Not in Precious Metals Alone) As the town developed a post office was established in 1882, and in 1884 an "English Nobility Colony" was located near the present town by a group of Englishmen who bought a block of land and built several log cabins.

The weather is unusually hot and humid. Of course the mosquitoes are extremely bothersome. The sun is beating down on the teepee, where the feverish Captain Clark is lying, making it unbearable. In an attempt to relieve some of his discomfort, Captain Lewis has the troops construct a small willow hut. After an afternoon thunderstorm, the hunters arrive with two elk and eight large whitetail deer. Sacajawea, having familiarized herself with the three forks area, tells the party their camp is on the exact location where her people, the Shoshone, were attacked by the Minnetares five years earlier. Four men, four women, and several boys were killed. Several attempted to escape up the southwest fork but were caught. She, four boys and a number of other females were taken captive and later traded to other tribes or taken to the Mandan as slaves. Surprised by her lack of outward emotion, Captain Lewis writes, *"...I cannot discover that she shews any immotion of sorrow in recollecting this event; if she has enough to eat and a few trinkets to wear I believe she would be perfectly content anywhere."*

Lewis proposes the building of an *"establishment"* in this location. He writes, *"this affords one of the best winter pastures on earth for horses or cows, and of course will be much in favour of an establishment should it be necessary to fix one at this place."* (Many traders and trappers that followed the Expedition to the western boundary of the Louisiana Purchase shared Lewis' sentiments. Having not encountered the wrath of the Blackfeet, he had no way of knowing what the future held for the three forks area.)

Fur Trade

Fur trading had become a lucrative business in the eastern thirteen states prior to the exploration of the vast area known as the Louisiana Purchase. Fashionable felt hats drove the United States, European and Oriental markets. France, Spain and England shared a long time interest in exploring the area west of the Mississippi River. President Jefferson attempted to put an exploratory venture together several years before he commissioned Lewis and Clark to lead the Corps of Discover west. His dream was to find the first river route connecting the United States to the Pacific Ocean for the establishment of a continental fur trade. By the turn of the century, the British had explored the Pacific coast and much of present day western Canada. The French had trapped the Hudson River valley and beyond for hundreds of years. It was no surprise for the Expedition to find Frenchmen at Mandan Village. The Spanish were pushing from the south. Regarding the British as the greatest threat, President Jefferson sought to challenge their claim to the market below the forty-ninth parallel. With the purchase of the Louisiana Territory from France and congressional approval for an expedition in 1803, the President was well on the way to realizing a life-long dream. The Expedition was organized. It would change the West forever. The journal entry of Lewis on July 31, 1805, previews things to come as this new territory is opened up to traders, trappers and settlers. It states, "when we a have plenty of fresh meat I find it impossible to make the men take any care of it, or use it with the least frugality. tho' I expect that necessity will shortly teach them this art." Prior to the arrival of the "white" man, the land and streams teemed with wildlife.

Captain Meriwether Lewis, on his return to St. Louis in 1806 wrote, "that portion of the continent watered by the Missouri and all its branches...is richer in beaver and otter than any country on earth." [25] Immediately greed drove the westward expansion. Pelts became the currency of the West! They bought tobacco, whiskey, guns and other supplies needed to survive in the wilderness. While the hides of buffalo, deer, elk, and bear were necessary for clothing, shelter, tools, and weapons, this market did not begin to compete with that of beaver and otter.

John Colter, John Potts, George Drouillard and Peter Weiser, members of the Corps of Discovery, returned to the upper Missouri watershed to guide, trap and hunt. Colter led the way when he joined two Illinois trappers near the mouth the Yellowstone, August 12, 1806. Forrest Hancock and Joseph Dickson were working their way up the Missouri in the summer of 1806 when they met the party of Lewis and Clark returning from the Pacific. As members of both parties exchanged information, Colter was caught up in the trapper's plans. He asked for an early discharge in order to accompany them. The Captains presented Colter's request to the Corps. No one objected. So, with the condition that no similar request be made by any member of the Expedition, permission was granted. With well wishes and the gift of a few supplies, the threesome headed upstream. Colter trapped with the Illinois trappers through the fall and winter of 1806-1807. Heading home once again, he had reached the Platte River before he met the enterprising, entrepreneur Manuel Lisa with fifty frontiersmen traveling upstream in two keelboats. Three of the fifty were former members of the Lewis and Clark Expedition. Lisa and Colter's old friends, Drouillard, Potts and Weiser persuaded him to join the company and return to what is known as present day Montana. Acting as a guide, Colter recommended Lisa build a trading post on the Yellowstone at the mouth of the Bighorn River. In the fall of 1807, Lisa had the men of his company construct the first white settlement in Montana. He named it Fort Raymond, after his son. That name did not endure and it was soon called Fort Manuel. With the onset of winter, pelts would be prime. Wasting no time, Lisa sent men in every direction of the Missouri watershed to explore and map streams rich in fur bearing animals. They were to open doors for future trade relations with various tribes and set the stage for Manuel Lisa's westward expansion. Colter left the fort in the winter of 1807-1808 and headed for the upper reaches of the Yellowstone Valley. After traveling over five hundred miles and exploring much of northwestern Wyoming, Yellowstone Park, parts of Idaho and Montana, he returned to Fort Manuel. Discovering Union Pass and mapping many other places which still bare his name, Colter became a legend in his own time.

Captain Clark used much of the information provided by Colter to construct his map of the west. When Colter told of the steaming water shooting thousands of feet into the air, pools of bubbling mud, boiling calderas and other sites he had seen in the great northwest, he was immediately given the reputation of a deranged lunatic. As a result, Yellowstone Park was nicknamed "Colter's Hell". However, one person of notable character, believed him.

When Daniel Boone was 80 years old, thinking he had to see the sights Colter had told him about, walked from his home in Femme Osage, Missouri to what is today Yellowstone Park and back again.

Manuel Lisa's St. Louis, Missouri, Fur Company thrived and made many trips up and down the Missouri. In no time, Lisa had a branch of his company operating in the three forks area. But as the number of trappers and sour trade deals increased so did the Indian's hostility for the "white" man. No one knows for sure what sparked the hostile flame. There is much speculation to support the theory that when whites fought for the Blackfeet's long time enemy, the Crows, relations immediately deteriorated. Colter had three encounters with the Blackfeet, in two of which he was a party to a group of Crows moving into the three forks area. To kill or be killed – he fought with the Crows. In 1808, the Blackfeet attacked the camp at the three forks – stealing, burning, torturing and killing. Eight men lost their lives; among them was John Potts. Colter was captured, stripped of his shoes and clothes and told to run for his life. Naked and weaponless, he ran barefoot over sharp stones, prickly pear cactus, through willows and rushes. Outrunning all but one of many pursuers and knowing he was being overtaken, Colter stopped and turned quickly to face his enemy. With blood pouring down his face, he startled his attacker, throwing him off balance. Colter grabbed the Indian's lance and killed him. With several Blackfeet still following, he ran until he reached the Jefferson River where he dove in and hid under some floating logs until after dark. He continued his escape overland for approximately two hundred and fifty miles, arriving at Fort Manuel seven days later – tired, torn, hungry and naked. Colter's last encounter also took place at the three forks. Five of his companions were killed by the Blackfeet. Colter wrote, "If God will only...let me off I will leave the country day after tomorrow – and be damned if I ever come into it again. [26]
True to his word, he returned to St. Louis in 1810 and died a poor man three years later. George Drouillard was killed near the three forks in 1810. When members of the party told of the Blackfeet's brutality, Lisa gave up the idea of establishing a post there. The Blackfeet continued to hold trappers out of the headwaters area for many years. However, Lisa, Astor, Ashley, Chouteau and others trapped and traded their way to wealth in other locations. Fashion saved the beaver and otter when felt hats were no longer stylish. By 1840, silk was the new craze – making the silk worm the new endangered species!

July 29, 1805. The hunters, out early, return with four deer and a live young sandhill crane which does not yet fly. Amused by it, Captain Lewis gathers the scientific information he desires, then sets it free to join many adults of the same species in the surrounding meadows. Observing several other animals, including a large number of kingfishers, mallards, ants, grasshoppers, and crickets, Lewis, who is apparently trying his hand at fishing, records, *"we see a great abundance of fish in the steam of which we take to be trout but they will not bit any bate we can offer them."* Many anglers find this statement to be true almost two hundred years later.

Captain Clark's fever is back to normal but still feeling sore and achy, he takes *"the barks"* prescribed by Captain Lewis and eats some venison. Well enough to fulfill President Jefferson's directive to take readings at every significant geographical finding, he makes some celestial observations – Latitude 45 degrees 22 minutes 34 seconds North. Captain Lewis writes, *"the men have been busily engaged all day in diding (dressing) skins and making them into various garments all are leather dressers and taylors."*

July 30, 1805. After resting for two days, taking necessary observations, exploring the headwaters and stockpiling food, the Corps of Discovery load the canoes and proceed up the Jefferson River in search of the Shoshone and the Pacific Ocean!

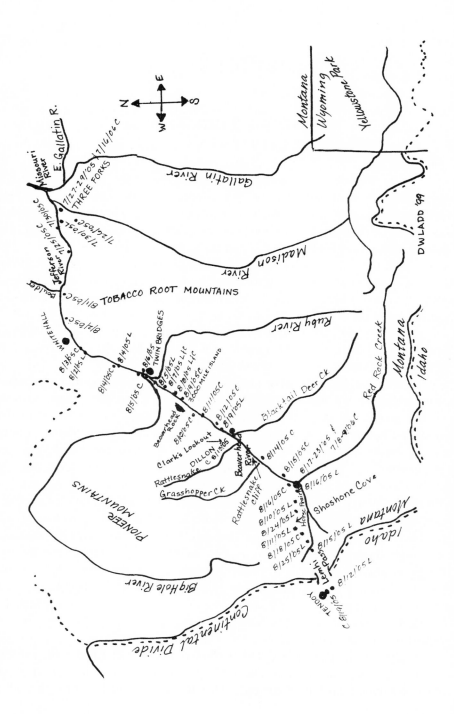

Chapter Eight

FROM THE THREE FORKS
TO THE CONTINENTAL DIVIDE

The rest period was short, but long enough for the party to mend their moccasins and their spirits. However, Captain Clark was still weak and recovering from his illness, two men had tumors, one suffered a dislocated shoulder which had been "relocated", another a stone bruise, and Sergeant Gass had injured his back. Besides which, all the party was hungry.

Did the men miss the abundant game of the prairies to the east? Yes! Game was shy and scarce in this country; no buffalo, some elk, deer and antelope, occasional beaver, geese, ducks, some trout, but rather a meager repast to offer these meat-eating, hard-working men and a dog. On July 31, 1805, Lewis wrote that there was no meat and noted that when there was plenty of fresh meat the men would not take care of it, or use it frugally, *"though I expect that necessity will shortly teach them this art."*

The two captains were anxious to find the Shoshone and somewhat disturbed that, as yet, there were no recent Indian signs. Sacajawea assured them that her people did range these lands and were probably fishing west of the mountains before their fall trek over the pass and across the plains to hunt buffalo. While Captain Clark led the canoes up the Jefferson River, Captain Lewis, with Sergeant Gass, Drouillard and a lame Charbonneau, set out to find the Shoshone in a land Sergeant Gass described as a *"howling wilderness."* A map of the Jefferson River with its side channels resembles a tangled skein of yarn, so it was easy for the explorers to be distracted into a side channel and travel several miles out of their way. That day, August 1, 1805, was hot, the road was rough, there was no shade, scarcely a breath of air, and they were thirsty. Lewis was also weakened by a bout with dysentery and the results of his "cure-everything medication", a dose of salts. Still, in spite of his discomfort, he wrote a lengthy description of the blue grouse and also the pinyon jay which he observed that day. He and Drouillard were lucky enough to spot and kill two elk, most of which they left for the boatsmen struggling up the river.

Struggling they were. The Jefferson River was filled with rapids, crowded islands, and shoals. The men had to haul the canoes over them sometimes two to three hundred yards. They towed, they walked through mud in

Looking west at the confluence of the Madison River (at the left) and the Jefferson River at the point where these rivers are joined by the Gallatin to form the Missouri River. The Corps took the Jefferson on its pursuit of the Continental Divide. (Photo by Pat Hastings)

icy water up to their chests. They tripped, they slipped on sharp stones that bruised and cut their feet, and they fell. But they "*proceeded on*." From the three forks they passed the point where Sacajawea had been captured by the Hidatsa, and they named a creek *Philosophy River* (Willow Creek). The travelers passed caverns which they did not see, but which are now named for them, the present Lewis and Clark Caverns near Cardwell, Montana. The travelers observed a river which they called *Frazer's River* (South Boulder River) and another the *Reuben Fields Valley* (Boulder River). On August 1, 1805, Captain Clark's thirty-fifth birthday, his party camped near Jefferson Island opposite North Boulder River and named a creek *Birth Creek* (Whitehall Creek) in honor of their captain. The journals record that on August 2, 1805, the men and Sacajawea nearly suffocated in the valley from the heat of the day, but that the nights were so cold as to require at least two blankets. A typical Montana "two dog night!" Sergeant Gass added "*disagreeably cold.*" Thunderstorms and hail interrupted the journey, and at one point the men protected themselves from the hail with willow boughs. Beaver dams choked their passage, and anyone who has tried fishing amidst beaver dams will sympathize with Lewis when on July 31, 1805, while walking ahead on the *Star* or right side of the river, he "*saw a vast number of beaver in many large dams ...maid in various bayoes of the river...distributed three or four miles on this side of the river over an extensive bottom of timbered and meadow lands intermixed.*" To avoid these dams Captain Lewis headed for the high plain " *with much difficulty and waiding many beaver dams to my waist in mud and water. I would willingly have joined the canoes but the brush were so thick, the river crooked and bottoms intercepted in such manner by the* beaver *dams, that I found it uceless to attempt to find them.*"

Beaver Dams

Captain Lewis: August 2, 1805 "several ...wer five feet high and overflowed several acres of land; these dams are formed of willow brush mud and gravel and are so closely interwoven that they resist the water perfectly. The base of this work is thick and rises nearly perpendicularly on the lower side while the upper side or that within the dam is gently sloped. The brush appear to be laid in no regular order yet acquires a strength by the irregularity with which they are placed by the beaver that it would puzzle the engenuity of man to give them."

Still the question taunted them, "Where were the Indians?" When Captain Clark recognized a track where an Indian had ascended to a point where the Expedition's camp would have been visible to him , the Americans now knew that they had been discovered, but the observer had run off. Reuben Fields killed a panther, their first, which measured seven and a half feet and which they commemorated by naming *Panther Creek* (Pipestone). That same day, August 3, 1805, Sergeant Gass lost a tomahawk in thick brush where the deep grass was *"so thick it was impossible to walk without risking falling down."* Captain Lewis response? *"I regret the loss of this usefull instrument.however, accedents will happen in the best of families"*.

On August 4, 1805, Captain Lewis and his advanced scouts came to "the Forks of the Jefferson." Another decision point! Coming in from the east is the Ruby River which the captains named *Philanthropy*. The middle fork, which is now listed as the Beaverhead, they called the Jefferson, and a few miles downstream and coming in from the west is the Big Hole River which Lewis considered not navigable, but called it *Wisdom*. After carefully examining these three streams, Lewis decided on the middle fork, which was gentle and appeared navigable. Subsequently, he wrote a message to Captain Clark instructing him to take the middle fork. Sergeant Gass attached the note to a willow at the forks. Then Captain Lewis and his scouts decided to explore the <u>west</u> fork, which is the present-day Big Hole River, and proceeded in that direction but planned to cross over to the middle fork and to eventually meet Captain Clark's party toiling up that stream.

Meanwhile the boats, led by Captain Clark, were two days travel behind Captain Lewis' party. They passed Waterloo and Silver Star and on August 5, 1805, in the late afternoon they arrived at the west fork, the Big Hole River. There was no note. When Captain Clark perceived that Lewis and the scouts had gone up the west fork he directed his boatmen up the west fork too. The passage was so difficult that the men had to cut their way through the willows. Clark was feverish, another tumor was developing on his ankle, and he was fretful and frustrated that he could not walk. At this point these stout-hearted men were *"so fatigued that they wished much that navigation was at an end so they might go by land."* Meanwhile Charbonneau and Gass could go no further and Captain Lewis sent them back to set up camp on the middle fork. Lewis continued on up the west fork with Drouillard. The two climbed a steep mountain spur, viewed the valley and could see the middle fork meandering for about twenty miles and concluded that they had made the proper decision. On their return Drouillard fell, sprained his finger and hurt his leg painfully. Even so, these two indomitable men walked twenty-five miles that day.

August 6, 1805. While Drouillard was hunting he encountered Clark and his party struggling up the west fork, and informed them that they should have been on the middle fork. What a costly error! Consequently, they turned about to return to the forks, but on the return a canoe overset wetting the baggage and damaging and losing many valuable articles. Also Joseph Whitehouse was thrown from his canoe and injured as the boat ran over him. In his journal Captain Lewis noted that had the water been two inches lower Whitehouse would have been crushed. Furthermore, Shannon was lost. The young soldier had been dispatched to hunt and knew nothing of the change of plan. Drouillard was sent to find him, but was unsuccessful. The trumpets were sounded; the guns fired. Shannon did not appear. However, the mystery of the missing note was solved when the travelers learned that the tree upon which the note was attached had been chewed down by a beaver. Perhaps someday, much later, someone would tell the tale around a campfire and chuckle over this incident, but on this day a dispirited, worn and weary crew likely had rough words for that beaver and wondered what would befall them next.

After drying out the baggage the men decided that a single canoe would hold all that remained, and consequently, they secured one canoe in the thickets, packed everything in the other and continued on past present Twin Bridges and up the middle fork.

Twin Bridges, Montana
The little community of Twin Bridges is located near the confluence of the Ruby, the Beaverhead and the Big Hole River. Lewis and Clark gave these

three rivers the names Philanthropy, Philosophy and Wisdom, respectively, the cardinal virtues honoring President Jefferson. The little settlement was first known as "The Bridges".

Dillon, Montana

Dillon is regarded as the natural hub for the entire southwestern corner of Montana. It originated as a railroad town to serve the mines of Butte. First known as Terminus, it was renamed in 1869 for Sidney Dillon, president of the Union Pacific Railroad. Historically, Dillon was near the crossroads of the Lewis and Clark Expedition, of Chief Joseph and his Nez Perce Band, and of Henry Plummer and the outlaws of Bannack and Virginia City. Dillon, once the largest wool shipping point in Montana, is surrounded by ranches older than the town and is the home of Western Montana College. The Beaverhead County Museum, the Visitor Center and the local chapter of the Lewis and Clark Heritage Foundation are active in preserving the history and memorablia connected with the Lewis and Clark Expedition.

Up to this point it had taken all of Clark's diplomatic skills to encourage and to *"passify"* his crew, but on August 8, 1805, Sacajawea

The Beaver's Head Rock between the towns of Twin Bridges and Dillon, Montana, was already a widely-known landmark when the Lewis & Clark Expedition first saw it, but it gave the Corps affirmation that they were in the homeland of Sacajawea's people. It is now one of the most famous natural features in the United States. (Photo by Pat Hastings)

recognized an Indian landmark in the distance, which her people called *"beavers head"* because of its resemblance to the head of a swimming beaver. Immediately the spirits of the party lifted as she assured them that they would soon find her people at their summer camp. The geese had begun to fly, a sure sign of autumn, and an anxious Captain Lewis, determined to find the Indians if it took him a month. However, on August 8, 1805, he did take the time to *"accomplish some wrightings...lest any accident should befalle me on the long and rather hazardous route I am about to take."*

Beaver's Head Rock

This rock, a landmark for the Indians for centuries, is located between Twin Bridges and Dillon, Montana. In 1969-70 the Rock was being blasted to provide rip-rapping. The seventy-one acre site was purchased by the state of Montana in 1975 to protect its historical significance. It is listed on the National Register of historic places.

Sacajawea is responsible for the name "Beaverhead" which includes Beaverhead County, Beaverhead River, and Beaverhead Mountains.

Clark's Lookout near Dillon, Montana. From this rock on August 13, 1805, Clark looked back at the Beaver's Head Rock and plotted the course of the Big Hole River (which he called the Wisdom River) to the south of a gap in the mountain from which the Beaverhead River emerged. (Photo by Jeanne O'Neill)

Shannon arrived on August 9 to the relief of all. The captains agreed that Lewis should proceed ahead to find the Indians. Subsequently, Captain Lewis: *"slung my pack"* and with Drouillard, Shields and McNeal went in search of the Shoshoni Indians. An ailing and frustrated Captain Clark wrote, *"I should have taken this trip had I been able to march, from the rageing tumer on my ankle."*

Clark's Lookout

Clark's Lookout is one of the few places on the Lewis and Clark Trail where it it is possible to stand on the exact spot that Captain Clark stood when he climbed this seventy-foot limestone cropping above the Beaverhead River on August 13, 1805, to take compass readings: one to Beaverhead Rock, a second to the Wisdom River, (the Big Hole), a third to the "gap of the Wisdom River" or where the river leaves its canyon. (Now called Clark Canyon). Clark's Lookout is owned by the State of Montana and is listed in the National Register of Historic Sites. It is, as yet, unmarked, but is located north of Dillon.

Captain Lewis and his trio went ahead, passed a creek they named McNeal (now Blacktail Deer Creek) and camped August 9th, near Dillon,

The upper reaches of the Beaverhead River (called the Jefferson by Meriwether Lewis on August 12, 1805) are shallow and the men were struggling to draw the canoes over the shallows. (Photo by Jeanne O'Neill)

Rattlesnake Cliffs near Dillon, Montana. Captain Lewis wrote on August 10, 1805, "...from the number of rattlesnakes about the clifts at which we halted we called them the rattle snake clifts." (Photo by Jeanne O'Neill)

Montana. On the 10th they found an Indian trail which led them to Rattlesnake Cliffs named so for the cliffs' inhabitants. Soon they arrived at a split in the Beaverhead River, the Two Forks which is today's Horse Prairie Creek coming in from the west and Red Rock River, which arises near Yellowstone Park and is now acknowledged to be the true headwaters of the Missouri River.

Rattlesnake Cliffs

These cliffs which were later seen by Captain Clark and his crew about which Clark wrote, " In walking on Shore I saw several rattles Snakes and narrowly escaped at two different times. This mount I call rattle Snake mountain not one tree on either side". Ordway reported, "Cap Clark was near being bit by a rattle Snake which was between his legs as he was fishing." August 15, 1805.

Today a park exists at the base of the cliffs and a monument there reads:

"Beaverhead Canyon Gateway
Ryans Canyon
The waters of the Beaverhead River opened this

southern gateway to Montana through which have passed
Ancient Indian Trail
Lewis and Clark Expedition 1805-1806
First missionary, Father DeSmet 1840
Great Beaverhead Wagon Trail Road 1866-1880
chartered by James Ryan and William Sturgis
First Railroad into Montana, the Utah and Northern, 1881.

When Lewis and his men came upon an Indian road, it led them into a *"handsome level valley"* which divides Horse Prairie Creek from the west and Red Rock River from the east. Red Rock arises near Yellowstone Park and is now acknowledged to be the true headwaters of the Missouri River. On August 10, Captain Lewis left a note for Captain Clark advising him to stay here in this valley as the streams were not navigable. This site is now submerged under the waters of the Clark Canyon Reservoir south of Dillon, Montana. Lewis and his three companions continued up Horse Prairie Creek into a valley which the captain described *"as a beautiful and extensive plain 10 miles long...5 to 6 miles in width...surrounded by roling or high wavy plains...the mountains surround the whole in an apparent circular manner forming one of the handsomest coves I ever saw."*

He named it Shoshone Cove and noted that there was little wood, but more prickley pear and bearded needlegrass. Shoshone Cove is located at Grant, Montana.

Clark Canyon Reservoir

A once thriving little cattletown called Armstead lies under the waters of the Clark Canyon Reservoir twenty miles south of Dillon. In 1964 the residents of Armstead yielded to the United States Government which dammed the Beaverhead River for the purpose of flood control and irrigation. The Bureau of Land Management administers the dam, but the fishery located there is controlled by the state of Montana. Eighty-thousand visitors a year visit Clark Canyon Reservoir which is open to recreation including fishing boating, canoeing, water skiing, swimming, hiking, bird watching, and picnics, including gatherings and reunions. An island in the reservoir is called Armstead Island. A memorial to Sacajawea is located near the campgrounds.

The Lewis and Clark Expedition stopped here, cached their goods, met with the Shoshoni Indians who traded them horses. They called the spot Camp Fortunate.

Captain Clark's brief entry for the same day, August 10, 1805, reported that they proceeded past a remarkable cliff about 150 feet high which the Indians call Beavers head. Hard rain with hail forced the men to protect themselves with willow branches. One deer killed that day. Total miles: **four.**

August 11, 1805. The trail that Lewis and his trio of scouts had been following disappeared. Lewis instructed Drouillard to walk about a half mile on his right, and Shields to walk a half mile on his left. McNeal walked beside him while all of them searched for the trail. After traveling about five miles toward the mountain pass which was their goal, Lewis spotted an Indian, brought up his spyglass and recognized a Shoshone Indian riding an *"eligant horse"* toward them about two miles distant. The captain signaled his two men to stop, but neither caught the signal and continued to walk toward the horseman, who was observing them about a mile away. Lewis stopped too and waved his blanket three times at the Indian, which he hoped was a sign of friendship, but the Indian only watched suspiciously. The captain then took some trade items and walked slowly toward the Indian. The native turned and rode on. A frantic Lewis shouted *"Ta-ba-bone"* a word which he had obtained from Sacajawea and which he hoped meant "white man" in Shoshone. The Indian did not react. Drouillard and Shields continued walking. A frantic Lewis shouted at them to stop. Drouillard caught the signal, but Shields did not hear and continued walking. Lewis stripped up his shirt sleeve to show white skin, yelled *"ta-ba-bone"* again, but the Shoshone only turned away whipped his horse and disappeared. A disappointed and angry Lewis

The site of Camp Fortunate where the Corps of Discovery encamped from August 17 to August 24, 1805, is now inundated under the waters of the Clark Canyon Reservoir south of Dillon, Montana. (Photo by Jeanne O'Neill)

berated Shields in true army fashion and wrote of the Indian, *"and with him vanished all my hopes of obtaining horses."*

A heavy rain not only nearly obliterated the tracks of the Indian, but soaked the travelers to the skin. However, they continued tracking, knowing that they were approaching the Shoshone. The next day, August 12, 1805, Captain Lewis and his scouts did come across another Indian road which they followed and which *"took us to the most distant fountains of the mighty Missouri in surch of which we have spent so many toilsom days and wristless nights."* McNeal stood astride the little rivulet and exulted, *"thanking his God that he had lived to bestride the mighty and heretofor endless Missouri."* Shortly afterwards they passed through a gap in the mountains now known as Lemhi Pass which crosses the Continental Divide and separates Montana from Idaho. Lewis: August 12, 1805, *"we proceeded on to the top of the dividing ridge from which I discovered immence ranges of high mountains still to the West of us with their tops partially covered with snow."* Was Meriwether Lewis apprehensive at the thought of having to cross those "immence" mountains? If so, he did not mention it as he was so caught up in the exultation of having crossed over the Continental Divide to the Columbia drainage. On the Idaho side they found a creek where Lewis exulted again *"where I first tasted the water of the great Columbia River".*

Lemhi Pass

The name, Lemhi, is from the Book of Mormon. When Mormon missionaries established a Fort on a branch of the Salmon River in 1885, they named it Fort Lemhi. Three years later the Shoshoni and Bannock Indians drove the Mormons out, but the name remains on a stream and on the pass between Idaho and Montana. The subgroup of Shoshoni Indians that originally lived in this area are sometimes referred to as "The Lemhi".

Captain Lewis did succeed in obtaining horses from the Shoshone and in engaging them to assist the main party over the Lemhi Pass into Idaho. When Sacajawea encountered these Indians she was overjoyed. These were her people, the tribe from which she had been kidnapped, and in an almost unbelievable scenario she recognized her brother among the Shoshone, no less than the chief, Cameahwait. This poor and hungry tribe welcomed the Americans and shared what little they had, only berries and fish.

August 26, 1805, was very cold. *"Ice near 1/4 inch thick"* Fall was approaching and the captains were anxious to get on with their journey. The Corps of Discovery continued over Lemhi Pass, and crossed the Continental Divide into uncharted territory on their way to the Columbia River and the Pacific Ocean. Just ahead of them, however the snow-capped Bitterroot mountains jutted skyward, offering these worn, but hardy men yet another challenge.

Red Rock Lakes National Wildlife Refuge

RED ROCK LAKES NATIONAL WILDLIFE REFUGE; the home of the rare trumpeeter swan is an important nesting and wintering habitat for this bird which was threatened with extinction only a few years ago. The refuge, established in 1935, provided protection and solitude to these majestic birds. By the 1960's their numbers had increased to almost 1,500. Situated eighty-five miles southeast of Dillon in the Centennial Valley, the Refuge spans over 43,500 acres, including more than 14,000 acres of lakes and marshes and is also home to other waterfowl including the sandhill crane, great blue heron, and Barrow's goldeneye.

A Trumpeter Swan. Large flocks of swans, both trumpeter and whistling, migrated over Montana, and although not identified as such or distinguished from the whistling swan were likely to have been seen by the members of the Lewis and Clark Expedition.

Remarkable Woman of Armstead, Montana:
Laura Tolman Scott, Historian and Naturalist

Laura Tolman Scott was born in August 6, 1857, at Marlborough, New Hampshire, of colonial ancestry from English forebearers. She came to the Redrock Valley of Montana in 1883 with her husband, Walter Scott, where they reared their four children. Upon Walter's death in 1920, she moved to Armstead, Montana, where she died in 1937.

Mrs. Scott is perhaps best known for her outstanding work in connection with the marking of historical spots. In 1914, she became a member of the state committee of preservation of historic spots of the Daughters of the American Revolution, and because of her untiring effort, she was recognized as having contributed more than any person in the marking of the Lewis and Clark pathway across Montana. Such sites are Pompey's Pillar near Billings, Giant Springs at Great Falls, and Camp Fortunate at Armstead (a site once known as Two Forks of the Jefferson – the junction of the Horse Prairie and Redrock Rivers). Another site is at Lemhi Pass, an area dedicated in 1935 to the memory of Sacajawea – "interpreter, guide and counselor to Lewis and Clark".

Mrs. Scott's life was rich and filled with many interesting hobbies. Her collection of pressed wildflowers is one of the most artistic and beautiful in existence. These are presently on exhibit at the Beaverhead Museum in Dillon, Montana.

Lupine
Jean Clary

Corps of Discovery Flags

After the United States purchased the Louisiana Territory in April of 1803, the western expedition which the United States had been planning since the previous November, took on a more profound objective. Now this proposed enterprise which was to become known as the "Lewis and Clark Expedition", would have the duty of making peace with all the Indian nations along its trail, and to inform these natives of the newly acquired sovereignty of the United States government over them and their lands[1]. Upon receiving the United States flags and medals, as symbols of their allegiance, the chiefs of the tribes were to display the flags and wear the medallions.

The Expedition took along United States flags of three sizes[2]. Apparently there was only one very large flag, a number of flags of a second size, and at least nineteen flags of a small size. Actually, they were used in a variety of ways. We are fortunate that Private Joseph Whitehouse recorded in his journal many of the occasions when the flag was used. For example, when the Captains were preparing for a council meeting with the Indians, the flag was hoisted. On August 28, 1804, the party camped to wait the arrival of some Indians in order to council with them. "We raised a pole on order to hoist our flag."[3] Another time, on September 5, 1805, where the Expedition was camped with the Salish at Ross' Hole, Whitehouse wrote, "we hoisted our large flag this morning. About 10 o'Clock our officers held a Council with the flathead nation..."[4]

However, most of the flags were given to Indian chiefs as peace gifts, along with medals and other items. While at the Mandan villages, Lewis gave a speech to the chiefs on October 29, 1804. (The United States flag had been hoisted the day before.) When the council was over, "he gave presents among them of Goods & Cloathing and to each Nation he gave an American Flag".[5] On October 17, 1805, Lewis and Clark met with some Indians along the Columbia River. Our officers gave the principal men meddles a flag & Some other Small articles"[6]. A prime example of the flag used as a symbol of peace was when Lewis finally met the Shoshone tribe. In his notes of August 13, 1805, he describes setting aside his pack and rifle; then he took the flag, unfurled it and advanced alone towards some women, but they disappeared behind a hill. Later that day he finally met Chief Cameahwait. "I gave him the flag which I informed him was an emblem of peace among whitemen and now that it had been received by him it was to be respected as the bond of union between us."[7] It is interesting how one flag even became a peace symbol _between_ two tribes. The Captains had given a flag of peace to the Cayuse Indians. As a result of this, the Cayuse, who had long been enemies of the Shoshones, later planted the flag at a trading rendezvous and made a permanent peace with those Indians.[8]

On occasion a flag would be used as a trade item. Once an old flag was used as trade for some otter skins. Then, while still in the area of the Nez Perce, west of the Bitterroot Mountains, the men exchanged one of their horses along with a small flag to procure an excellent sorrel horse[9]. Another use of the flag was for celebration. On Christmas day, 1804 the men were permitted to fire the three "cannons" at the raising of the flag.[10]

And lastly, above the Great Falls, the party being anxious to encounter some of Sacajawea's people, and flags flew from the canoes. A few days before arriving at the "Three Forks", Whitehouse wrote, "We hoisted our flag on board our Canoes and proceeded on."[11]

We have read what became of many of the medium and small flags, but what about the large flag? By March 16, 1806, a week before the Expedition left Fort Clatsop for the homeward journey, their stock of trading merchandise was nearly depleted. Even their large flag had been made into robes. Lewis wrote, "two handkerchiefs would now contain all the small articles of merchandize which we possess; the balance of the stock consists of 6 blue robes one scarlet . . . five robes made of our large flag, and a few old cloathes trimed with ribbon."[12]

What did the Expedition's flags look like? Let's make a quick review of our country's flag. The design of the early flags of the thirteen states were arranged in some different ways. The Congressional Journal of June 14, 1777, notes, "RESOLVED: that the flag of the United States be made of thirteen stripes, alternate red and white; that the union be thirteen stars, white in a blue field, representing a new constellation"[13]. There was no ruling on the arrangement of the stars, although they were generally arranged in rows. It depended on the person sewing it together. Uniformity in design and proportions was not legislated until 1912.

Then, when the States of Vermont were admitted into the Union in 1791 and Kentucky in 1792, two more stars and two more stripes were added to the flag. On January 13, 1794, legislation was signed by George Washington stating, "That from and after the first day of May, 1795, the flag of the United States be fifteen stripes, alternate red and white, and that the union be fifteen stars white, in a blue field."[14] Even though Tennessee and Ohio joined the union in 1796 and 1803, respectively, the flag remained with the fifteen stripes and stars design for twenty-three years, from 1795-1818. The flag of this design accompanied Lewis and Clark.

In some flags of this period the stars were staggered in five rows of three stars each, as shown here, while the other flags were arranged in three horizontal rows of five stars each, one directly above the other. Interestingly, the flag with the fifteen stars, staggered, was the design which flew over Fort McHenry, Maryland, during the bombardment the night of September 13-14, 1814, and inspired Francis Scott Key to write what became our national anthem, "The Star Spangled Banner". The design of the flags which the Lewis and Clark Expedition carried did, indeed, have many aspects of historical significance. Two such flags can be found flying today, at Fort McHenry and at Fort Clatsop in Oregon.

To bring us up to date, in 1818 our flag design was returned permanently to thirteen stripes and a star to represent each state presently in the Union. As new states entered, additional stars were added, which created new star arrangements. In 1959 Alaska and Hawaii entered, bringing the number of states and stars to fifty, producing the twenty-seventh flag-design change.[15]

Chapter Nine

SACAJAWEA

Sacajewea was a Lemhi Shoshoni from the area near the Continental Divide in Montana and Idaho. She had been captured by an Hidatsa raiding party near Three Forks in Montana about four or five years before becoming part of Lewis and Clark's Journey of Discovery. Toussaint Charbonneau, a French Canadian independent-trader living among the Hidatsa, purchased her for a second wife. (Some say he won her in a gambling match.) Charbonneau was hired as an Hidatsa interpreter for the Expedition with the expectation that one of his Shoshoni wives would accompany him on the journey. Charbonneau's second wife, Sacajewea, made the journey with him. She was invaluable in communicating with the Shoshoni who had horses which the Expedition needed for travel over the mountains and the portage to the Columbia River or waters leading to it.

Much has been written about the young Indian woman who had been abruptly and violently uprooted from her family when only nine or ten years old, and then taken prisoner to live hundreds of miles away from her homeland. She was pregnant and, perhaps, barely a teenager when Charbonneau was hired by Lewis and Clark. Various scholars estimate her age at that time to be between thirteen and eighteen years old.

On February 11, 1805, Captain Lewis helped deliver her son, Jean Baptiste. The young girl's labor was difficult. Lewis said, *"it is worthy of remark that this was the first child which this woman has boarn, as is common in such cases her labor was tedious and the pain violent."* To ease and hasten the delivery, a portion of the rattle from the rattlesnake was given to her. It was broken into small particles and added to water. Lewis said, *"Whether this medicine was truly the cause or not I shall not undertake to determine, but I was informed she had not taken it no more than ten minutes before she brought forth."*

Less than two months afterward, Sacajewea, with little Baptiste in a cradle-board strapped to her back, began the long journey across the country. Along with the rest of the party she endured all of the hardships, dangers and fatigues on the route to the Pacific and back. She was perhaps more lonely, as she had to keep her own counsel within the Expedition, being the only woman, the only mother and Indian.

Sacajewea's life captures the imagination and still inspires many writers, artists and others. An opera, poems, books, essays, paintings, sculptures, statues, rivers, creeks, mountain peaks, parks, etc., have been dedicated to her, written about, or named for her. She is an admired and respected historical figure.

The documented information concerning her life, however, is extremely slim. There are no physical descriptions of her, no sketches or life-paintings, no accounts of her early life, and very little information about her life following the Lewis and Clark journey. The verifiable information consists of journals written by people of that time-period. Possibly because there is so little information it has led to speculation and conjecture about aspects of her life. There are questions and controversies concerning the pronunciation and spelling of her name, when and where she died, and her contribution to the Expedition as guide or interpreter.

According to linguistic scholars, her name traces its roots to the Hidatsa tribe, among whom she lived a great part of her life. It is formed from two words: *tsakáka* means "bird," *wea* means "woman." *Ts* often changes to *s*, and *k* to *g* in Hidatsa. Hence *Tsakáka*wea changes to *Sacagawea*, or *Sakakawea*. There is no "j" in Hidatsa.[1]

Sacajawea as envisioned by sculptor Robert Scriver in the official Montana state statue in Fort Benton, Montana. See photo of entire statue on Page 48. (Photo Courtesy Dale A. Burk)

"About five miles above the mouth of shell river a handsome
river of about fifty yards in width discharged itself into the shell river
(on the stard. or upper side)...this stream we called <u>Sâh-câ-ger-we-âh</u>
or bird women's River, after our interpreter the Snake [Shoshoni]
woman." (May 20, 1805, Lewis)

Sacajewea was the spelling adopted by most Western states. It was said
to mean "boat launcher" in Shoshoni, but many linguistic scholars find no
historical justification for the word or its meaning. The 1814 edition of Biddle's
narrative edition of the Expedition journals used the "j" spelling. It has become
the most popular spelling and pronunciation.

Currently the Bureau of American Ethnology, the National Geographic
Society, the U. S. National Park Service, the Encyclopedia Americana, and many
Lewis and Clark scholars support the Sacagawea spelling and pronunciation.

– – – – –

The question of the length of Sacajewea's life and her burial site are also
debated. Some believe she separated from Charbonneau and lived a long life after
their journey to the Pacific. They believe she did not die until 1884 in Wind
River, Wyoming, where she was buried with ceremony. This theory of her later
life was supported by oral testimonies.

The journals of two men who lived during that time period contend with
that view, however. Journalist H. Brackenridge wrote (in 1811) that he had
recently traveled [from St. Louis] with Charbonneau and his sickly "Shoshoni
wife." The following year on December 20, 1812, a clerk of the fur trading
company for which Charbonneau worked wrote, "this evening the wife of
Charbonneau, a Snake (Shoshoni) Indian died of a putrid fever. She was a good
and the best woman in the fort. Aged about 25 years. She left a fine infant girl."
(This would be at Fort Manuel near today's Kenel, South Dakota.) An additional
argument was written by Capt. Clark. On an 1825-28 census list concerning
persons from the Expedition were notations written in his hand of who was living
and dead. Next to Sacajewea's name was written, "Dead." Also among Clark's
personal papers were court documents showing his adoption of Sacajewea's two
children.

Regrettably, Lutting's journal was not published until 1920, and Clark's
written document in 1955. Some controversy might have been averted if they had
come to light sooner.

Also an issue of debate is Sacagawea's role in the Expedition as guide
or interpreter. She is recorded as guiding the party twice. Both times were on the
return trip through Montana in July, 1806, when she was in the mountain
territory of her childhood. She alerted Clark to an old Indian route through Big
Hole Pass. This was a shorter route to the cache they were retrieving which had
been buried the previous year near the junction of Trail Creek and the two forks

of the Beaverhead River. She also recommended to Clark what is now Bozeman Pass for the travel route from the Gallatin Valley to the Yellowstone River. Clark said of her easier and more direct route,

"The Indian woman who has been of great service to me as a pilot through this country recommends a gap in the mountain more south which I shall cross." (July 13, 1806, Clark)

In August, 1805 on the route to the Pacific she was not a "pilot" but she recognized land features of her childhood territory and cheered the exhausted and "indisposed" men with the news, because arriving in Shoshoni territory meant they would soon have horses and would begin a new part of their journey.

"She recognized the point of a high plain (Beaver Head)...and assures us that we shall either find her people on the river, or the river immediately west of its source." (August 7, 1805, Lewis)

- - - - -

Charbonneau, her husband, had been hired as an interpreter. She was included on the journey not merely because she was his wife. The Captains were aware of the benefits she could provide the Expedition when they met her people. Shoshoni was her native tongue and she could undoubtedly ease the initial contact and reception with the Indians, and aid the Corps in the bartering for horses which were vital for the journey. Lewis speaks of her importance to the Expedition when she was gravely ill at Great Falls.

"Found the Indian woman extemely ill and much reduced by her indisposition. This gave me some concern as well for the poor object herself, then with a young child in her arms, as from the consideration of her being our only dependence for friendly negociation with the Snake Indians on whom we depend for horses to assist us in our portage from the Missouri to the Columbia river." (June 16, 1805, Lewis)

The August negotiations with the Shoshoni were friendly. The presence of Sacajewea eased the mounting tension among the Indians, who were on edge about the possibility that the Expedition might be a raiding party. Her presence with the party of men was a sign of peace.

The party of Shoshoni the Expedition encountered turned out to be Sacajewea's own band, and further, the chief was her brother. The Expedition witnessed a tender, emotional reunion, and the first council meeting halted many times because of her tears.

As the Corps' Shoshoni interpreter she was part of a communication chain of five people. Each phrase or request from Capt. Lewis was translated into French and then to Hidatsa before reaching Sacajewea, who translated it into Shoshoni for her brother Chief Cameahwait. His response would go back the other way. Drouillard, who knew intertribal sign language, was usually on hand for assistance when necessary. Through that chain of communication the Expedition bartered for and acquired horses, sought and received geographical information, gained intelligence about tribes ahead, and received baggage carriers and guides for the journey ahead. Sacajawea interpreted in the same fashion among other Indian villages on the journey where there were Shoshoni captives who had learned their captor's language.

The young mother was helpful to the Expedition in other ways. She shared her skills and traditional abilities throughout the journey. There were many references to her gathering food for the Expedition. The wild fruits and roots she brought, such as wild licorice, white apple, wild artichokes, currents, plums, cherries, fennel and gooseberries were helpful additions to the men's diet. She knew how these vegetables and fruits should be used, what they were good for, and how they would affect the body. At Fort Clatsop, where game was meager, she showed that elk shank bones could be turned into food through cracking and boiling them and obtaining a quantity of tallow as an addition to their meals. Her ability and skill to fashion moccasins and leather clothing was useful to the party. The young woman was not stingy or small-minded and she moved to lend assistance and aid when needed. She took off her blue-beaded belt and gave it to Lewis and Clark when they wanted to purchase a chief's robe made of beautifully fashioned sea-otter skins. They had no more blue beads, which was the only payment the chief would consider for the barter. She retrieved most of Lewis and Clark's papers, maps and other articles which washed out of the white pirogue when a sudden squall tipped the boat. With little Baptiste on her back, she balanced herself over the choppy water to remove as many floating articles as she could, and bring them back into the boat. Lewis wrote admiringly of her effort to save what she could,

"The Indian woman to whom I ascribe equal fortitude and resolution, with any person on board at the time of the accident, caught and preserved most of the light articles which were washed overboard."
(May 16, 1805, Lewis)

Capt. Clark said,

"this accident had like to have cost us deerly; for in this perogue were embarked our papers, Instruments, books, medicine, merchandize...in short nearly every article indispensibly necessary for the success of the enterprize in which we are now launched to the distance of 2200 miles."

– – – – –

There is little information to indicate Sacajewea's personality or nature, but the glimpses which we are afforded are appealing.

On Christmas Day (1805), which was "Big Medicine," Clark received two dozen white weasel tails from her. On another occasion she gave him a piece of bread she had saved for her baby. Her presence with little "Pomp" must have softened the tone and character of the camp. Having a mother and child around the campfire would lighten and moderate the camp's tenor, possibly consoling some of the men who missed home. The gentle Indian girl trudged, climbed, starved, endured biting cold, violent storms and blazing sun on the long journey with only one request. She wanted to see the enormous fish (whale) that was beached on the sandy coast near Fort Clatsop. Captain Lewis wrote about her desire,

"The Indian woman was very importunate to be permitted to go and was therefore indulged; she observed that she had traveled a long way with us to see the great waters, and that now that monstrous fish was also to be seen, she thought it very hard she could not be permitted to see either." (January 6, 1806, Lewis)

Sacajewea shared the labor and hardships of the journey during her sixteen months and several thousand miles with the Expedition, and her presence helped in many ways to make the historical journey successful. She became the story's heroine, not because she was spectacularly brilliant or stunningly beautiful, but because she did what had to be done or needed doing.

She carried on her traditions by doing what was useful and what she had been trained to do: gathering and preparing food; caring for her child; making moccasins and clothing and teaching others these crafts; giving allegiance to and sharing skills with her community, which at this point was the Corps of Discovery; and finally, "enduring" through the harsh land traveled by the Expedition and respecting its resources. She carried out these acts with steadiness and dependability, and what someone who had been with her (Mr. Brackenridge) called a "mild and gentle disposition." She never received any compensation for her service to the Expedition. Clark said after the journey, "Sacajewea deserved a greater reward for her attention and services than we had in our power to give her."

The young Indian woman is worthy of legend.

While those who who laid the woman to rest in 1884 who is buried beneath this headstone on the Wind River Reservation in Wyoming were sure she was the Shoshone woman who had accompanied Lewis and Clark, most historians believe otherwise. Captain Clark himself had written in a mid-1820's Expedition census report that Sacajawea was dead, fully sixty-four years before the woman buried at this site died. (Photo Courtesy of Clem Stechelin)

Chapter Ten

WESTWARD TO THE PACIFIC

Equipped with all the information the Shoshone's had to offer, with horses to pack and ride over the mountains, with Old Toby and his son to guide them, the Expedition was ready for their march through the Bitterroots. The travelers now had to cross the first ranges of these mountain, those *"immence mountains"* which threatened to derail the whole adventure. Although the Shoshones had warned them of the difficulties of their proposed route and suggested that they retrace their steps and approach the valley from the Big Hole side along a well-known Indian trail, the Ne-mee-poo, the Captains would not consider the longer but easier route. With a hint of arrogance they proclaimed that their men could go wherever Indian squaws could go. Consequently, from August 31 to September 4, 1805, the men and Sacajawea struggled in cold wet, foggy and freezing weather, over rocky terrain, jagged cliffs, and slippery mountainsides as *"steep as roofs'*. They cut their way through thickets, waded in icy streams and went to sleep cold and hungry. Game was scarce and as excellent as the hunters were, they could not provide enough food for their exhausted party. Horses slipped and fell down mountainsides, injuring themselves and adding to the trials besetting the Corps. But on September 4, 1805, the travelers dropped into a mountain meadow where a tribe of Ootlashoot Indians of the Salish nations were preparing to join their friends, the Shoshone, to band together and hunt buffalo on the prairie lands occupied by the fearful Blackfeet. Fortunately for the Americans, the Salish, also known as Flatheads, greeted them warmly, shared what little food they had, and traded fresh sturdy Salish horses for the poor worn-out Shoshone ponies.

The Americans camped alongside these friendly Indians at this meadow, now called Ross' Hole near Sula, Montana. The Captains again repeated their message of peace, the sovereignty of the United States, and promised that upon their return from the Pacific they would send traders who would provide arms and material goods in exchange for beaver pelts and animal hides from the Indians. Once again the native Americans, who could have killed them and stolen their arms and trade goods, rescued the men and Sacajawea from what could have been the terminus of the Expedition.

These views are to the west from Lemhi Pass into the drainage of the Columbia River in what is present-day Idaho. In the distance are the mountains through which the Corps of Discovery would have to pass to reach the Pacific Ocean. (Photo by Pat Hastings)

Ross' Hole

Ross Hole, named for Alexander Ross who was stranded here by deep impassable snow with a party of fifty-five Indian and white trappers, eighty-nine women and children and 392 horses from March 12, 1825, to April 15, 1825. This important campsite of the Expedition and the Salish Indians has not yet been marked or memorialized, but is located near Sula, Montana, eighteen miles south of Darby on Highway 93.

On September 7, 1805, the two groups parted, and the Expedition, refreshed and anxious, continued its trek through the beautiful Bitterroot Valley of Montana, past where the present communities of Darby, Hamilton, Victor, Stevensville, and Florence are located. Near present-day Lolo they camped on the banks of a clear creek coming in from the west, Lolo Creek. The campsite is known as Traveler's Rest and is located about eleven miles south of Missoula, Montana.

On September 11, 1805, the Expedition started over what would become the most dangerous and the worst part of the whole journey. What should have been only a "five-sleep" trip into the meadows of Idaho turned into a nightmare lasting twelve grueling days. Old Toby led them along Lolo Creek, over Lolo Pass which divides Montana from Idaho. Although Old Toby was probably conscientious, he was unfamiliar with the rough and rocky trail and he led the Corps on a detour over mountains down to the Lochsa River. There was no game as the Indians had predicted; consequently, the hungry men killed and roasted a colt. The next day they had to climb the steep tortuous path back to the Nez Perce trail which followed the high mountain ridges. By the 16th of September, 1805, Clark, who was no whiner, wrote in his journal, *"I have been wet and as cold in every part as I ever was in my life, indeed I was at one time feafull my feet would freeze in the thin Mockersins which I wore."* By the 18th of September, a week into this tortuous journey, the captains decided that Captain Clark would take six hunters, forge ahead in search of game, and attempt to locate the Indians. On the 20th he did meet the Nez Perce, persuaded them to sell him some food, salmon and bread from roots and sent these provisions back to the main party. Again the Indians proved to be life-savers to the Expedition. Although the starving men gorged themselves on this food that was foreign to them and became desperately ill with dysentery, they did recover slowly and stayed for a week and a half with the hospitable Nez Perce.

Leaving their horses in the care of the Indians, the Corps resumed its journey in five dugouts they had constructed and put into the Clearwater River in Idaho on October 7, 1805. Now the canoes swept along with the river current. However, there were rapids which tore at and split one of the canoes, rocks that

On August 12, 1805, Captain Meriwether Lewis wrote in his journal, "Here I first tasted the water of the great Columbia river." He was just to the west of the Continental Divide on what is now known as Lemhi Pass when he had that drink of water in a small, clear stream. (Photo by Pat Hastings)

swamped and sunk another canoe. Still they made good time and were joined by two Nez Perce chiefs, Twisted Hair and Tetoharsky. At this point Old Toby and his son decided to return to the mountains and left the Expedition without a good-bye or without being paid. The travelers passed other Indians camping on the river banks catching and drying salmon. These river Indians ate dog and dried fish and so did the men of the Expedition. Although Lewis relished the dog meat, Clark never did. He stayed with the fish.

A week passed and on October 16, they reached the Columbia River, that great river which at last would bring them to the Pacific. When they met the Yakimas and Wanapams Indians, the Captains gave them gifts and recited the peace speech although now the Expedition had passed from United States Territory and had no claim to this land. A friendly meeting occurred with Chief Yelleppit and his Walla Walla Indians who welcomed the strangers and delighted in the music Pierre Cruzatte teased out of his old fiddle. However, when the Expedition came upon the Umatillas, those natives were frightened and terrorized by the approach of the white men. But here again Sacajawea's presence was an indication to the fearful Indians that this party was not intent on war.

The journey continued. There were many rapids to portage and Indian villages to visit where the Captains repeated the peace talks. Music proved to be the common denominator as Cruzatte and George Gibson played their fiddles, the men danced and sang with the Indians and that most interesting of all spectacles, York performed. Again there were portages, a difficult one around the Great

Chute of the Columbia, the Cascades, on November 1, where the men carried baggage on their backs over slippery rocks. Although the travelers were constantly wet and cold from the interminable rain, and growing disagreeable from the fleas infesting their blankets, their goal was near. On November 7, 1805, Captain Clark wrote more enthusiastically than was his usual style, *"Ocian in view! O! the joy."* However, he was seeing not the ocean, but the estuary of the Columbia which reached some twenty miles from its mouth. It was not until late November that the party was able to find and decide upon a winter camp site near present Astoria, Oregon. On December 7, 1805, they began to build their winter campsite, Fort Clatsop, named after their neighbors, the Clatsop Indians.

The Vote: November 24, 1805

Of note was the election of November 24, 1805 to determine the location of the winter camp. Each member of the Expedition was polled including Sacajawea and York. This was the first time in United States history that a woman, who was a Native American, and a black man, who was also a slave, were extended the privilege of voting.

D. LADD '99

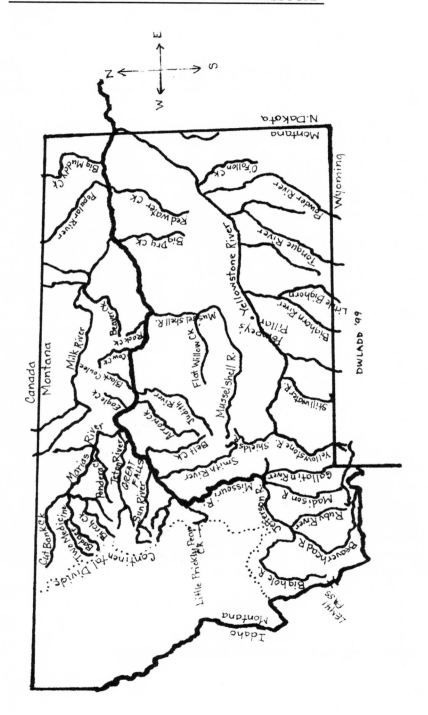

Chapter Eleven

THE RETURN TRIP

After a wet and dismal winter when the Captains extended their knowledge of the geography and of the coastal Indians from whom they bartered for food, the men once again put the canoes into the water and headed upstream on the Columbia for the return journey, March 23, 1806. After some disagreeable encounters with the Indians on the river whom they found to be bothersome, untrustworthy and pilferers, a nearly explosive situation occurred when some Indians stole Seaman and brought down the wrath of Captain Lewis. Seaman was returned. Near The Dalles, Oregon, they succeeded in trading their canoes for pack horses and went overland to the villages of their friends, the Nez Perce. There they waited impatiently for the snowpack on the Bitterroots to melt. Finally, on June 10, 1806, they set out against the advice of the Nez Perce, who warned them that the snow was still too deep. The Indians were right, and after struggling through drifts twelve to fifteen feet high, the men were forced to make a retrograde march, the only one of the whole excursion. Finally, they did succeed in crossing *"those immence mountains"* with the help of young Nez Perce guides, of whom Captain Lewis admitted that they were surrounded by mountains and without the assistance of their guides could never have found their way. *"...Those Indians are most admirable pilot,"* Lewis wrote on June 27, 1806. On June 29th the men enjoyed the comforting baths of the hot springs at Lolo, and the next day the entire party reached Travelers' Rest again, where they paused for a couple of days and prepared for the continuation of the journey home.

The Corps of Discovery was once again in Montana. The Captains had decided on a plan both courageous and daring. They would split the party at this point. Captain Lewis would take nine men and proceed up the present Clark Fork River to the Blackfoot and over the Continental Divide to the Great Falls of the Missouri, with the intention of exploring the Marias River in the hope of finding a trade route to the north that would compete with the British fur trade in Canada. Meanwhile Captain Clark would lead the remainder of the party and horses back through the Bitterroot Valley, across the Divide into the Big Hole Valley and on to the Three Forks. There he would dispatch Sergeant Ordway and a contingent of nine men to travel down the Missouri to the camp at White Bear, where they would assist Sergeant Gass and his men in portaging the Great Falls. Then Captain Clark and the remaining men, the horses and Sacajawea with little Pomp, would proceed down the Yellowstone River, exploring and mapping until they would rendevous with Captain Lewis and his men at the mouth of the Yellowstone. It was a daring plan as both parties would be traveling in hostile Indian territory. Would their good luck hold out? They must have believed so and obviously were confidant in their own skills and courage, as well as those of their men. They planned to rendevous in six weeks.

Traveler's Rest

Charles "Chuck" Campbell, a student of the Lewis and Clark Expedition, describes Traveler's Rest as a hub from which three spokes emerge. The first spoke tracks the Bitterroot River down which the Corps of Discovery traveled the east side of the river in September 1805. Captain Clark's party then traveled up this route on the west side of the river on the return, July, 1806. The second spoke leads west over Lolo Pass following the trail of the Nez Perce into Idaho. The third spoke leads northeast following the "buffaloe trail" up the Blackfoot River, across the Continental Divide to the Dearborn River and on to the Great Falls of the Missouri.

Captain Lewis Explores the Marias

On July 3, 1806, Captain Lewis and Captain Clark split the party for the return trip. Were there feelings of apprehension and concern for the safety of these travelers who had bonded into an intimacy akin to family? Captain Lewis wrote, *"I took leave of my worthy friend and companion, Cap Clark and the party that accompanyed him. I could not avoid feeling much concern on this occasion."*

With nine men, seventeen horses and five Nez Perce guides, Captain Lewis proceeded down the Bitterroot River to its junction with the Clark Fork west of Missoula, Montana. About two miles below the junction the Indians indicated a good place to ford the swift-running water, although somewhat hazardous when Captain Lewis was swept off a raft and had to swim to safety. Finally, after directing the Captain to the *cokalahiskit,* or the Big Blackfoot River, where the Nez Perce assured him he would find the well-beaten *"buffloe road"* to the Great Falls of the Missouri, the guides parted from Captain Lewis' group with what Olin Wheeler referred to as "mutual esteem and regret."

Lewis' party then continued along the Blackfoot River, sometimes diverting from the stream to the upper ridges along the Indian trails. Their Nez Perce guides had warned them of the *"Pahkees"*, their enemies, whom they were likely to encounter on the journey and feared for the safety of their white friends. Consequently, the men maintained a constant guard, but no incidents occurred. On July 7, 1806, the party passed over the Continental Divide, *"the dividing ridge between the waters of the Columbia and Missouri"*, Lewis and Clark

Pass, misnamed because Clark never saw it. Currently, Montana Highway 200 runs southeast from this pass over another named Rogers Pass. However, Highway 200 follows an old Indian trail which tracks from the Sun River Valley to Missoula, the same trail Lewis and his men traveled. They were now back in the United States on the Rocky Mountain Front, which spills over onto the prairies of central Montana. Patrick Gass, *"came to a fine spring the water of which run into the Missouri."* Soon they were again observing abundant game, where buffalo numbered in the tens of thousands, pursued by the ever-hungry wolves. Large herds of elk were visible and bears again appeared. There was meat, good buffalo meat for the hungry men and a dog and skins to replace their worn and tattered clothes and moccasins.

On July 11th, the travelers arrived at the White Bear Islands, and the next day they crossed the river to their old camp. Seven horses were missing. Drouillard went in pursuit and did not return for three days, but without the horses which were presumably stolen by the Indians. Suspicion rested upon the Tushshepahs.

Alone In The Wilderness

Olin Wheeler wrote in his classic book, "The Trail of Lewis & Clark," "One thing to be noted on all the operations of the expedition was the fearlessness and absolute independence of action of these men when sent out on such errands as this. Singly and in pairs they penetrated into the unknown wilds, hunting, following lost horses, seeking trails, etc. apparently not knowing hesitation or fear, and risking ambushment attack and death."

Here, at the Great Falls, their enemies, the mosquitos were waiting. *"The musquetoes, who now infes us in such myriads that we frequently get them into our throats when breathing, and the dog even howls with the torture they occasion."* This is the last time Seaman is mentioned in the journals.

What Happened to Seaman?

We do not know Seaman's ultimate fate. Part of the mystery and aura of the Expedition is the question of Seaman's fate. Captain Lewis' big Newfoundland dog was a true member of the Corps of Discovery. The Captain paid twenty dollars for him, and he and this faithful companion arrived at Camp Wood together. Sometimes referred to as "Scannon" due to the spelling in the journals, Seaman contributed his share to the adventures of the Expedition. He hunted squirrels for Captain Lewis, who fried them for his dinner, (September, 1803), antelopes and a goose (April, 1805), deer, (May, 1806, and again, July, 1806). He was a sentinel who frightened a stampeding buffalo from camp (May, 29, 1805), alarmed by grizzlies and barked all night (June 17, 1805) and provided entertainment for the Indians (August 27, 1805).

Seaman suffered from thistles puncturing his feet (July 25, 1805) and was tortured by mosquitos, the last mention of him. Captain Clark referred to Seaman as "our dog was so Heeted and fatigued ...Send him back to the Creek."(August 25, 1804). Captain Lewis refused to sell his dog and when Seaman was stolen by some Indians (April 11, 1806) the captain threatened to have them shot if the dog was not returned. Seaman was severely bitten by a beaver (May 29,m 1805) and Lewis feared for his life. Present-day Monture Creek in Powell County, Montana was originally named "Seaman's Creek" by Captain Lewis. Since no mention is made of Seaman after July 15, 1806, conjectures have been presented that he could have been a victim of a ferocious animal. It is unlikely he was with Lewis on the Marias or he would have warned his master of the approach of the stealthy Indians. Surely, Lewis would not have abandoned his prized dog on the trail. "Therefore the evidence, such as it is, points to the conclusion that he was with the party when it arrived at St. Louis. Whatever his fate. Seaman is part of our country's history. With fidelity and courage he participated in an historic event which had a profound effect on our nation's future," wrote Ernest Osgood and Donald Jackson in "The Lewis and Clark Expedition's Newfoundland Dog."

Then on July 17th, Captain Lewis embarked on a most bold and dangerous plan, a reconnaissance of the Marias River where he still hoped to discover a waterway to the west coast or at least into Canada. He took with him, George Drouillard, always his right-hand man, and the fearless brothers, Joseph and Reuben Fields, to penetrate into the Blackfoot stronghold – four men, alone. Although there was sign of Indians having camped in the vicinity, Lewis and his men encountered no one as they traveled up the north fork of the Marias which is now Cut Bank Creek. When the Captain assured himself that Cut Bank Creek diverted west, not north, he judged it did not originate in Canada, and another hope was lost. Also, rations were meager, mush of cous, mixed with tainted bear grease. The buffalo had moved on. The weather remained unfriendly, *"the air has become extremely cold...wind...rain...renders our position extremely unpleasant."* Lewis, frustrated that he could not obtain any astronomical observations, named this site Camp Disappointment. It is located on the present Blackfeet Reservation.

Cut Bank

Cut Bank, near the border of the Blackfeet Reservation, was named for the "river which cuts through the white clay banks" by the Indians. Cut Bank is the county seat for Glacier County. Oil and gas were discovered there in 1960. A monument to Meriwether Lewis is situated about twenty-two miles west of Cut Bank, but the northernmost point reached by this expedition lies a few miles farther north.

The travelers now turned about to return to their rendevous with the remaining party, which was making its way downstream of the Missouri from the Great Falls. Drouillard was scouting ahead when, on July 26, 1806, Lewis spotted about thirty horses with several riders looking down toward the river, presumably at Drouillard. Bad news! Indians, probably the Blackfeet. However, Lewis, always in command of a situation, approached the Indians with peaceful gestures, shook hands and invited them to join their encampment that evening in the vicinity of the Two Medicine River. As Lewis, Drouillard, and the Field brothers sat around the campfire smoking with the eight Indians, who were Piegan Blackfeet, the Captain, through Drouillards's sign, gave the Indians the peace talk, and also informed them that he had been with the tribes to the west and had made peace with them. He had also promised the Nez Perce, Salish, and Shoshone that he would send American traders to them. Now, Lewis informed these strangers, it would be advantageous for the Blackfeet to trade with traders from the United States rather than with the British; then there would be peace among all the tribes. What did this mean? To the Blackfeet it meant that their day of controlling the Plains through their superior weaponry was being threatened. The western tribes were about to be armed by the Americans.

Early the next morning the Indians attempted to steal the rifles of the white men. A fracas occurred in which Reuben Fields stabbed one Indian to death. When the other Indians attempted to run off the Americans' horses, Captain Lewis pursued them. One of the Indians turned on the captain, who then shot him in the abdomen with his pistol and was rewarded with a bullet whizzing past his ear, a parting volley from the fallen man. The remaining Indians, pursued by the Field brothers, fled with some of the horses. However, fearing that the Blackfeet would soon be tracking them, the Field brothers returned, and the four men saddled up the horses, including four of the Indian ponies, and set fire to the Indians' belongings. Then, before they left, Captain Lewis placed a medal around the neck of one of the dead Indians *"that they might be informed who we were."*

The Americans rode hard and fast, pushing the horses as much as they dared toward the mouth of the Marias. They stopped only to graze the horses and continued on until two a.m. when they halted for some needed sleep. The next morning, though so stiff and sore they could hardly stand, the four men continued their ride toward the river. Upon arriving at the banks of the Missouri, in another amazing stroke of luck, Captain Lewis and his companions *"had the unspeakable satisfaction to see our canoes coming down."* With joyful shouts they hailed the

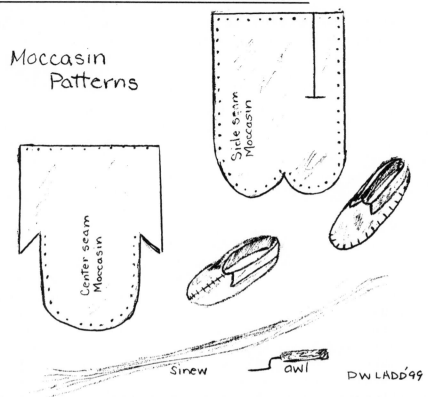

Moccasins of The Types Used By The Corps of Discovery

Moccasin (mok a sin, a word of Algonquian origin) is a heelless shoe made from soft leather, usually deerskin. The type of moccasin worn seemed to be determined by terrain. Prairie moccasins were usually made of strong bison skin for protection against cactus spines and rocks. They were usually double soled with tough skins, which made them more difficult to sew. Forest moccasins had thin leather, which was better for damp forest floors. They dried easily, were flexible, and were easy to carry (as opposed to heavy European shoes or boots).

The two-piece style moccasin was worn most often on the plains. It had a soft leather, U-shaped piece for the top of the foot. The sole came over the toes and sides of the foot where it met and was seamed to the upper U-shaped piece. When the sole wore out it could be replaced unlike the one-piece moccasin. The one-piece style appears to be the older style which was replaced early in the nineteenth century. Some tribes, however, still preferred those of one piece. To make the one-piece moccasin, the hide was folded lengthwise and cut to the shape of the foot, forming the sole and the upper portion in just one cutting. It was then sewn along one side. The one-piece style was generally used with an added flap of an inch to six inches high sewn around the ankle and held with thongs. It was most often preferred for winter wear and used with the fur turned to the inside.

Some tribes decorated the moccasins with beads of bone and porcupine quills dyed various colors. Later, European glass beads were used and combined with quill work. Characteristic tribal designs were evident. Northern Plains Indians preferred geometric designs. Flower designs appeared shortly after missionaries arrived. Many tribes preferred little decoration on their moccasins, while others were more lavish in their adornment. Usually the ones used everyday were plain. The tools used for sewing the moccasins were an awl of pointed bone for making holes, strips of sinew for thread, and a knife for cutting.

North American Indians, and later traders, settlers, and hunters wore moccasins. They are worn now as house shoes, and casual shoes made of heavy, stiff leather with seams imitating the true soft moccasin.

---

river party, unsaddled and dismissed their horses, and scrambled into the canoes. They had traveled over a hundred miles in twenty-four hours.

Near the mouth of the Marias they opened their caches to find that much of the contents of the first one had been ruined. The other caches had held, and as they loaded the canoes, Sergeant Gass and Private Willard arrived with the horses. Now all of the men under Captain Lewis were reunited and eager to meet Captain Clark and his contingent which was now, supposedly, moving down the Yellowstone River. The journey was rapid and on August 7, 1806, they reached the mouth of the Yellowstone and were rewarded and relieved to find a note written by Captain Clark, *"a few miles further down on the right hand side."* However, before they joined their fellow travelers, an unfortunate accident disabled Captain Lewis. While elk hunting on August 11th, the captain was shot in the buttocks by Pierre Cruzatte, the one-eyed boatman, who mistook his captain for an elk. The wound was very painful, and the following day, when the canoes arrived at Clark's camp, Lewis was not in sight. A worried Captain Clark feared for his friend and was much relieved to find him lying on his stomach in the canoe. From this time on, Captain Clark cared for Captain Lewis and took over the job of journaling. Captain Lewis wrote his last entry, August 12, 1806. *"As wrighting in my present situation is extremely painfull to me I shall desist untill I recover and leave to my friend Capt. C the continuation of our journal."*

On The Yellowstone With Captain Clark

When the two captains parted at Traveler's Rest, July 3, 1806, Captain Clark moved up the west side of the Bitterroot River with twenty men, Sacajawea and Pomp, and fifty horses. The river was in spring runoff, high and turbulent and too dangerous to cross. The men struggled against the current, water hurled down from those *"awful mountains"*. As they forded the turbulent creeks, horses slipped and fell, baggage was sodden. Still these hardy and experienced travelers managed to make good time. On the Fourth of July, they celebrated Independence Day in honor of *"my country"* as Captain Clark stated and *"partook of a Sumptious Dinner of a fat saddle of venison and mush of cows"* while they remembered the previous fourth of July at the Great Falls of the Missouri when they drained their last keg of whiskey. When John Shields found the trail by which the Salish passed over the Continental Divide into the Big Hole Valley, Captain Clark *"determined to make the attempt and follow their trail if possible."* On July 6, 1806 they crossed from the Bitterroot Valley into the Big Hole Valley. Fields of blue camas were in bloom. They were on their way home.

Subsequently, however, the Salish chief, Charlo, son of Victor, once lamented. *"We were happy when he (the white man) first came. We first thought he came from the light; but he comes like the dusk of evening now, not like the dawn of morning. He comes like a day that has passed, and night enters our future with him."*

Now the Indian roads scattered, and it was to Sacajawea that Captain Clark and the men looked for guidance. From now until July 15, 1806, Sacajawea proved her worth as guide. She remembered her childhood days of digging for roots in this valley with her people. As the travelers moved down the Big Hole Valley toward Camp Fortunate, along the river they had named Wisdom, the Big Hole. They stopped at the springs Clark called "hot springs." Sergeant Ordway described it as *"we come to a boiling hot Spring at the edge of this plains which is large and handsom...I drank some of the water found it wel-*

Ruffed grouse DWL 1999

tasted. But so hot that I cannot hold my hand in [it] a Second of time. Captain Clark wrote that they had cooked some meat in the hot water and found that the thicker portion about the size of his three fingers cooked in twenty-five minutes.

Jackson Hot Springs, Montana
Jackson, a tiny community located in the middle of the rich ranch country of the Big Hole Valley, which boasts of 10,000 haystacks, was named for Anton Jackson, the first postmaster, 1896. It is a community catering to summer tourists and fishermen, hunters and winter sports enthusiasts.

Captain Clark continued to move up the Big Hole Valley, which he called the *"hot springs Vally,"*

Wisdom
This little community in Beaverhead County, Montana is named for the river which flows through the town. Originally called "Crossings", it obtained a post office in 1883, called itself "Wisdom" and became a center for trade for the hay farms and ranches in valley. A nearby creek is named Wise River as is a community in the vicinity. It is possible the name was also derived from the Wisdom River.

The travelers were in a hurry to reach their destination, Camp Fortunate, where caches containing tobacco awaited the nicotine-starved men. Captain Clark wrote that they now took leave from the *"butiful extensive vally which I call the hot springs Vally"* Once again Captain Clark traveled over gold-rich lands along Willards Creek which is the famous Grasshopper Creek where the really big strike in Montana was made by William Eads in 1862.

Bannack
Bannack, first spelled Bannock, was named after the local Bannock Indians. After gold was discovered on Grasshopper Creek, Bannack grew to become the largest city in Montana (pop. 8,000) and became the first territorial capitol of the state in 1864. The sheriff of Bannack, Henry Plummer, operated an outlaw gang of road agents who terrorized the area from Bannack to Alder Gulch and were responsible for the death of more than a hundred men. The Plummer gang's reign of terror ended at the hands of the Vigilantes and consequently, for many of them, at the end of a rope. Bannack is now an interesting mining ghost town owned by the state of Montana.

On July 8, 1806, Clark's party reached Camp Fortunate, where the men rushed to remove the saddles from their horses and partake of the pleasure of chewing and smoking their tobacco. Here they spent two frosty days *"grass stiff Frozend,"* while they repaired the canoes, and packed the baggage from the cache. Sergeant Ordway was detailed to gather up the stray horses. The party resumed its journey along the Jefferson River, passed Beaver Head Rock on July 11th, and two days later reached the Three Forks. They wasted no time. After sharing a meal together the party split. Sergeant Ordway took nine men in six canoes and traveled down the Missouri River to join Captain Lewis' group and assist with the portage around the falls, all according to plan. It took seven days for the Ordway detachment to reach White Bear camp, and by the 26th of July 1806, the portage was complete, and the men continued down the Missouri and met up with Captain Lewis and his three companions, again as planned. No delays. They were going home.

Now Sacajawea directed Captain Clark. *"The Indian woman who has been of great service to me as a pilot through this country recommends a gap in the mountain more south which I shall cross...* and he did on July 15th. On the same day, they arrived at the Yellowstone River near present Livingston, Montana. In his journal Captain Clark noted that the horses were suffering from very sore feet, so this ingenious group made moccasins for them out of green buffalo skins.

The Americans were now entering the home of the Crow Indians, the most skillful horse thieves of all the plains tribes. Clark's Indian ponies were accustomed to chase any animal they encountered. Consequently, it was no easy task to keep them in line. On July 21st the travelers awoke to find that half the horses were gone. The best trackers could not find them, consequently, the presumption arose that the Indians had stolen them. A full guard was put on the remaining horses which were then detached with Sergeant Pryor, accompanied by Shannon, Windsor, and Hall to the Mandan villages to be used in trade when the Expedition arrived there. Sergeant Pryor was also detailed to take a letter to a Mr. Hugh Heney, whom the captains had met at Fort Mandan, and whom they hoped to engage in an effort to persuade some of the Sioux Indian chiefs to return to Washington with the Expedition.

Meanwhile the men constructed two canoes, lashed them together, and lowered them into the Yellowstone River. They were on their way to the Missouri. Game was abundant for eating and for skins, which was fortunate for Sergeant Pryor and his companions who lost all the horses to the Crow Indians near present-day Hardin, Montana. Finding themselves stranded without horses in the wilderness, what did they do? They packed their baggage on their back, hiked to the river, killed a buffalo, constructed bull boats from the buffalo skin, and floated down the Yellowstone hoping to meet up with their Captain. On July 26th a bold and vicious wolf bit Sergeant Pryor's hand while he was asleep and attempted to grab Windsor. Fortunately, Shannon shot the wolf. Again, tragedy avoided. Good fortune was still smiling.

Pompey's Pillar

On July 25, 1806 Captain Clark arrived at a remarkable rock which he named "Pompey's Tower" and which he described "as 200 feet high and 400 paces in circumference, and only accessible on one side, which is from the N.E.,... On the top there is a tolerable soil about 5 or 6 feet thick covered with short grass...the natives have engraved on the face of this rock the figures of animals, near which I marked my name and the day of the month and year. From the top of this tower I could discover two low mountains and the Rocky Mountains covered with snow." This rock was a campsite for the Indians for centuries, and is now a National Historic Monument under the management of the Bureau of Land Management. Clark's carved signature, Wm. Clark, July 25, 1805, is protected by shatter-proof glass. This is the only site along the Lewis and Clark Trail which bears physical proof of the presence of the Lewis and Clark Expedition.

Along the Yellowstone River east of Billings, Montana, stands a mighty tower of rock that is known today as Pompey's Pillar. On Juy 25, 1806, Captain William Clark wrote "I have engraved on the face of this rock...which I marked my name and the date of the month and year." He also named the rock "Pomp's Tower" in honor of Sacajawea's child, Pomp. (Photo by Pat Hastings)

Buffalo! Captain Clark had to land and wait for one hour to let the buffalo cross the river *"this gang of buffalo was entirely across and as thick as they could swim."* That evening, August 1, 1806, the travelers camped upon an island. *"Two gangs of buffalo crossed a little below us, as noumerous as the first."*

Bear! The next day a large bear raised himself up from a sandbar as the canoes passed, plunged into the water and swam toward them. *"We shot him with two balls and he returned to shore badly wounded. In the evening I saw a very large bear take the water above us. I ordered the boat to land on the opposit shore. When the bear was in a few paces of the shore I shot it in the head."* August 6th a white bear, a grizzly, pursued the canoe. They all fired into the bear, did not kill him, but wounded him, and he escaped to the opposite shore.

Mosquitoes! *"So troublesome that the men complained that they could not work their skins. Clark could not hunt in the bottoms, those insects being so numerous and tormenting as to render it impossible for a man to continue in the timbered lands. The evenings, nights and mornings are almost unendurable...I could not keep them off my gun long enough to take sight, and by that means Missed."* after sighting a bighorn animal.

Again they named the rivers and streams: Shields River, named after that valuable gunsmith and metalworker, John Shields, has retained the name. "Clarks Fork of the Yellowstone" remains Clarks Fork, not to be confused with the Clark Fork near Missoula, Montana. Although "Pryor's River" became Dry Creek, "Pryor's Creek" remains Pryor's Creek. The Bighorn River is still the Big Horn River. The Tongue River was named by the Indians.

Elk! July 29th, 1806, the captain reported so many elk that they remained in sight the whole day. At one point near Billings, Montana, Clark wrote, *"for me to question or to give an estimate of the wild animals on this river...would be incredible. I shall therefore be silent on the Subject further.*

Beaver! Immense numbers of beaver, so many that the flapping of their tails kept the men awake. Not for long . With the return of the Expedition tales of wealth to be had in fur trading spread rapidly, and the industrious little animals were trapped almost to extinction in less than forty years.

A Land Changed Forever

K. Ross Toole, the late Montana historian observed: *"When the Expedition left Montana in the first week of August, 1806, they left the land where they had made their most important discoveries and had survived their greatest crisis. In no other region did they split up and make such a wide and detailed study of the country; no traveler or resident of Montana today is far from some part of their route; they saw and mapped all the main drainage areas and removed the mystery of the terrain; they recorded rich resources;*

their most crucial tests were here. Lewis and Clark discovered the sources of the Missouri; transferred from the river to the land; negotiated with Indians, and charted the way through mountains which were much greater in scope than they were led to believe. Lewis and Clark left in their journals not only a story of hardship and courage, but a story of wealth. It was all there plain to see for anyone who cared to read it. Although they left only the ashes of their campfires behind, Montana would never be the same again."

Finally, on August 3. 1806, Clark's little band reached the Missouri, but again, their perennial enemy, the mosquito, made stopping unthinkable. On August 9th Sergeant Ordway's detachment joined them in their bull boats. The Captain left a note for Captain Lewis and continued on down the Missouri River where on August 11th they met two trappers, Joseph Dickson and Forrest Hancock, moving up to the Yellowstone in search of furs. On August 12 the Corps of Discovery was reunited, a time of rejoicing of thankfulness that all had returned safely. *"Now thanks to God we are all together again in good health,"* Patrick Gass wrote. Did that include Seaman?

They were in a hurry now, but took time to visit with their Indian friends, the Mandans and Hidatsa. To their disappointment the captains learned that the peace they had so vigorously encouraged on their visit in 1804 had not held, and the villagers were at war again. Captain Lewis was still recovering so the diplomatic duties were up to Captain Clark, who endeavored to persuade the chiefs to return to St. Louis and thence to Washington to meet the President. After some intense efforts Clark was successful in persuading the Mandan chief, Sheheke, also known as Big White, to accompany them. When they pushed their canoes into the Big Muddy this time, they were without Charbonneau, Sacajawea, Pomp and John Colter. Colter had asked to return to the fur fields with traders, Dickson and Hancock, and had been granted his request provided no other member of the Expedition asked the same. Touissant Charbonneau decided to remain with the Hidatsa, but he and Sacajawea agreed to Captain Clark's request to bring little Jean Baptiste to St. Louis when he was weaned from his mother. Captain Clark, who had become quite fond of little Pomp, promised to rear and educate the toddler in his home.

Finally, on August 17th, 1806, the Corps took final leave of their friends, the Mandans, and hurried toward St. Louis, stopping only to hunt and to visit with the fur traders whom they met going upriver. From them they learned that most Americans had given up hope of the Expedition returning and expected that they had died in the wilderness or had been captured and enslaved by the Spanish. The troublesome Teton Sioux did taunt them when Captain Clark refused to have a council, but after what James Ronda referred to as a "nasty verbal exchange" and a noisy one, the travelers continued downriver. On September 4, 1806, they stopped at the grave of their comrade, Sergeant Charles Floyd, found that his grave had been disturbed and was partially opened. They closed it, revered the memory of their friend and continued downriver through rain and wind and sunshine so glaring that the men complained of sore eyes. Besides news, the men received food and whiskey from the traders they met coming upriver in exchange for information. On September 20th they noticed cows grazing, a sure sign of civilization. At LaCharette they fired their guns and received a loud welcome cheer and at St. Charles they stopped and enjoyed the hospitality of the citizens who invited them into their homes. St. Louis came in sight about noon on September 23, 1806. The *"wrightingest explorers"* concluded the journals of the Corps of Discovery with the now famous entry of Captain Clark, September 26, 1806, *"a fine morning we commenced wrighting."*

Seaman.

BIBLIOGRAPHY

•All quotations from the Journals of Lewis and Clark are from the Reuben G. Thwaites Edition, 1904-5 Edition, unless otherwise noted.

•Alt, David and Hyndman, Donald W., *Roadside Geology of Montana,* Missoula, Montana: Mountain Press Publishing Company, 1992

•Alwin, John A. *Eastern Montana: A Portrait of the Land and Its People.* Montana Geographic Series #2, Montana Magazine Inc., Helena, Montana 1982

•Ambrose, Stephen E. *Undaunted Courage: Meriwether Lewis, Thomas Jefferson and the Opening of the American West.* New York: Simon and Schuster, 1996

•Anderson, Irving W., *A Charbonneau Family Portrait*, Fort Clatsop Historical Association, 1988

•Appleman, Roy E., ed. By Robert G. Ferris. *Lewis and Clark Historic Places Associated With Their Transcontinental Exploration (1804-06),* Washington, D.C. National Geographic, 1975

•Bakeless, John. *Lewis and Clark Partners in Discovery.* New York: William Morrow and Company, 1967

•Barth, Gunther. *The Lewis and Clark Expedition Selections From The Journals.* Boston/New York: Bedford/St. Martin, 1998

•Beaverhead Chamber of Commerce. *Southwester Montana Beaverhead County-Dillon,* Dillon, Montana

•Behnke, Robert J. *Native Trout of Western North America.* Bethesda, Maryland: American Fisheries Society, 1992

•Berthold, Mary Paddock. *Including Two Captains: A Later Look Westward*, Detroit: Harlo Press, 1975

•Bloom, Marshall. *Trout Line: News from the Montana Council of Trout Unlimited.* Hamilton, Montana: Ravalli Republic, Fall 1998, and Winter & Spring 1999

•Broder, Patricia J. *Great Painters of the Old American West.* Abbeville Press, New York, 1979

•Burk, Dale A., *A Brush With The West,* Stoneydale Press Publishing Company, Stevensville, Montana 1980

   New Interpretations, Stoneydale Press Publishing Company, Stevensville, Montana 1969

•Burroughs, Raymond Darwin, ed. *The Natural History of the Lewis and Clark Expedition.* East Lancing, Michigan: University Press, 1995

•Busch, Robert H. *The Wolf Almanac.* New York: Lyons & Burford, 1995

•Campbell, Charles V. *Westward Barriers: Guidebook for Routes Followed by Lewis and Clark Across the Rocky Mountains in 1805-6,* Missoula: Traveler's Rest Chapter Lewis and Clark Trail Heritage Foundation, 1994

•Catlin, George. *Life Among The Indians.* Bracken Books, an imprint of Random House, UK Ltd., London, 1996

•Chairmakers' Rush" MMO15OD' Music/BMD *"Lewis and Clark Sounds of Discovery,"* 1998

•Cheney, Roberta Carkeet. *Names On The Face of Montana,* Missoula. Mountain Press Publishing Co., 1983

•Chittenden, Hiram Martin. *The American Fur Trade of the Far West.* New York: Francis P. Harper, 1902

•Coues, Elliot, ed. *History of the Expedition Under the Command of Lewis and Clark.* New York: Dover Publications, reprint three volumes, 1965

•Cutright, Paul R. *Meriwether Lewis: Naturalist.* Portland, Oregon: The Oregon Historical Quarterly, 1968

  Lewis and Clark: Pioneering Naturalists. Lincoln and London: University of Nebraska Press, 1969

•DeVoto, Bernard, *Across the Wide Missouri,* New York,:Bonanza 1947

  The Course of Empire, Cambridge: The Riverside Press, 1952

  The Journals of Lewis and Clark, Boston: Houghton-Mifflin Co., 1953

•Dorgan, Darrell. *Lewis & Clark at Fort Mandan.* Film/cassette featuring Stephen Ambrose, Gerard Baker, Ken Burns, Dayton Duncan North Dakota Lewis & Clark Bicentennial Commission, 1999

•Dorn, Robert D. *Vascular Plants of Montana.* Cheyenne, Wyoming: Mountain West Publishing, 1984

•Duncan, Dayton and Burns, Ken. *Lewis & Clark, The Journey of The Corps of Discovery.* New York: Alfred A. Knopf, 1997

•Fanslow, Julie. *The Travelers Guide to the Lewis and Clark Trail,* Helena: Falcon Press Inc., 1994

•Fifer, Barbara and Soderberg, Vicki. *Along The Trail With Lewis and Clark,* Great Falls, Montana: Montana Magazine, 1998

•Fisher, Everett. Remington and Russell. Published by Gallery Press, a division of W.H. Smith Publishers, Inc., New York, (Produced by Bison Book Corp., Greenwich, CT) 1985

•Fritz, Harry. Meriwether *Lewis and William Clark and The Discovery of Montana.* Supplement publication *We Proceeded On,* Vol. 10 #4, 1984

  Montana Land of Contrast. Windsor Publications, Inc., Woodland Hills, California, 1984

•Garver, Frank Harmon. *Lewis & Clark in Beaverhead County.* Reprint from the Dillon Examiner of Dec. 10, 1913, Beaverhead Printers, Dillon, Montana, 1964

•Griggs, Jack L. *All the Birds of North America.* New York: Harper Collins Publishers, Inc., 1997

•Hall, Raymond E. & Nelson, Keith R. *The Mammals of North America.* 2 Vols. New York: Ronald Press Co., 1959

•Harris, Burton. *John Colter His Years in The Rockies,* University of Nebraska Press, Lincoln and London, 1993

•Hawke, David Freeman. *Those Tremendous Mountains: The Story of the Lewis and Clark Expedition.* W. W. Norton & Company, New York-London, 1985, 1998

•Henderson, Junius & Craig, Elberta L. *Economic Mammalogy.* Springfield, Illinois: Charles C. Thomas, 1932

•Hollmann, Clide. *Five Artists of the Old West*. Hastings House Publishers, New York, 1965

•Howard, Ella Mae. *Lewis and Clark Exploration of Central Montana*, Lewis and Clark Interpretive Association, 1998

Hull, Bette Meine and Tourism and Recreation Department of Western Montana College of the University of Montana. *Lewis and Clark in Beaverhead County*, Travel Montana, Department of Commerce, and Gold West Country

•Hungry Wolf, Beverly and Adolf. *Indian Tribes of the Northern Rockies*. Summertown, Tennessee Book Publishing Company, 1989

•Hunt, Robert R. *The Blood Meal. We Proceeded On*. Great Falls, Montana: Trail Heritage Foundation, Inc., Vol. 18, No. 3, August, 1992

  We Proceeded On, "Merry to the Fiddle: The Musical Amusement of the Lewis & Clark Party, Vol. 14, No. 4, November 1988

•Jackson, Donald, ed. *Letters of the Lewis and Clark Expedition, with Related Documents; 1783-1854*, 2nd ed. Urbana: University of Illinois Press, 1978

•Jacobsen, Judy and Merrill, Andrea. *Montana Almanac,* Helena: Falcon Press, 1997

•Kessler, Donna J. *The Making of Sacajawea, A Euro-American Legend*. The University of Oklahoma Press, Tuscaloosa and London, 1996

•Lavender, David. *The Way to the Western Sea,* New York: Harper and Roe, 1988

•MacGregor, Carol Lynn. *The Journals of Patrick Gass: Member of the Lewis & Clark Expedition*. Missoula, Montana: Mountain Press Pub. Co., 1997

•MacGregor, Carol, ed., *The Journals of Patrick Gass, Member of the Lewis and Clark Expedition,* Missoula: Mountain Press Publishing Company, 1997

•Madsen, Brigham D. *The Lemhi: Sacajawea's People,* Caldwell, Idaho: The Codon Printers, 1979

•McRae, W.C. and Judy Jewell. *Montana Handbook,* Chico, California: Moon Publications, Inc., 1999

•Martin, Edwin T. *Thomas Jefferson: Scientist*. New York: Henry Schuman, 1952

•Mirsky, Jeannette. *The Western Crossings*, New York: Knopf, 1946

•Montgomery, David R. *Indian Crafts and Skills*. Horizon Publishers and Distributors, Inc., 1985

•*Montana's Historic Spots Interesting,* The Montana Free Press, Dillon, Montana, March 31, 1929

•Montana Power Company. *Know the Facts, Play Safe at Montana Power's Historic Dams,* Butte, Montana.

  Missouri-Madison Hydroelectric Project, Butte, Montana: Renewable Technologies, 1991

•Montana State University. *Trees and Shrubs of Montana*. Extension Service Bulletin 323, 1995

•Moss, James A. *The Flag of the United States: its History and Symbolism.* Washington, D.C.: The United States Flag Association, 1933

•Moulton, Gary. *The Journals of Lewis and Clark Expedition,* University of Nebraska Press, 1983-97

•Mussulman, Joseph A. *We Proceeded On: "The Greatest Harmony: Medicine Songs on the Lewis and Clark Trail"*

•Myers, Rex C. & Ashby, Norma B. *Symbols of Montana.* Helena, Montana: Montana Historical Society Foundation, 1989

•Nabokov, Peter, and Easton, Robert. *Native American Architecture,* Oxford University Press, New York and Oxford, 1989

•Nell, Donald F. and Taylor, John E. *Lewis and Clark in the Three Rivers Valley 1805-06.* Tucson, Arizona: Headwaters Chapter Lewis and Clark Heritage Foundation, Inc. and Patrice Press, 1996

•O'Driscoll, Patrick. *Mending The Big Muddy,* USA Today, June 7, 1999

•Osgood, Ernest S. and Jackson, Donald. *The Lewis and Clark Expedition's Newfoundland Dog,* Lewis and Clark Trail Heritage Foundation, Inc., *We Proceeded On,* supplement publication, No. 12. July 1997

•Peterson R. T. *Peterson Field Guides: Western Birds.* Boston and New York: Houghton Mifflin Co., 1990

•Quaife, Milo M. *The History of the United States Flag.* New York and London: Harper & Row, 1961

Edited *The Journals of Captain Meriwether Lewis and Sergeant John Ordway.* Madison, Wisconsin: Western Historical Collections, State Historical Society of Wisconsin, 1916

•Ramey, Rob Roy & Wehausen, John D. *Morphometric Analysis of Horn and Skull Variation in Mountain Sheep: Northern Regions of Ovis canadensis.* Boulder, Colorado: University of Colorado, June 1996

•Ronda, James P. *Lewis and Clark Among the Indians,* Lincoln: University of Nebraska Press, 1984

Voyages of Discovery Essays on the Lewis and Clark Expedition, Montana Historical Society Press, Helena, Montana, 1998

The Core of Discovery. We Proceeded On, Vol. 25, No. 1, February 1999

•Saindon, Bob. *The Flags of the Lewis and Clark Expedition. We Proceeded on.* Great Falls, Montana: Trail Heritage Foundation, Inc. Vol. 7, No. 4, Nov. 1981

•Salisbury, Albert and Jane. *Two Captains West,* Bramhall House, New York, MCML

•Schmidt, Thomas. *National Geographic's Guide to the Lewis and Clark Trail,* Washington, D.C.: The National Geographic Society, 1998

•Smith, Phyllis. *Bozeman and The Gallatin Valley, a History,* Twodot (Falcon Publishing Company), Helena, Montana 1996

•Snyder, George. *In the Footsteps of Lewis and Clark,* National Geographic Society, 1970

•*Story of the Great American West,* Reader's Digest Association, Pleasantville, New York, 1987

•Swenson, David. *Sounds of Discovery.* Music, Line notes by David Swenson. Chairmakers Rush, a division of MaKoche Recording Company, Bismarck, North Dakota

•Teale, Edwin Way. *Audubon's Wildlife, A New Look at the Birds and Animals,* Viking Press, New York, 1964

•*The Buffalo Hunters,* by the editors of Time-Life Books, Alexandria, Virginia 1993

•Thayer, Tom. *Missouri River Country of Montana and North Dakota, Montana,* Montana Speaks, Billings, Montana: Montana Guide Books, 1997

•Thompson, Curt. *Floating and Recreation on Montana's Rivers,* Lakeside, Montana: Curt Thompson, 1993

•Thorp, Daniel. *Lewis & Clark, An American Journey.* Metro Books, an imprint of Friedman/Fairfax Publishers, 1998

•Tirrell, Norma. *Montana,* Oakland: Compass American Guides, Inc. 1991

•Thwaites, Reuben G., ed. *Original Journals of the Lewis and Clark Expedition.* (8 Vols.) New York: Dodd and Mead and Company, 1904

•Toole, K. Ross. *Montana: An Uncommon Land,* Norman: University of Oklahoma Press, 1959

•United States Corps of Engineers. *Let Us Try. The Construction History of Fort Peck Dam (video)*

•United States Forest Service. *Mann Gulch – Remembering Those Who Died*

•Van West, Carroll. *A Traveler's Companion to Montana History,* Helena: Montana Historical Society Press, 1988

•Walcheck, Ken. *Audubon Bighorn Sheep: The Riddle of Existence.* Montana Outdoors, Helena, Montana: Department of Fish, Wildlife and Parks, Jan-Feb 1980

•Wernert, Susan J., ed. *North American Wildlife.* Pleasantville, New York: Reader's Digest, 1982

•Wetmore, Alexander. *Song and Garden Birds of North America.* Washington, D.C.: National Geographic Society, 1964

•Wheeler, Olin D. *The Trail of Lewis and Clark, 1804-1806,* New York: G.P. Putnam and Sons, 1926

•Wissler, Clark. *Indians of the United States.* Anchor Books, New York, 1966

•Young, Michael K. ed. *Conservation Assessment for Inland Cutthroat Trout: U.S.D.A. Forest Service General Technical Report.* Fort Collins, Colorado: Colorado State University, Feb. 1995

FOOTNOTES

A listing of annotated footnotes for those chapters in which the writers utilized them.

Chapter Six: PIONEERS IN NATURE
1. Edwin T. Martin, *Thomas Jefferson: Scientist.* (New York: Henry Schuman, 1952) p. 3-4
2. Paul R. Cutright, *Meriwether Lewis: Naturalist.* (Portland, Oregon: The Oregon Historical Quarterly, 1968) p. 1-2
3. Donald Jackson, ed., *Letters of the Lewis and Clark Expedition, with Related Documents: 1783-1854, 2nd ed.* (Urbana: University of Illinois Press, 1978) p. 63
4. Paul R. Cutright, *Lewis and Clark: Pioneering Naturalists.* (Lincoln and London: University of Nebraska Press, 1969) p. 9
5. Ibid., p. 74
6. Hiram Martin Chittenden, *The American Fur Trade of the Far West.* (New York: Francis P. Harper, 1902) p. 820
7. Reuben G. Thwaites, ed., *Original Journals of the Lewis and Clark Expedition.* 8 Vols. (New York: Dodd and Mead and Company, 1904 Vol. I, p. 4
   Additional quotes from the Thwaites journals will be footnoted only as "Thwaites".
8., 9., 10., Ibid.
11. Jackson. P. 260-261
12. Thwaites
13. Robert H. Busch, *The Wolf Almanac.* (New York: Lyons & Burford, 1995) p. 168
14., 15., 16., 17., 18., 19. Thwaites
20. Carol Lynn MacGregor, *The Journals of Patrick Gass: Member of the Lewis & Clark Expedition.* (Missoula, Montana: Mountain Press Pub. Co., 1997) p. 211
21. Gary Moulton, ed., *The Journals of the Lewis and Clark Expedition,* Vol. 9 p. 115
22., 23., 24. Thwaites
25. Moulton, Vol. 4, p. 84
26., 27., 28., 29. Thwaites
30. Alexander Wetmore. *Song and Garden Birds of North America.* (Washington, D.C.: National Geographic society, 1964) p. 293
31. Rex C. Myers. *Symbols of Montana.* (Helena, Montana: Montana Historical society Foundation, 1989) p. 14
32., 33., 34. Thwaites
35. Jackson. p. 78
36., 37. Thwaites
38. Cutright. p. 158.
39. Robert J. Behnke, *Native Trout of Western North America.* (Bethesda, Maryland: American Fisheries Society, 1992) p. 3
40. Michael K. Young, ed. *Conservation Assessment for Inland Cutthroat Trout: U.S.D.A.* Forest Service General Technical Report. (Fort Collins, Colorado: Colorado State Univ., Feb. 1995) p. 5
41. Ibid. p. 11
42., 43., 44., 45. Thwaites

46. Robert R. Hunt. *The Blood Meal. We Proceeded On.* (Great Falls, Montana: Trail Heritage Foundation, Inc., Vol. 18, No. 3, Aug., 1992) p. 7
47. Ibid. p. 11
48., 49., 50., 51. Thwaites
52. Milo M. Quaife, ed. *The Journals of Captain Meriwether Lewis and Sergeant John Ordway.* (Madison, Wisconsin: Western Historical Collections, State Historical Society of Wisconsin, 1916) p. 380
53., 54., 55., 56. Thwaites
57., 58., 59., 60., 61. Thwaites
62. Montana State University. *Trees and Shrubs of Montana.* (Extension Service Bulletin 323, 1995) p. 33
63. Moulton. Vol. 9, p.162
64., 65., 66. Thwaites
67. Cutright. p. 369

Chapter Seven: DUE SOUTH ON A WESTWARD JOURNEY
All quotes in this chapter are from the Thwaites edition of the journals unless otherwise noted.
1. Originates in the Castle Mountains and flows northwest for one hundred twenty five miles through limestone cliffs of the Big Belt and Little Belt Mountains. The name originally Smith's River has remained unchanged for almost two hundred years except for eliminating the *s*.
2. A landmark for Lewis on his return in 1806. Depicted in many of Charlie Russell's paintings.
3. Known today as Half Breed or Lone Pine Island.
4. Probably buffalo berries.
5. Possibly a Sundance Camp.
6. Volcanic rock found in the Adel Mountains located between Cascade and Wolf Creek.
7. Flows out of the Scapegoat Mountains east for approximately sixty-five miles. With the exception of the 's, this name has endured the test of time. Westward, it leads to the Lewis and Clark Pass – a direct route to the Columbia River system.
8. Lewis and Clark's Medicine River, present day Sun River.
9. The Indian stripped the bark to the cambium layer and chewed the sweet, sap-filled inner layer for nourishment.
10. Helena Valley – Prickly Pear Creek feeds Lake Helena – there are discrepancies in the journals and on the maps regarding this stream.
11. Probably passed over Scratchgravel Hills. Below a thin layer of gravel, these hills contained gold nuggets until 1920 when earlier settlers, using rakes and plows, had scratched them clean. The West might have been settled much earlier had Lewis and Clark known of the rich deposits in nearby hills and mountains.
12. To protect his feet from the briars, Captain Lewis sewed buffalo rawhide soles on his moccasins.
13. There is conflicting information on the maps and in the journals. This is thought by some to be present day Spokane Creek.
14. Under the backwater of Canyon Ferry Dam.
15. Lewis' Woodpecker. Captain Lewis' original specimen given a variety of scientific names, is in a zoology museum at Harvard University.
16. New to science. They called these pheasants but they were probably mountain blue grouse, scientific name – Dendragapus obscurus.
17. It is known today as Beaver Creek.
18. Present day Duck Creek.

19. Lewis was probably correct. The western garter snake is common and enters water when frightened.

20. A short distance from the three forks, this campsite was probably near present day Trident.

21. Probably set as a warning to other Indians in the area.

22. The west fork originates in Yellowstone Park. Over one hundred miles long, it snakes through one of the most scenic areas in Montana. The east fork originates in the Bridger Mountains and joins the west fork approximately twelve miles prior to its entrance into the Missouri.

23. The Jefferson originates in southwest Montana at the confluences of the Big Hole and Beaverhead Rivers. It winds for eighty three miles before joining the Madison and Gallatin to form the Missouri.

24. The Madison, one hundred and thirty three miles long, has its headwaters in Yellowstone Park. It passes through a broad valley before joining the Jefferson and Gallatin at the Three Forks.

25. Harry W. Fritz, <u>Montana, Land of Contrast</u>, (Woodland Hills, California, 1984) p.21

26. Reader's Digest, *Story of the Great American West*, Pleasantville, New York, 1987, p. 89

INDEX

H
Hauser Dam, 130
Hidatsa, 27,29,30,31,39,44,49,70,73,87,94
Holter Dam, 130,137,141
Holter Lake, 138

I
Insects, 123,124

J
Jackson Hot Springs, 195
Jefferson, President Thomas, 13,17,27,56,69,76,77,84,131,135,153,154,157,163
Jefferson River, 115
Judith River, 36,121,128

L
Last Chance Gulch, 146
LePage, Baptiste, 39, 75,131,134,124,125,126,129,131,133-
137,140,141,143,144,146,
149-154,156,157,160,161,162,165,169,187,188,190,191,193,197
Lemhi, At, 112
Lemhi Pass, 129,169,182,184
Lewis' Lookout, 153
Lewis, Meriwether 13,16,17,23,26,27,29,31,32,34,35,40-47,49,51,55-
60,62,63,67,70,71,73-77,79,82,83,89,93,94,115,117,120,123,124
Lewis Woodpecker, 110
Lisa, Manuel, 87
Loma, 41
Louisiana Purchase 15,24

M
Mandan, 18,20-26,29,30,39,66,69,76,149,154,199
Mandan Village, 87,93,94,95,127,129
Mann Gulch Fire, 142
Marias River, 27,39,93,120,125,126,188,190
  Maria, Woods, 41,42,44,120
McNeal, Hugh, 113,169
Medicine River 44,59,60,94
Milk River 31,44,121
Missouri River 13,16-
20,27,28,30,33,39,41,42,44,47,49,64,65,71,79,81,87,89,94,96,115,122,127,129,130
,131,135,
137,142,148,160,166,197
Missouri River Breaks, 34,91
Moccasins, 192

LISTING OF BOOKS

Additional copies of *LEWIS AND CLARK ON THE UPPER MISSOURI,* and many other of Stoneydale Press' books on outdoor recreation, regional history, or historical reminisces centered around the Northern Rocky Mountain region, are available at many book stores and sporting goods stores, or direct from Stoneydale Press. If you'd like more information, you can contact us by calling a Toll Free number, *1-800-735-7006,* or by writing the address at the bottom of the page. Here's a partial listing of some of the books that are available:

Historical Reminisces/Other

Lewis & Clark In The Bitterroot, By The Discovery Writers With a Foreword by Dale A. Burk, 208 pages, color section, the story of the Lewis & Clark Expedition's travels through the Bitterroot Mountains of Montana and Idaho, available in hardcover and softcover editions.

Seaman: The Dog Who Helped Explore America, By R. W. "Rib" Gustafson, 70 pages, softcover, in text and illustration, a children's perspective on Seaman, the Newfoundland Retriever that accompanied the Lewis and Clark Expedition on its epic journey.

Indian Trails & Grizzly Tales, By Bud Cheff Sr., 212 pages, available in clothbound and softcover editions.

They Left Their Tracks, By Howard Copenhaver, Recollections of Sixty Years as a Wilderness Outfitter, 192 pages, clothbound or softcover editions (One of our all-time most popular books.)

More Tracks, By Howard Copenhaver, 78 Years of Mountains, People & Happiness, 180 pages, clothbound or softcover editions.

Copenhaver Country, By Howard Copenhaver. A delightful collection of stories from out of the Ovando, Montana, and Bob Marshall Wilderness areas in Montana by a noted storyteller, 160 pages, clothbound and softcover editions.

Mules & Mountains, By Margie E. Hahn, the story of Walt Hahn, Forest Service Packer, 164 pages, clothbound or softcover editions.

Montana's Mineral County In Retrospect, By Margie E. Hahn, historical look at rich history of western-most part of Montana, many historical photographs, 160 pages, softcover only.

A Brush With The West, By Dale A. Burk, 140 pages, clothbound, perspective on role of art on historical and contemporary perspectives of place in the West and the Northern Rockies.

New Interpretations, By Dale A. Burk, 204 pages, softcover, insightful third edition of development of western art in Montana from the time of Russell and Seltzer into the late 1960s.

Mules Across The Great Wide Open, *By Jody Foss, 288 pages, compelling narrative by Jody Foss on trip by mules she, her sister, and another companion made from Park City, Utah, north into Wyoming and then across Montana and Idaho into eastern Washington.*

Lolo Creek Reflections, *By The Lolo Woman's Club. A facsimile reprint of a historic book chronicling the settlement of the historic Lolo Creek and famous Lolo Trail area in western Montana. Early-day photographs.*

The Bitterrooter, *By George Hayes. A novel about the struggles of life in the early part of the 20th Century as settlers were battling to establish homes in a literal wilderness. Softcover, 144 pages..*

Outdoor Books

The Elk Mystique, *By Mike Lapinski, large format book of color photographs and text about the history and mystique of the wapiti, the American elk by one of nation's top outdoor writers. A gorgeous all-color book with many photos of elk in the wild.*

Self Defense For Nature Lover, By Mike Lapinski. Subtitled "Handling Dangerous Situations With Wild Critters," *this timely and helpful book is a detailed guide to self defense in terms of potential outdoors dangers involving mountain lions, grizzly bears, black bears, etc.*

The Woodsman and His Hatchet, *By Bud Cheff, Eighty years on back country survival by an expert whose secrets of common sense wilderness survival are described in detail, 112 pages, softcover only.*

So You Really Want To Be a Guide, *By Dan Cherry. The latest and single most authoritative source on what it takes to be a guide today. This book is an excellent guideline to a successful guiding career. Softcover edition only.*

Field Care Handbook For The Hunter & Fisherman, *By Bill Sager & Duncan Gilchrist, 168 pages, comb binding, many photographs and illustrations. The most comprehensive field care handbook available.*

Cookbooks

Camp Cookbook, *Featuring Recipes for Fixing Both at Home and in Camp, With Field Stories by Dale A. Burk, 216 pages, comb binding*

Cooking for Your Hunter, *By Miriam Jones, 180 pages, comb binding*

That Perfect Batch: The Hows & Whys of Making Sausage and Jerky, *By Clem Stechelin, 116 pages, comb binding.*

Venison As You Like It, *By Ned Dobson. This book covers the details for utilizing wild game in roasts, steaks, hamburger, chili, chops, casseroles, sausages, etc. Over 200 recipes.*

STONEYDALE PRESS PUBLISHING COMPANY
523 Main Street • Box 188
Stevensville, Montana 59870
Phone: 406-777-2729